FOUCAULT AND FEMINISM

For Marian and Michael McNay

FOUCAULT AND FEMINISM:
Power, Gender and the Self

Lois McNay

Northeastern University Press
BOSTON

First published in England in 1992 by Polity Press, Cambridge,
in association with Blackwell Publishers, Oxford. First
published in 1993 in the United States of America by Northeastern
University Press, by agreement with Polity Press.

Library of Congress Cataloging-in-Publication Data

McNay, Lois.
    Foucault and feminism : power, gender and the self / Lois
McNay.
        p.   cm.
    Originally published: Cambridge, England : Polity Press, 1992.
    Includes bibliographical references.
    ISBN 1–55553–152–0 (alk. paper)   ISBN 1–55553–153–9
(pbk. : alk. paper)
    1. Foucault, Michel—Contributions to feminist theory.
2. Feminist theory.   3. Sex role.   4. Power (social sciences)
5. Self.   I. Title.
HQ1190.M39   1993
305.42′01–dc20   92–27536

Composed in Palatino by Graphicraft Typesetters Ltd., Hong Kong.
Printed in Great Britain by T. J. Press (Padstow) Ltd, Cornwall.

This book is printed on acid-free paper.

Contents

Acknowledgements

I would like to thank John Thompson for his excellent advice and encouragement. I would also like to thank Henrietta Moore for her stimulating critical comments.

Introduction

Currently, many left-wing thinkers, ranging from literary critics to political theorists, appear to be grappling with a basically similar dilemma. This dilemma revolves around the implications of poststructuralist thought – and its most recent mutation into theories of the postmodern – for emancipatory politics. The engagement between poststructuralism and other types of radical criticism has been going on for several years now. The poststructuralist attack on traditional forms of thought and, in particular, on orthodox notions of rationality and the unified subject has had deepseated effects on many types of cultural and social critique. Whilst there have always been some critics on the left who have rejected out of hand the insights of poststructuralist thought, the convergence has been, on the whole, positive and stimulating.

However, what distinguishes the most recent dilemma is that many previously sympathetic radical thinkers have begun critically to withdraw in varying degrees from some of the post-structuralist tenets they used to espouse. The questions that are now being asked tend to turn around two central, interrelated themes. Firstly, where does the poststructuralist deconstruction of unified subjectivity into fragmented subject positions lead in terms of an understanding of individuals as active agents capable of intervening in and transforming their social environment? Secondly, what are the implications of the postmodern suspension of all forms of value judgement, of concepts such as truth, freedom and rationality, for emancipatory political projects which necessarily rest on certain 'metaphysical' assumptions about what constitutes oppression and freedom?

The tensions that have always existed between poststructuralist theory, whose 'relativist' logic tends to lead to a 'retreat from politics' (see Fraser 1984), and the normative demands of more politically engaged forms of critique have, in some cases, reached breaking point. Thus, in *New Left Review*, Kate Soper argues that left-wing thinkers must make explicit their suspicions about the 'self-indulgent quality' of postmodern scepticism and return to 'an open commitment to certain political principles and values' (Soper 1991: 123).

Feminists have not been exempt from this dilemma either. Indeed, perhaps more than any other group of thinkers, feminists are particularly involved because the crossover between feminist theory and poststructuralism has been especially vibrant and productive. The poststructuralist philosophical critique of the rational subject has resonated strongly with the feminist critique of rationality as an essentially masculine construct. Moreover, feminists have drawn extensively on the poststructuralist argument that rather than having a fixed core or essence, subjectivity is constructed through language and is, therefore, an open-ended, contradictory and culturally specific amalgam of different subject positions. This argument has been used in various ways by feminists – particularly socialist feminists – to criticize the tendency amongst certain radical feminists to construct women as a global sisterhood linked by invariant, universal feminine characteristics, i.e. essentialism.

Despite these important theoretical convergences, however, feminists are beginning to question anew how far they can draw on poststructuralist thought. Once again the fundamental problem is the extent to which a philosophical form of critique that rejects any type of certainty or value judgement conflicts with, or even undermines, feminist politics whose principal aim of overcoming the subordination of women necessarily rests on certain basic value judgements and truth claims.

It is against the general background of these debates that I conduct my investigation into the implications of the work of the French philosopher and historian Michel Foucault for feminist social theory. As a major figure in the poststructuralist canon, any consideration of Foucault's work will almost inevitably have to take into account the questions being thrown up in the current debate. Even more so, because, perhaps to a greater extent than any other poststructuralist thinker, feminists have drawn on Foucault's work.

The engagement between feminist theory and the thought of Michel Foucault has tended to centre around the work of his middle years, most notably *Discipline and Punish* and the first volume of *The History of Sexuality*. In these works, Foucault presents a theory of power and its relation to the body which feminists have used to explain aspects of women's oppression. Foucault's idea that sexuality is not an innate or natural quality of the body, but rather the effect of historically specific power relations has provided feminists with a useful analytical framework to explain how women's experience is impoverished and controlled within certain culturally determined images of feminine sexuality. Furthermore, the idea that the body is produced through power and is, therefore, a cultural rather than a natural entity has made a significant contribution to the feminist critique of essentialism mentioned earlier.

However, despite the extent to which Foucault's idea of the body has been used in feminist theory, feminists are also acutely aware of its critical limitations. Again, these limitations centre upon the difficulties of assimilating a primarily philosophical form of critique into feminist theory which is rooted in the demands of an emancipatory politics. For the emphasis that Foucault places on the effects of power upon the body results in a reduction of social agents to passive bodies and does not explain how individuals may act in an autonomous fashion. This lack of a rounded theory of subjectivity or agency conflicts with a fundamental aim of the feminist project: to rediscover and re-evaluate the experiences of women.

With this in mind, a central aim of this book is to show how Foucault's little-considered final work – *The Use of Pleasure, The Care of the Self* and various interviews and articles – goes some way to overcoming the limitations of his earlier work on the body through the elaboration of a notion of the self. The development of a concept of the self derives, in part, from Foucault's own recognition of the analytical limitations of his partial account of the individual as a passive body. Not only does such a limited model deny the potential for agency and self-determination, but it also leads to an understanding of power in purely negative terms as prohibitory and repressive – although, in principle, Foucault contests such conceptions with his idea that power is a productive and positive force. He complements his earlier analysis of technologies of domination, therefore, with an analysis of technologies of subjectification. Foucault defines these technologies of the self as a certain number of practices and techniques through which individuals *actively* fashion their own identities. Such an idea permits Foucault to explain how individuals may escape the homogenizing tendencies of power in modern society through the assertion of their autonomy. At the same time, however, Foucault avoids

defining autonomy in essentialized terms as, for example, the realization of an individual's prediscursive or innate potential, because,
in the final instance, these practices are always determined by the
social context.

Foucault's final work on the self represents a significant shift
from the theoretical concerns of his earlier work, and also seems to
overcome some of its more problematic political implications. Individuals are no longer conceived as docile bodies in the grip of an
inexorable disciplinary power, but as self-determining agents who
are capable of challenging and resisting the structures of domination
in modern society. Such a shift in emphasis also calls for a renewed
exploration of the implications of his idea of the self for feminist
theory. However, despite the fact that Foucault's work on the self
has been widely available in English translation for some time now,
it has received relatively little attention from both within and outside
feminist circles. Even very recent studies of Foucault's work concentrate in the main upon his theories of power and the body
rather than on his notion of the self. This neglect may be explained
in part by the somewhat esoteric and dry manner in which Foucault
offers up his theory of the self in a study of ancient Greek and
Roman behaviour. As a result, a large proportion of the little attention his work has received has been from scholars of antiquity who
often dispute the accuracy of Foucault's interpretation of his classical sources. It is my aim, then, to consider the implications of
Foucault's work on the self in relation to his *œuvre* as a whole and
in relation to feminist theory.

I argue that Foucault's work on the self is worth serious consideration by feminists because, on certain points, it converges in an
interesting fashion with some of the theoretical issues that are
currently dominating areas of feminist debate. For example, the
idea of a process of active self-fashioning, which lies at the heart of
Foucault's theory of practices of the self, parallels, in certain respects, recent attempts by theorists such as Teresa de Lauretis to
model the subjectivity of women in terms other than those of passive
victims of patriarchy. Similarly, Foucault's work on ethics of the
self resonates with feminist critiques of some of the essentializing
assumptions that underlie radical feminist work on 'feminine' or
'mothering' ethics.

I hope to show, on the one hand, how Foucault's work on the
self opens up areas of theoretical debate – closed off by his earlier
work on the body – for renewed consideration by feminists. On the
other hand, I show how at significant points, especially in the linking
of practices of the self to issues of gender, Foucault's work is flawed

and how feminist theory on similar issues, such as identity and autonomy, is, in some respects, more insightful. Obviously, to a certain extent, the flaws in Foucault's work can be connected to his sudden death so soon after initiating such a significant change in his intellectual interests. However, despite the unfinished nature of his final work, I show how some of its flaws are linked to Foucault's failure to resolve fully some of the more problematic theoretical elements of his earlier work, such as his undifferentiated theory of power. Thus while trying to break into new intellectual ground, the legacy of these unresolved problems hinders his last work.

Another central aim of my examination of Foucault's work is to re-assess the charge often made against him that he is an 'anti-Enlightenment' thinker. I show how Foucault's theory of practices of the self, rather than representing a rejection of Enlightenment values, represents an attempt to rework some of the Enlightenment's central categories, such as the interrelated concepts of autonomy and emancipation. This reading of Foucault's work is not, as some commentators may argue (Poster 1984; Rajchman 1985), an attempt to force his work into inappropriate categories, because Foucault himself saw his final work as running in a tradition of Enlightenment thought rather than running counter to it. By establishing such a continuity between Foucault's work and the Enlightenment, I also wish to cast doubt on a predominant trend in recent Foucault commentary which argues that his work is a paradigmatic example of 'postmodern' thought (e.g. Harstock 1990; Hekman 1990; Hoy 1988). Undoubtedly, there are elements in his work which accord with what are held to be some of the central theoretical tenets of postmodern thought, in particular Foucault's rejection of systematic forms of knowledge which rest on universal truth claims. However, I show how a close reading of Foucault's last work confounds any straightforward equation with postmodern thought by revealing the presence of themes and concepts usually associated with the thought of modernity.

My argument that Foucault can not be so easily categorized as a postmodern thinker inevitably touches on the recent debate about the possibility of formulating a postmodern feminism. To schematize, the general points of convergence being debated are, on the one hand, how the postmodern rejection of 'metanarratives' and the corresponding stress on the specific and the category of 'difference' can correct some of the essentialist and universalizing tendencies that still hamper certain types of contemporary feminism. For example, the emphasis on the constitutive powers of discourse reminds feminists that the problem of feminine identity

is better approached as an historically and culturally specific construct rather than as an innate phenomenon. Internal feminist critiques of the essentialist tendencies of some types of feminism have
been well established for some time, but there is still a need for
such forms of critique in the early 1990s. For if Michèle Barrett
(1988) is right, socialist feminism has been in decline and increasingly feminism is identified publicly with the essentialist forms of
feminism presented by writers such as Mary Daly, Adrienne Rich,
Carol Gilligan and some of the 'new French' feminists.

If postmodern thought is seen to contribute to the critique of
essentialism within feminism, then the other side of the debate is
that a feminist perpective may contribute an awareness of issues
connected to gender which, on the whole, is absent from most
postmodern thought. The postmodern preoccupation with difference either bypasses the question of sexual difference altogether
or, as Rosi Braidotti (1988) points out, renders sexual difference a
metaphor of all difference, thus turning it into a general philosophical term which bears little relation to the concrete issues of
gender or to the historical presence of real-life women.

Needless to say, within the feminist debate on postmodernism
there is no consensus of opinion. A few feminists are optimistic
about the possibility of formulating a postmodern feminism (Fraser
and Nicholson 1988; Hekman 1990). Other feminists are entirely
opposed to the possibility of a fruitful convergence between the
two strands of thought, arguing that the postmodern deconstruction
of categories such as subjectivity and agency denies women the
chance of articulating and analysing their experiences, just as they
are beginning to realize the possibility of overcoming their
marginalization (Benhabib 1990; Harstock 1990). Many feminists
adopt a line between these two positions and accept that there is
a need for feminists to develop theoretical tools able to deal with
difference in a non-essentializing way, but, at the same time, remain
sceptical about the relativist implications of a postmodern stance
on feminist politics.

My conclusions about the viability of formulating a postmodern
feminism can be related to the more general issue of the compatibility of theories of difference with the feminist interest in sexual
difference. Whilst there are undoubtedly fruitful points of convergence, I am sceptical about the necessity of having to formulate
such a variation of feminism in order for feminists to be able to
come to terms with the issue of difference. The category of difference – or the differences within sexual difference – has, for a while,
been an important topic of debate within feminism as a result of

criticisms from black and Third World feminists about the ethno-centric and middle-class nature of much feminist theory, which assumes that the struggle against gender oppression is primary regardless of the economic and political conditions under which many women live. Consequently, Western feminists have been trying to break down some of the universalizing categories they have previously employed and are attempting to develop tools capable of relating gender issues to the equally fundamental cate-gories of race and class.

Concern with the question of the primacy of sexual difference has led some feminists to postmodern theories of difference as a potential source of more sophisticated analytical tools. However, in my view these varying theories of difference are not only not coextensive, but they also conflict in several fundamental respects. Furthermore, there is a danger that many feminists, in their desire to construct a correspondence between feminist theory and post-modern theory, overlook these points of conflict. In the final analysis, I believe that feminists cannot afford to relinquish either a general theoretical perspective, or an appeal to metanarratives of justice. I contend that gender issues cannot be fully comprehended without an understanding of general social dynamics, nor can gender op-pression be overcome without some appeal to a metanarrative of justice. The adoption of such general theoretical perspectives does not necessarily preclude feminists developing a greater sensitivity to difference.

It is in this area of a potential crossover between feminism and theories of the postmodern that I hope to show how a reconsidera-tion of Foucault's work on the self by feminist theorists has much to offer. For many of the themes of recent feminist theory, espe-cially those that voice an anxiety concerning postmodernism and its apolitical nature, find parallels in Foucault's later work. Just as the presence of emancipatory themes in Foucault's work on the self hinder its categorization as postmodern, so the fundamental emancipatory aims of feminism hinder its assimilation into a post-modern variant. Ultimately – in spite of arguments against subject/object dualisms, the rational subject, etc. – feminism has never abandoned the politics of progression and personal emancipation.

My scepticism about the possibility of a feminist postmodernism arises not only from what I see as certain incompatibilities between the categories of difference and sexual difference, but also from what I perceive as the false polarization that the debate on moder-nity and postmodernity has established between theory and practice, metanarratives and action, the general and the particular. Such

false antagonisms obscure the fact that it is not only possible to
articulate a greater sensitivity to difference within a general
theoretical perspective, but also that the establishment of certain
collective aims and norms is necessary to ensure an atmosphere
of tolerance and equality in which differences can be expressed.
By abandoning any normative perspective, it is not clear how a
postmodern position of *laissez-faire* could ensure against an environment of hostility and predatory self-interest in which the more
powerful repress the less privileged. I believe that if, in the future,
feminists are to deal more adequately with the question of difference, it is necessary for them to look beyond the artificial polarities
of the modern/postmodern debate and explore ways in which
theory can be made compatible with the local.

Despite a shared unease about aspects of postmodern thought,
especially concerning the subject and subjectivity, certain theoretical problems with Foucault's work on the self prevent too close
a convergence with the feminist project. My main criticism of
Foucault's final work is that there is an unresolved tension between his commitment to emancipatory social change and his refusal to outline the normative assumptions upon which such change
should be based. Like other postmodern theorists, Foucault is reluctant to establish normative guidelines for his ethics of the self
because he believes that the laying down of norms inevitably has
a normalizing effect on the individual's freedom to act. However,
in the final two chapters, partly through a comparison with the
work of Habermas, I show how Foucault wrongly confuses the
establishment of basic norms, which serve as a safeguard against
the abuse of power and the domination of weaker individuals,
with the imposition of inappropriate political demands and aims
on individuals. Whilst the latter is to be avoided, the former is
necessary if ethics of the self is not to retreat into a form of unregu-
lated introversion. On the one hand, the idea of practices of the self
is informed by a strong political commitment and Foucault clearly
intends what he sees as the autonomous practices of individuals
to feed into some wider process of social transformation. It is this
belief in the potential of independent critical thought and action to
lead to social transformation that links Foucault's work to a tradition
of Enlightenment thought. Yet, on the other hand, by failing to
establish any basic normative guidelines or collective aims for
practices of the self, it is unclear how the self can be called out of
the self on to a plane of generality where it is reminded of its
responsibilities to other individuals in society.

Despite the limitations of Foucault's theory of the self, it nevertheless represents an important contribution to social theory. For as Anthony Giddens (1979) has pointed out, within social theory there is a marked skewing to the structure side of the agency/structure duality. Of particular significance is the fact that Foucault elaborates his theory of the self without recourse to psychoanalytic theory. At the most fundamental level, most psychoanalytic models posit a basic sense of self which is constituted at an early age and continues into adult life cutting across divisions of race, class and ethnicity. Against this invariant notion of identity, Foucault's account of the self emphasises the variety of ways in which identities are constituted. Given the enormous influence of Lacan's rereading of Freud upon the work of feminist and other theorists in France, this resistance to psychoanalysis makes Foucault's work even more interesting. On the whole, however, I deliberately avoid a comparison of Foucault's work on the self with psychoanalytic accounts of identity, mainly for reasons of space but also because there is extensive discussion of such issues elsewhere (for example, Braidotti 1991; Forrester 1980).

This book is divided into five chapters. Each chapter deals with a theme which has figured significantly in recent feminist theory. The first chapter focuses on feminist discussions of the 'body' and relates these to Foucault's earlier theory of the relation between the body and power. On the one hand, I argue that Foucault's account of the body as a radically contingent entity helps to overcome tendencies to essentialism and biologism which have hampered feminist definitions of the body. On the other hand, however, I argue that Foucault does not devote enough attention to the overdetermining effects of gender upon the body. Another more serious problem with Foucault's account is that he tends to understand individuals solely as bodies and he, therefore, excludes a consideration of other aspects to the experiences of individuals in modern society. Such a one-sided emphasis conflicts with the feminist project of rediscovering and revaluing the experiences of women. In the second chapter, I consider the extent to which the idea of practices of the self overcomes some of the problems with Foucault's earlier notion of individuals as 'docile bodies'. I focus on the notions of power and autonomy and link this to parallel developments within feminist theory to avoid positing women as innocent victims of systems of oppression.

Having introduced the notion of practices of the self, the following three chapters centre on a detailed examination of some of the theoretical implications of this theory. In the third chapter, I compare Foucault's idea that practices of the self can translate into a modern ethics with recent feminist theories of 'feminine' or 'mothering' ethics. Whereas some theories of feminine ethics tend to reify the categories of masculinity and femininity, I argue that Foucault's theory of ethics presents feminists with the challenge of thinking through the differences within sexual difference. In the fourth chapter, I examine some of the ambiguous normative implications of Foucault's theory of the self and I link these ambiguities to his ambivalent relationship with Enlightenment thought. I continue this line of enquiry in the final chapter in relation to Foucault's one-sided emphasis on the self which leads to a conception of the individual as an isolated entity, rather than explaining how the self is constructed in the context of social interaction.

By exploring a specific set of theoretical issues in Foucault's work from a feminist perspective, I aim to make the general point that the feminist concern for sexual difference should not be elided as closely as it has been with the poststructural emphasis on difference. However, although the critical approach I adopt is one that tends to focus on points of tension and conflict, this is not meant to be a purely negative assessment. Indeed, I believe that the uncovering of tension and conflict is healthy in that it prevents closure, sustains reflexivity and continually pushes the debate between feminist and poststructuralist theory on to new and challenging ground.

1

Power, Body and Experience

INTRODUCTION

In this chapter, I intend to explore the significance of Foucault's theory of the body for feminist critique. There are two strands to my argument. On the one hand, I show how Foucault's theory of power and the body indicates to feminists a way of placing a notion of the body at the centre of explanations of women's oppression that does not fall back into essentialism or biologism. In this respect, Foucault's work has been the main impetus behind many interesting and original studies into the regulatory mechanisms which circumscribe the sexualized body. Yet, on the other hand, I hope to show that if feminists are to make use of Foucault's account of the body there are several theoretical problems which need to be overcome.

One such problem is that, in his elaboration of the body, Foucault neglects to examine the gendered character of many disciplinary techniques. This is a problem that has been widely noted by feminists; for example, Rosi Braidotti claims that 'Foucault never locates woman's body as the site of one of the most operational internal divisions in our society, and consequently also one of the most persistent forms of exclusion. Sexual difference simply does not play a role in the Foucauldian universe, where the technology of subjectivity refers to a desexualized and general "human" subject' (Braidotti 1991: 87). For many feminists, Foucault's indifference to sexual difference, albeit unintended, reproduces a sexism endemic in supposedly gender-neutral social theory. Silence – no matter how diplomatic or tactical – on the specificity of sexual difference does not distinguish Foucault's thought significantly from the gender blindness and biased conceptual habits of more traditional theoretical discourses. As Schor puts it: 'What is to say that the discourse of sexual indifference/pure difference is not the last or, (less triumphantly) the latest ruse of phallocentrism?' (Schor 1987: 109).

Having considered the status of the gendered body in Foucault's work, I go on to argue that a more serious problem with Foucault's notion of the body is that it is conceived essentially as a passive entity, upon which power stamps its own images. Such a conception of the body results in a problematic one-dimensional account of identity. In respect to the issue of gendered identity, this unidirectional and monolithic model of power's operations on the body leads to an oversimplified notion of gender as an imposed effect rather than as a dynamic process. In terms of identity in general, the reduction of individuals to passive bodies permits no explanation of how individuals may act in an autonomous and creative fashion despite overarching social constraints. For feminists – and, indeed, social theorists in general – this is a particular problem given that a significant aim of the feminist project is the rediscovery and revaluation of the experiences of women.

GENEALOGY, THE BODY AND THE CRITIQUE OF THE SUBJECT

The idea of the body is a concept central not only to the work of Michel Foucault, but to much of what is categorized as poststructuralist thought. The reason for the predominance of the idea of the body is that it is one of the central tools through which poststructuralists launch their attack on classical thought and its linchpin the rational subject or cogito. To schematize, the poststructuralist argument holds that the notion of a rational, self-reflective subject, which has dominated Western thought since the Enlightenment, is based on the displacement and/or derogation of its 'other'. Thus the notion of rationality is privileged over the emotions, spirituality over the material, the objective over the subjective. One dualism of central importance to classical thought is the Cartesian opposition between mind and body. This dualism privileges an abstract, pre-discursive subject at the centre of thought and, accordingly, derogates the body as the site of all that is understood to be opposed to the spirit and rational thought, such as the emotions, passions, needs. By prioritizing the first term in the series of dualisms, classical thought thus controls the parameters of what constitutes knowledge and monitors the extent and kind of discourses that are allowed to circulate.

It is the opposition between mind and body which, of all the dualisms, has become the focus of the deconstructive manoeuvres of the poststructuralists and the pivotal point of their attack on classical systems of thought and the philosophy of the subject. In regard to this opposition, a main concern has been to unpack the concept of the stable and unified subject by demonstrating how the ideas of rationality and self-reflection, which underlie it, are based on the exclusion and repression of the bodily realm and all that which, by analogy, it is held to represent – desire, materiality, emotion, need and so on. The category of the body, then, has a tactical value in so far as it is used to counter the 'ideophilia' of humanist culture. As Nancy Fraser puts it: 'The rhetoric of bodies and pleasures . . . can be said to be useful for exposing and opposing, in highly dramatic fashion, the undue privilege modern western culture has accorded subjectivity, sublimation, ideality and the like' (Fraser 1989: 62).

Foucault first employs a notion of the body in the essay 'Nietzsche, Genealogy, History', where he attacks traditional forms of history which he regards as being dominated by certain metaphysical concepts and totalizing assumptions derived from a philosophy of the subject. Firstly, he argues that traditional or 'total' history is a 'transcendental teleology'; events are inserted in universal explanatory schemas and linear structures and, thereby, given a false unity. The interpretation of events according to a unifying totality deprives them of the impact of their own singularity and immediacy: 'The world we know is not this ultimately simple configuration where events are reduced to accentuate their essential traits, their final meaning, or their initial and final value. On the contrary, it is a profusion of entangled events' (Foucault 1984e: 89). Secondly, Foucault sees traditional history as falsely celebrating great moments and situating the self-reflective subject at the centre of the movement of history. Privileging of the individual actor places an emphasis on what are considered to be immutable elements of human nature and history is implicitly conceived in terms of a macroconsciousness. Historical development is interpreted as the unfolding and affirmation of essential human characteristics (Foucault 1984e: 85). Following on from this, history comes to operate around a logic of identity which is to say that the past is interpreted in a way that confirms rather than disrupts the beliefs and convictions of the present. The disparate events of the past are filtered through the categories of the present to produce 'a history that always encourages subjective recognitions and attributes a form of reconciliation to all the displacements of the past' (Foucault 1984e: 86).

Finally, traditional forms of historical analysis seek to document a point of origin as the source of emanation of a specific historical process or sequence. Foucault attacks the search for origins as an epistemologically problematic quest for ahistorical and asocial essences. The search for the origin of a particular historical phenomenon implicitly posits some form of original identity prior to the flux and movement of history. In turn, this original identity is interpreted as an indication of a primordial truth which precedes and remains unchanged by history or 'the external world of accident and succession' (Foucault 1984e: 78–9). For Foucault, however, 'what is found at the historical beginning of things is not the inviolable identity of their origin; it is the dissension of other things. It is disparity' (Foucault 1984e: 79). Thus, if the origin of the concept of liberty is analysed, we find that it is an 'invention of the ruling classes' and not a quality 'fundamental to man's nature or at the root of his attachment to being and truth' (Foucault 1984e: 78–9).

Against what are seen as traditional types of history, Foucault poses the notion, derived from Nietzsche, of 'effective' history or genealogy. Adopting Nietzsche's conception of the primacy of force over meaning, Foucault opposes 'the hazardous play of dominations' and 'the exteriority of accidents' to the conception of an immanent direction to history. History is not the continuous development and working through of an ideal schema, rather it is based on a constant struggle between different power blocks which attempt to impose their own system of domination. These different systems of domination are always in the process of being displaced, overthrown, superseded. The task of the historian is to uncover the contingent and violent emergence of these regimes in order to shatter their aura of legitimacy. The structuring of social relations is perceived in terms of warfare (Foucault 1980: 90–1, 114). 'Humanity does not gradually progress from combat to combat until it arrives at universal reciprocity, where the rule of law finally replaces warfare; humanity installs each of its violences in a system of rules and thus proceeds from domination to domination' (Foucault 1984e: 85).

The representation of history as a series of discontinuous structures is directed against the philosophy of history and, in particular, the Marxist aim of comprehending the totality of past and present from the standpoint of a future yet to be realized. An understanding of history as a series of struggles between different forces is also directed against the dialectical idea of the self-reflective subject as the pivot of historical development. Rather than seeing history as a process of reconciliation of the contradictions between subject and object via the human actor's interaction with and reflection upon the world, Foucault views the forces in history acting upon and through the human body in a manner which resists incorporation into a totalizing historical perspective. The replacement of the self-thematizing subject as the pivot of history with a notion of the body results in a change in the historian's methodology. Historical development is no longer hermeneutically interpreted in terms of the meanings it reveals but is understood as a conflict between different power blocks, i.e. permanent warfare. As the centre of the struggle for domination, the body is both shaped and reshaped by the different warring forces acting upon it. The body, then, is conceived of in radically anti-essentialist terms; 'Nothing in man – not even his body – is sufficiently stable to serve as a basis for self recognition or for understanding other men' (Foucault 1984e: 87–8). The body bears the marks, 'stigmata of past experience' upon its surface;

> The body is the inscribed surface of events (traced by language and dissolved by ideas), the locus of a dissociated self (adopting the illusion of a substantial unity), and a volume in perpetual disintegration. Genealogy as an analysis of descent, is thus situated within the articulation of the body and history. Its task is to expose a body totally imprinted by history and the processes of history's destruction of the body (*Foucault 1984e: 83*).

Effective history takes the examination of the body as its starting point and thus analyses the effects of power in their most specific and concrete form. Correlative to this attention paid to the power relations inscribed on the body, the genealogist focuses on events in their singularity. The genealogist tries to rediscover the multiplicity of factors and processes which constitute an event in order to disrupt the self-evident quality ascribed to events through the employment of historical constants and the ascription of anthropological traits. The aim of effective history is not to systematize but to disperse and fragment the past; 'History becomes effective to the degree that it introduces discontinuity into our very being – as it divides our emotions, dramatizes our instincts, multiplies our body and sets it against itself' (Foucault 1984e: 88).

It is this idea, that the body and the way it is worked upon by power is the proper focus of history, that is the underlying principle of Foucault's two later studies, *Discipline and Punish* and *The History of Sexuality*. Foucault replaces a method based on the hermeneutic elucidation of contexts of meaning, and a correlative anthropological stress on the subject as the mainspring of history, with an examination of the way in which the body is arbitrarily and violently constructed in order to legitimize different regimes of domination.

FEMINISM AND THE BODY

It is Foucault's notion of the body as the point where power relations are manifest in their most concrete form which, in the last few years, has made a significant contribution to feminist thinking on the body. Of all poststructuralist work on this theme, Foucault's has received probably the most attention because of his insistence on the body as an historical and culturally specific entity (Bartkowski 1988). This insistence on the body as an historically specific entity distinguishes Foucault's theory from those of other theorists, such as Derrida, where the body is a metaphorization of the more general philosophical problem of difference. For feminists, this stress on specificity is important because, as Rosi Braidotti has argued, the representation of the more general philosophical issue of difference in the metaphor of the feminine body allows poststructuralist thinkers to bypass altogether the question of sexual difference as it relates to the experiences of women:

> The notion of 'sexual difference' has been subjected to such inflationary value that it has led to a paradoxical new uniformity of thought. 'Postmodern' ... 'deconstructive' ... and other kinds of philosophers have first of all sexualised as 'feminine' the question of difference and secondly have turned it into a generalised philosophical item. As such it is clearly connected to the critique of classical dualism ... Yet it is not directly related to either the discursivity or the historical presence of real-life women (*Braidotti 1989: 89*).

A similar criticism of the poststructuralist tendency to metaphorize the feminine has been made by Alice Jardine in *Gynesis* (1985). The displacement of classical modes of thought based on dualism and the consequent dislocation of the subject has led post-structuralists to posit a space of unrepresentability or difference – or hetereogeneity, the body, madness, the unconscious, etc. – that new modes of thinking, writing and speaking should try to trace. This space of 'otherness' and instability where identity is unfixed is, according to Jardine, generally feminized. However, this putting into discourse of 'woman' – 'woman in effect' as Jardine calls it – is problematic for feminists. Firstly, it is not clear to what extent the supposedly radical equation of woman with that which cannot be contained within discourse is very different from traditional stereotypes of woman as unknowable and unrepresentable. Secondly, it is difficult for feminists to make the links between this metaphorized idea of woman and the experiences of women as active subjects; indeed, the idea of woman-in-effect may negate the experiences of 'real' women altogether.

One of the most important contributions that Foucault's theory of the body has made to feminist thought is a way of conceiving of the body as a concrete phenomenon without eliding its materiality with a fixed biological or prediscursive essence. The problem of conceptualizing the sexualized body without positing an original sexual difference is one that has preoccupied feminist theorists. On a fundamental level, a notion of the body is central to the feminist analysis of the oppression of women because it is upon the biological difference between the male and female bodies that the edifice of gender inequality is built and legitimized. The idea that women are inferior to men is naturalized and, thus, legitimized by reference to biology. This is achieved through a twofold movement in which, firstly, women's bodies are marked as inferior by being compared with men's bodies, according to male standards (*homme manqué*) and, secondly, biological functions are conflated with social characteristics. In many respects, masculine characteristics can be seen to be related to dominant perceptions of the male body, i.e. firmness, aggression, strength. However, man, unlike woman, is understood as being able to transcend being defined in terms of his biological capacities via the use of his rational faculties. In contrast, women, as de Beauvoir notes, are entirely defined in terms of their physical capacities:

> When woman is given over to man as his property, he demands that she represents the flesh purely for its own sake. Her body is not perceived as the radiation of a subjective personality, but as a thing sunk in its own immanence; it is not for such a body to have reference to the rest of the world (*de Beauvoir 1972: 189*).

This derogation of the female body through comparison with the male body, and the consequent definition of femininity through reference to biological capacities, leads to a series of different strategies of corporeal oppression: the restriction of sexuality within the framework imposed by the opposition of masculinity and femininity, the subjection of women in confinement to medical power, the contemptuousness of menstruation, the construction of female sexuality as 'lack' or frigidity, etc.

THE PROBLEM OF ESSENTIALISM

Although a notion of the body is central to a feminist understanding of the oppression of women, it needs to be thought through carefully if what is regarded as patriarchal logic – the definition of the social category of woman in terms of biological functions – is to be subverted and not compounded. This conflation of the social existence of women with their biological functions is a problematic tendency of some types of feminism, most notably radical feminism and some of the 'new French' feminisms. The theoretical difficulties inherent in these approaches have been widely commented on and need only be considered briefly here (see Butler 1990a; Plaza 1978; Soper 1989 and 1990). The work of the French feminist Annie Leclerc exemplifies the problems inherent in such an approach to the body. Leclerc argues that women must reappropriate their bodies from patriarchal forms of control and, thereby, learn to revalue them outside of the framework of male norms and standards. By recovering a positive image of their biological selves, women will find fulfilment in what Leclerc regards as their 'innate' caring and nurturing functions:

Washing dishes, peeling vegetables, cleaning clothes, ironing . . . Menial, gloomy, thankless, futile, degrading work? . . . A varied, multiple occupation, work that can be done while singing or day dreaming, work which, like all happy tasks, is obviously meaningful, work where one produces with one's own hands all that life requires . . . How can work that produces immediate results, results which are carried forward in the very task itself, be thankless? The house takes on a festive air, the meal smells good, the child burbles contentedly while showing off its silky little bottom, and an hour's dreamy efforts grant the trousers another year's wear (*Leclerc 1987: 75–6*).

Whilst most feminists would agree that there is a need to re-value women's physical way of being in the world, in particular the task of reproduction, the shortcomings of Leclerc's approach are clear. Her notion of femininity is based on a sentimentalized image of motherhood which comes close to reinforcing patriarchal conceptions of gender difference. Moreover, the elevation of the maternal function as the essence of femininity excludes many women, who are not mothers, from the category of 'true woman-hood'. As Soper trenchantly observes about this extreme difference feminism: 'it is particularly offensive and arrogant – to the point in fact of operating a kind of theft of subjectivity or betrayal of all those who fail to recognize themselves in the mirror it offers' (Soper 1990: 15).

An appeal to difference, which is based in an essentialism of the female physique, reinforces traditional notions of a male/female divide and 'leaves woman once again reduced to her body . . . rather than figuring as a culturally shaped, culturally complex, evolving, rational, engaged and noisy opposition' (Soper 1990: 13). Because the category of the 'natural sexed body' only makes sense in terms of a binary discourse on sex, in which men and women exhaust the possibilities of sex and relate to each other as complementary opposites, the category of sex is always subsumed under a discourse of heterosexuality. Christine Delphy makes a similar point in her attack on Leclerc in *Parole de Femme*. Delphy argues that Leclerc confuses biological males and females with the social categories of men and women. This derivation of absolute psychological differences from the fact of physical distinction leads to a hypo-statization of the categories of masculine and feminine. It also results in a reductionist account of the human subject whose functioning is explained by reference 'to a few cells' (Delphy 1987: 89).

To compound this, Leclerc overlooks the complex nature of the oppression of women by reducing it to a simple case of misrecognition. If the caring and nurturing qualities of women were valued more highly by both men and women then, she argues, the oppression of women would disappear. As Delphy notes, Leclerc's explanation is idealist in that it bypasses an examination of the concrete mechanisms of oppression altogether and inverts cause and effect through the argument that devaluation leads to exploitation rather than the other way round. The caring and nurturing aspects of women's work are undervalued not simply because of ideological misrecognition but, according to Delphy, because the domestic realm is a major site of the exploitation of women's labour. By neglecting to analyse the specificities of women's subordination,

Leclerc produces a biologically reductionist and romanticized vision of liberation that is centred around the freeing of women's
bodily functions, which are held to define entirely women's capacities as social actors. As Delphy observes, Leclerc finishes by
reinscribing dominant and oppressive ideologies of femininity in a
new 'feminist' context.

It must be noted briefly here that Leclerc's brand of essentialist
feminism is not necessarily representative of the work of the other
'new French' feminists. In particular, there has recently been some
debate about the essentialist nature of the category of the 'body'
in the work of Luce Irigaray. Some feminists argue that Irigaray's
'rewriting' of the female body is both a parody and displacement
of patriarchal strategies which have defined and controlled the
female body. Irigaray's redefinition of the feminine does not represent, therefore, a simplistic retreat to a natural female body, but
rather it indicates a way in which women may block the patriarchal logic that invariably constructs the feminine body in negative
terms and thereby women may come to control the discourse of
biology for their own strategic ends. In short, for some feminists
Irigaray's articulation of a female sexuality through a notion of the
biological body is purely strategic rather than essentialist (see Fuss
1989: 55–72; Gatens 1991: 100–21).

This reassessment of the work of Irigaray often goes along with
a more general questioning, amongst feminists and other theorists,
of the term essentialism. Essentialism, it is argued, is not necessarily
as reactionary a position as is often assumed. Thus, Rosi Braidotti
argues that nowadays a feminist who is interested in sexual difference 'cannot afford not to be essentialist' (Braidotti 1989: 93).
Similarly, in a reading of Irigaray, Paul Smith holds up her essentialism as an exemplary 'moment of contestation' and goes on
to conclude that 'the charge of essentialism . . . does not necessarily
or always amount to the damning criticism it is supposed to be.
Within the logic of feminism's still evolving constitution essentialist
claims are perhaps becoming more and more important' (Smith
1988: 144). Following on from Smith, Fuss argues that the process
of laying claim to an essence is not necessarily a reactionary political
manoeuvre. Since, in traditional Western metaphysics, woman has
no essence, the act of describing a feminine bodily essence undoes
'Western phallomorphism' and offers 'women entry into subjecthood' (Fuss 1989: 71).

Nevertheless, despite these renewed debates over the interpretation of the bodily essentialism in French feminism in particular
and the status of the concept of essentialism in general, feminists

– in my view – are still justified in their suspicion of essentialist approaches to the feminine body. An interesting approach to the question of essentialism has been suggested by Diana Fuss who argues that rather than labelling a text as essentialist and therefore bad, feminists should ask instead if a text is essentialist, what motivates its deployment, how and why is it invoked and, most importantly, what are its political effects (Fuss 1989: xi). It is this question of the political effects of essentialist feminisms that brings us to the heart of the resistance from socialist feminists and others to them. For despite the greater sophistication of Irigaray's rewriting of the body over Leclerc's, both lead ultimately to a feminist politics that remains within the realm of the aesthetic and psychosexual. As Butler points out, many women simply do not identify with a notion of femininity based on an aestheticized and non-phallic version of the body and hence, rather problematically, risk being written off as 'male-identified' or 'unenlightened' (Butler 1990a: 30). Furthermore, many feminists believe that such a narrowly aesthetic feminist politics that constantly takes women back to their bodies does not adequately address the social oppression of women and associated issues of power, history and politics. As Ann Jones puts it, 'Feminists may still doubt the efficacy of privileging changes in subjectivity over changes in economic and political systems; is this not dangling a semiotic carrot in front of a mare still harnessed into phallocentric social practices?' (Jones 1985: 107).

OVERCOMING ESSENTIALISM

Although the oppression of women is based on the appropriation of their bodies by patriarchy, it does not follow, therefore, that oppression derives from the body or sex, or that the notion of a natural sexual difference can be used to explain gender inequalities. Rather, the 'natural' body must be understood as a device central to the legitimation of certain strategies of oppression. As Monique Plaza puts it, 'If the category of sex has such an important position in patriarchal logic, this is not because sex gives its shape to the social; it is because the social is able to make sexual forms seem obvious and thereby hide oppressive systems' (Plaza 1978: 9). If one is to avoid positing an original sexual difference, which is represented *a posteriori* in social practices and, thereby, reduces the social to an effect of biological impulses, then it is necessary to recognize that diverse sexual differences are overdetermined in order to produce a systematic effect of sexual division. It is not necessary to posit a single bodily cause of feminine subordination. Once the female sex has come to connote specific feminine characteristics, this 'imaginary signification' produces concrete effects throughout diverse social practices. These concrete effects are not the expression of an immutable feminine essence. However, they react, in turn, by contributing to the maintenance and reproduction of this symbolism and, thus, perpetuate the myth of immutable feminine qualities (see Laclau and Mouffe 1985: 118).

An example of such a concrete effect arising from an ideology of femininity is given by Michèle Barrett. Barrett argues that the 'imaginary signification' of femininity is often in contradiction with the actual economic organization of the household. Thus, although a woman may contribute significantly to a household's economy, the ideology of female dependence within the context of the nuclear family is powerful enough to alter perceptions of the woman's contribution. (Barrett 1980: 214–15). It is possible, therefore, as Laclau and Mouffe argue, to 'criticise the idea of an original antagonism between men and women, constitutive of the sexual division, without denying that, in the various forms of construction of 'femininity', there is a common element which has strong overdetermining effects in terms of sexual division' (Laclau and Mouffe 1985: 118).

The sex/gender distinction represents an attempt by feminists to bypass some of the theoretical problems which arise from grounding a theory of gender inequality in an original sexual difference. If gender is the cultural meanings that the sexed body assumes, then a gender cannot be said to derive from the natural body in any one way: 'gender is neither the causal result of sex nor as seemingly fixed as sex' (Butler 1990a: 6). However, as Barrett points out, whilst the sex/gender distinction has been successful in bypassing the notion that one's biological makeup is one's social destiny, the social constructionist approach it leads to remains caught within a problematic opposition between the body understood as a biological category and gender as a social one (Barrett 1988: xxiv–xxvi). By privileging the gender side of this equation, the body is in effect neutralized and denied any salience whatsoever. Taken to its logical limit, the distinction between sex and gender suggests a radical discontinuity between sexed bodies and culturally constructed genders. Gender becomes a free-floating entity with the consequence that 'man and masculine might as easily signify a female body as a male, and women and feminine a male body as easily as a female one' (Butler 1990a: 6; see also Gatens 1991). Such a deconstruction of the polarized terms into which sexuality is forced – what Kristeva calls the 'demassification of difference' – may be the ultimate aim of some forms of feminism. However, in our present society, femininity invariably connotes the female body and, in order to reveal the differences within monolithic sexual differences, it is necessary for feminists to analyse the processes through which the female body is transformed into a feminine one. In other words, the female body and the feminine gender are not radically discontinuous as the sex/gender distinction implies.

The limits of purely sociological approaches to gender have been noted by feminists adopting a psychoanalytical perspective who argue that, by bypassing the corporeal reality of the body, the associated issues of desire and psychic impulses are not adequately tackled. Whilst accepting the materialist critique of psychoanalysis, that it tends to lack socio-historical specificity, Jacqueline Rose (1986) claims that what materialist accounts themselves lack is a way to explain the failure or instability of identity. Psychoanalysis achieves this through the category of the unconscious. Materialist approaches, however, regard the assumption of sexual identity in behaviourist terms as the relatively unproblematic internalization of social norms. Rose argues that it is this idea of the failure of identity as a norm of individual development which forges a link between psychoanalysis and feminism in that it is shown that women do not easily assume their subordinate feminine role: 'psychoanalysis becomes one of the few places in our culture where it is recognized as more than a fact of individual pathology that most women do not easily slip into their roles as women, if indeed they do at all' (J. Rose 1986: 91).

There is not space to consider psychoanalytic approaches to the body and identity in detail here. However, the psychoanalytic criticism of the sociological approach to gender indicates that, whilst it is necessary to avoid conceiving of the body in essentialist terms, corporeal reality cannot remain entirely untheorized. Like Rose, Rosi Braidotti and Parveen Adams are amongst those who have argued that the treatment of femininity and the body in terms of the internalization of social norms results in an impoverished account of sexual identity (see Adams 1989; Braidotti 1989). According to Braidotti, the idea of motherhood offers an accurate way of assessing 'the progress accomplished by feminist thought on biology and the female body' (Braidotti 1989: 96). Whereas in earlier forms of feminist thought, motherhood had to be rejected in so far as 'compulsory heterosexuality' had made made it the social destiny of all women,[1] nowadays, feminists regard it as both one of the main supports of patriarchal domination and also one of the strongholds of feminine identity. This understanding of motherhood illustrates an alternative feminist approach to the body which is understood as lying at the threshold of subjectivity but not in terms of a fixed biological essence, nor as the result of social conditioning:

> The 'body' is rather to be thought of as the point of intersection, as the interface between the biological and the social, that is to say between the socio-political field of the microphysics of power and the subjective dimension ... This vision implies that the subject is subjected to her/his unconscious; the driving notion of 'desire' is precisely that which relays the self to the many 'others' that constitute her/his 'external' reality (*Braidotti 1989: 97*).

By introducing such a notion of the 'libidinal' body into an account of identity, feminists seek to show how the sexualization of the female body is fundamental to the way in which women are socialized as individuals. The libidinal body is used to install a theory of desire and ambivalence into an understanding of how identity is constructed. The internalization of representations of the female body by women is fundamental to the formation of feminine identity, but this process must not be understood as being straightforward and unproblematic. It is by mapping the way in which the body circumscribes subjectivity that feminists can begin to describe how gender is constitutive of identity but, at the same time, never determines it completely.

IDEOLOGY AND DISCOURSE

The problems encountered in elaborating a theory of the body beyond the sex/gender distinction are paralled by problems that feminists have found with orthodox Marxist approaches to women's oppression in terms of the dualism of ideology/material base. Feminist dissatisfaction with orthodox Marxism is well documented and need only be elaborated briefly here (see Sargent 1981). To schematize, feminists argue that classical Marxism marginalizes women in two ways. Firstly, by privileging the labour/capital distinction, it renders women peripheral unless they are engaged in productive wage labour. Secondly, by emphasizing the primacy of economic determination, women's oppression is reduced to an ideological effect. The treatment of issues related to gender as sec-

ondary to class relations is regarded as inadequate by feminists for
dealing with the complex and deep-rooted nature of women's
interior position within society. The simple observation that there
are transhistorical similarities to some of the strategies of patriarchal oppression problematizes the Marxist argument that with
the abolition of the capitalist mode of production the 'ideology' of
women's secondary status will evaporate. The problem still remains,
however, of defining sexuality if it is not purely an ideological
effect (gender), nor a reflection of an original sexual difference
(natural sex).

Given this dilemma, the appeal of Foucault's theory of the body
for feminists is that it is formulated around a notion of discursive
practice rather than around an ideology/material distinction.
Foucault rejects theories of ideology primarily because they always
imply a pre-existent truth situated elsewhere which can be discerned
with the demystification of a given ideological fiction. Foucault
rejects the distinction between science and ideology and, therefore,
the idea that there are discernible, objective truths. For Foucault,
all science has an ideological function. The production of knowledge is always bound up with historically specific regimes of power
and, therefore, every society produces its own truths which have
a normalizing and regulatory function. It is not surprising then
that political economy 'has a role in capitalist society, that it serves
the interests of the bourgeois class, that it was made by and for
that class, and that it bears the mark of its origins even in its concepts
and logical architecture' (Foucault 1972: 185). By establishing a
connection between science and ideology, Foucault brackets the
whole question of validity and truth. Rather, it is the task of the
genealogist to discover how these discourses of truth operate in
relation to the dominant power structures of a given society. As
Foucault puts it, 'the problem does not consist in drawing the line
between that in a discourse which falls under the category of scienti-
ficity or truth, and that which comes under some other category,
but in seeing historically how effects of truth are produced within
discourses which in themselves are neither true nor false' (Foucault
1980: 118).

Related to his criticism of the assumed primacy of truth over
ideology, Foucault also refuses theories of ideology because they
always stand in a secondary relation to some prior determining
material realm. For Foucault, as for many social theorists, the reduction of cultural phenomena to secondary or derivative effects
of a primary economic realm is untenable (Foucault 1980: 118).

In place of a theory of ideology, Foucault substitutes a notion of discourse or discursive formation. This concept first appears in an early work, *The Archaeology of Knowledge*. The aim of Foucault's method of archaeology – the predecessor to geneaology – was to show the limits of the legitimacy of knowledge by demonstrating that all systems of knowledge were in fact statements or discursive events. In turn, these events or statements make up part of a discursive formation which has its own autonomous and deep-seated linguistic rules of formation. For Foucault, knowledge is not constituted by the human subject; instead he regards knowledge as an effect of a primarily linguistic discursive formation, i.e. a set of fundamental rules that define the discursive space in which speaking subjects exist.

> I have tried . . . to show that in a discourse . . . there were rules of formation for objects (which are not the rules of utilization for words), rules of formation for concepts (which are not the laws of syntax), rules of formation for theories (which are neither deductive nor rhetorical rules). These are the rules put into operation through a discursive practice at a given moment that explain why a certain thing is seen (or omitted); why it is envisaged under such an aspect and analyzed at such a level; why such a word is employed with such a meaning and in such a sentence (*Foucault 1989: 52*).

Thus, Foucault proposes that in all the human sciences there must be quasi-structuralist rules of formation which, unknown to the actors involved, regulate and determine the spectrum of speech acts which can be taken seriously at any given historical moment (see Foucault 1972: 76; see also Dreyfus and Rabinow 1982: 102).

Foucault's theory of the discursive formation which forms the unspoken background to all systems of knowledge is complicated and beyond the scope of this book (see Gutting 1989). Futhermore, in his later work Foucault rejected the degree of autonomy accorded to discourse by the archaeological method. Despite this, in *The Archaeology of Knowledge* Foucault first raises a notion that is to become more prominent in his subsequent work: the relation between discursive and non-discursive factors. This is to say that Foucault argues that the deep-seated discursive formations which determine the production of knowledge in a given period are intimately bound up with non-discursive factors defined as 'an institutional field, a set of events, practices, and political decisions, a sequence of economic processes that also involve demographic fluctuations, techniques of public assistance, manpower needs, different levels of unemployment, etc.' (Foucault 1972: 157). However, *The Archaeology of Knowledge* gives an idiosyncratic inflection to this relation between the discursive and the non-discursive by maintaining the priority of discourse through the argument that socio-historical factors are ordered around the episteme rather than vice-versa (Foucault 1972: 168).

However, with the subsequent shift from the archaeological to the genealogical method, Foucault comes to refute the autonomy of discourse, and non-discursive practices are understood as the elements which truly sustain and surround discursive ones. This is not to say that Foucault reverses the priority and falls back into a crude material determinism. Rather, the discursive and the material are linked together in a symbiotic relationship. Foucault's most well-known formulation of this symbiosis is the power/knowledge nexus. On the one hand, all knowledge is the effect of a specific regime of power and on the other hand, forms of knowledge constitute the social reality which they describe and analyse: 'power and knowledge directly imply one another; . . . there is no power relation without the correlative constitution of a field of knowledge, nor any knowledge that does not presuppose and constitute at the same time power relations' (Foucault 1977a: 27). The effects of the power/knowledge complex are relayed through different discourses: 'it is in discourse that power and knowledge are joined together' (Foucault 1978a: 100). Thus, discourse or a particular discursive formation is to be understood as an amalgam of material practices and forms of knowledge linked together in a non-contingent relation.

It is by linking the material and non-material together in a theory of discourse that Foucault hopes to bypass some of the problems which he sees as intrinsic to a theory of ideology. With respect to the problem of determinism, there is no prior determining moment in the theory of discourse because the effects of knowledge and power have a mutually determining and productive role (Foucault 1978a: 94–5). With respect to the problem of truth, discursive analysis does not seek to pierce a mystificatory realm of ideas in order to uncover an objective truth, rather discursive analysis seeks to examine the particular way power/knowledge complexes operate at a micro-social level in order to produce regimes of truth. Foucault's treatment of the issues of truth and validity will be dealt with in more detail in the final two chapters. Here, it must be noted that there is much debate about whether the notion of discourse does in fact succeed in bypassing some of the theoretical difficulties associated with the concept of ideology. Michèle Barrett argues that

the idea of discursive practices simply couches old debates about
the autonomy and materiality of ideology in new terms. Hence the
problems are simply deferred rather than solved: 'they have shifted
the discourse of ideology on to the terrain of the discourse of
discourse and while in their terms this may be as real an advance
as any other, to the critic of discursive imperialism it may seem a
nominal rather than a conceptual gain' (Barrett 1980: 88).

Setting aside this interesting debate, however, it remains that it
is precisely because Foucault has replaced a theory of ideology
with the more material and concrete notion of discourse that
feminists have been attracted to his idea of the body. For, as we
have seen, it is the body that is the principal target of the power/
knowledge relations transmitted through discourse. From this perspective, the question of sexuality cannot be addressed in terms of
an ideology of gender nor in terms of the colonization of the body's
natural forces. Rather, the question of sexuality and the body must
be looked at in terms of how the body is invested with certain
properties and inserted into regimes of truth via the operations of
power and knowledge. As Foucault puts it:

> To analyse the political investment of the body and the micro-
> physics of power presupposes, therefore, that one abandons –
> where power is concerned – the violence-ideology opposition,
> the metaphor of property, the model of the contract or of
> conquest . . . One would be concerned with the 'body politic', as
> a set of material elements and techniques that serve as weapons,
> relays, communication routes and supports for the power and
> knowledge relations that invest human bodies and subjugate them
> by turning them into objects of knowledge' (*Foucault 1977a: 28*).

THE FOUCAULDIAN BODY AND FEMINIST CRITIQUE

Following from his definition of discourse as an amalgam of the
material (power) and non-material (knowledge), Foucault presents,
in *The History of Sexuality*, a theory of the body and sexuality which
is both radically anti-essentialist but, at the same time, does not
deny the materiality of the body. Foucault begins by contesting the
conception of sex as a radically unconstructed or natural phenomenon. He argues that, rather than being the natural origin of desires, sex is in fact a cultural construct that is produced with the
aim of social regulation and the control of sexuality:

We must not make the mistake of thinking that sex is an autonomous agency which secondarily produces manifold effects of
sexuality over the entire length of its surface of contact with
power. On the contrary, sex is the most speculative, most ideal
and most internal element in a deployment of sexuality organized by power in its grip on bodies and their materiality, their
forces, energies, sensations, and pleasures' (*Foucault 1978a: 155*).

The construct of 'natural sex' performs a certain number of regulatory functions: firstly, it makes it possible to group together in
an 'artificial unity' a number of disparate and unrelated biological
functions and bodily pleasures; secondly, by unifying these disparate pleasures, it bolsters a regulatory notion of a 'natural' heterosexuality; finally, the notion of sex inverts the representation of
the relationship of power to sexuality, so that, rather than seeing
sexuality as a phenomenon produced and constructed through
the exercise of power relations, it is seen as an unruly force which
power can only attempt to repress and control:

> The notion of sex brought about a fundamental reversal; it made
> it possible to invert the representation of the relationships of
> power to sexuality, causing the latter to appear, not in its essential
> and positive relation to power, but as being rooted in a specific
> and irreducible urgency which power tries as best it can to domin-
> ate (*Foucault 1978a: 155*).

The inversion of the causal relation between sex and power blocks
any inquiry into the historical construction of sexuality which is
collapsed back into a manifestation of a natural sex. Furthermore,
the notion that power merely controls or represses an 'unruly'
sexuality – what Foucault calls the juridical representation of power
(Foucault 1978a: 88–91) – disguises the true 'productive' nature of
power. Power and sexuality are not ontologically distinct, rather
sexuality is the result of a productive 'biopower' which focuses on
human bodies, inciting and extorting various effects: 'We have not
only witnessed a visible explosion of unorthodox sexualities; but –
and this is the important point – a deployment quite different from
the law, even if it is locally dependent on procedures of prohibition, has ensured, through a network of interconnecting mechanisms, the proliferation of specific pleasures and the multiplication
of disparate sexualities' (Foucault 1978a: 49).

Foucault's radical idea of sex as a regulatory construct disrupts
binary distinctions between the natural and the cultural contained

in the sex/gender distinction. Gender is not to be conceived merely as the cultural inscription of meaning on a pregiven sex, but rather gender must also designate the apparatus of production whereby the sexes are themselves established. As Judith Butler puts it, 'gender is not to culture as sex is to nature; gender is also the discursive/ cultural means by which "sexed nature" or "a natural sex" is produced and established as "prediscursive", prior to culture' (Butler 1990a: 7). Foucault does not want to deny the material reality of anatomically discrete bodies, indeed, against the speculative nature of sex, he insists on the corporeal reality of bodies:

> the purpose of the present study is in fact to show how deployments of power are directly connected to the body – to bodies, functions, physiological processes, sensations, and pleasures; far from the body having to be effaced, what is needed is to make it visible through an analysis in which the biological and the historical are not consecutive to one another . . . but are bound together in an increasingly complex fashion in accordance with the development of the modern technologies of power that take life as their objective' (*Foucault 1978a: 151–2*).

However, what Foucault's model suggests is that it is impossible to know the materiality of the body outside of its cultural significations. The psychic impulses and drives of the body may form the threshold of sexual identity, but these drives are not pre-social, rather they are always already produced within the signifying network of gender. Since the body cannot be known in its unadorned essence, sexual liberation cannot be for Foucault sexuality without power relations: 'Where there is desire, the power relation is already present: an illusion, then, to denounce this relation for a repression exerted after the event; but vanity as well, to go questing after a desire that is beyond the reach of power' (Foucault 1978a: 81–2). Rather, sexual liberation consists in unhitching the notion of sexuality from the juridical fiction of a natural, heterosexual sex. Once we accept that desire and power are indissolubly linked, that sexuality gains its shape from historically specific power relations, then we can begin to imagine new forms of desire which are not hampered by the myth of a state of powerlessness. A political genealogy exposes the contingent and socially determined nature of sexuality and, thereby, frees the body from the regulatory fiction of heterosexuality and opens up new realms in which bodily pleasures can be explored: 'The rallying point for the counterattack against the deployment of sexuality ought not to be sex-desire, but bodies and pleasures' (Foucault 1978a: 157).

Foucault's theory of the body, which attempts to develop a notion of corporeal reality whilst not falling back into essentialist assumptions, has had a significant influence on feminist work upon the body. The significance of the Foucauldian body for feminism has been widely enough documented to consider it only briefly here.[2] Following Foucault's point that the sexual body is both the principal instrument and effect of modern disciplinary power, feminists have shown how the various strategies of oppression around the female body – from ideological representations of femininity to concrete procedures of confinement and bodily control – were central to the maintenance of hierarchical social relations. Although the female body is not a main focus of attention in *The History of Sexuality*, Foucault outlines briefly how, in the nineteenth century, the female body was controlled through a process of hysterization. By representing the female body as saturated with sex and inherently pathological, a certain knowledge was established which allowed for the regulation of desire and sexual relations with the ultimate aim of discipline and control of family populations. The female body is placed 'in organic communication with the social body (whose regulated fecundity it was supposed to ensure), the family space (of which it had to be a substantial and functional element), and the life of children' (Foucault 1978a: 104).

Feminist and other historical studies of the medical, psychiatric and educational institutions since the nineteenth century have developed Foucault's idea of the hysterization of the female body further (e.g. Beechy and Donald 1985). Lucy Bland (1981), for example, has argued that it is not simply that there was a proliferation of discourses around the female body, but that, at the same time, there were various splittings or differentiations produced in relation to women. These discourses are related in part to pre-existing, ancient beliefs about the nature of female sexuality, but they also brought into play a new relation between the female body and medical discourses. Women's sexuality became the object of hygienization, of the splitting of cleanliness and pleasure. Sexual pleasure in women was seen as perverse and, correspondingly, good women were not passionate and had no sexual desires. The good woman was fulfilled through her reproductive capacities and through the nurturing of children. Thus, Bland argues, it is not so much that a woman's body was 'saturated with sexuality' as Foucault claims, but that her body was suffused 'with the wild workings of her reproductive system rather than with wild sexual desire' (Bland 1981: 58–9).

Foucault's insight that sexuality is produced in the body in such a manner as to facilitate the regulation of social relations has not only provided the impetus for feminist studies into the relation between the female body and dominant conceptions of femininity. It also presents the potential for similar studies in relation to the question of masculinity and the male body. Recently, feminists have recognized that if the polarization of sexual difference in the categories of masculinity and femininity is to be broken down, it is necessary to examine the construction of male, as well as female, sexuality. As Helene Cixous says in *Laugh of the Medusa*, 'men still have everything to tell us about their sexuality' (quoted in Bartkowski 1988: 52). Bob Connell has done some work in this area, showing how the construction of masculinity is based, in a large part, on the physical sense of maleness and on the ordering of men's bodies in space (Connell 1983). Taking up Foucault's idea that, far from constituting the most intimate truth about oneself, the sexuality of the individual is in fact an instrument of social regulation, Jeffrey Weeks has shown how gay sexuality disrupts the distinction between public and private which structures modern understandings of sexuality. Public displays of gayness and the gay body, which are often central to gay and lesbian culture, cut across distinctions between home, family and work, and upset the conventional idea that sexuality belongs only to the most private and intimate of these spheres (Weeks 1985: 223). Although Foucault is not concerned explicitly with studying how dominant masculine characteristics, such as rationality, self-control and aggression, are specific effects of the disciplining of the male body, his study nevertheless suggests a potential way of analysing masculinity as a social and historical construct; for example, the analysis of contemporary masculinity in terms of the way it is still marked by its militaristic and disciplinary inheritance.

THE PROBLEM OF GENDER BLINDNESS

Whilst Foucault's work on the body has contributed significantly to feminist theories of the body and sexual identity, it must be recognized that the trade off has not been simply one way. Feminists have also drawn attention to certain inadequacies in Foucault's treatment of gender issues. One important criticism has been that Foucault's analysis does not pay enough attention to the gendered nature of disciplinary techniques on the body and that this over-

sight perpetuates a 'gender blindness' that has always predomin-
ated in social theory.

In her article on disciplinary power and the female subject, Sandra
Lee Bartky (1988) argues that Foucault's treatment of the body as
an undifferentiated or neutral gender is inadequate because it fails
to explain how men and women relate differently to the institutions
of modern life. If, as Foucault claims, there is no such thing as a
'natural' body and it is, therefore, impossible to posit a pre-given
natural sex difference, then he needs to elaborate on how the
systematic effect of sexual division is perpetuated by the techniques
of gender that are applied to the body. By analysing various
practices and discourses aimed specifically at women and the
different aspects of the 'feminine' body image, Bartky shows how
the female body is ordered and controlled within what she calls a
'disciplinary regime of femininity'. Bartky follows a well-known
criticism of the concept of disciplinary power; that it is generalized
from an analysis of the practices of 'total' institutions – the prison,
asylum, etc. – to other social institutions which do not operate in
such a closed way (see Giddens 1984: 153–4). Accordingly, Bartky
argues that the discipline of the feminine body is hard to locate in
so far as it is 'institutionally unbound'. This absence of a formal
institutional structure creates the impression that the assumption
of femininity by female subjects is either natural or voluntary:

> Feminine bodily discipline has this dual character: on the one
> hand, no one is marched off for electrolysis at gunpoint, nor
> can we fail to appreciate the initiative and ingenuity displayed
> by countless women in an attempt to master the rituals of
> beauty. Nevertheless, in so far as the disciplinary practices of
> femininity produce a 'subjected and practiced', an inferiorised,
> body, they must be understood as aspects of a far larger disci-
> pline, an oppressive and inegalitarian system of sexual sub-
> ordination. This system aims at turning women into the docile
> and compliant companions of men just as surely as the army
> aims to turn its raw recruits into soldiers (*Bartky 1988: 75*).

Bartky is undoubtedly right to criticize Foucault for neglecting
to consider in what distinct ways disciplinary techniques operate
on the female body inscribing physical effects, such as restricted
and hesitant body movement and posture, that compound the
secondary position or object status that dominant conceptions of
femininity ascribe to women. For Foucault, the female body seems
to possess no specificity apart from the male norm. Ultimately,

Bartky argues that this silence on the question of the production of female bodies reproduces, regardless of authorial intention, a sexism endemic in supposedly gender-neutral social theory. Foucault is 'blind to those disciplines that produce a modality of embodiment that is peculiarly feminine. To overlook the forms of subjection that engender the feminine body is to perpetuate the silence and powerlessness of those upon whom these disciplines have been imposed' (Bartky 1988: 64).

Other feminists have made similar criticisms about the gender blindness of Foucault's work. Patricia O'Brien claims that the problem with Foucault's analysis of prison regimes in *Discipline and Punish*, is that he does not consider how the treatment of male and female prisoners differed and how these differences related to dominant constructions of masculinity and femininity. For Foucault, the prisoner's body, indeed the disciplined body in general, is often implicitly assumed to be male. O'Brien acknowledges that, in certain respects, there was a close congruence in age, social background and occupation between prisoners of different sexes. Women were in prison mostly for the same categories of crime as men – the predominant category being thieving. However, in other respects O'Brien shows that there were substantial differences in the social perceptions of male and female criminality. Female criminality was perceived solely through the grid of what was regarded as the inferior biological makeup of women. It was explicitly linked to what were understood as fundamental traits of the feminine physiology – delicacy, nervousness, susceptibility. O'Brien shows how diverse categories of crime were labelled as 'menstrual psychoses'. Suicides and homocides amongst women were seen as 'organic maladies of the uterus' (O'Brien 1982: 68). Informing these attitudes towards the female criminal was an understanding of female sexuality as inherently pathological and regressive. As O'Brien puts it: 'The argument at its most extreme was that all menstruating, lactating, ovulating, pregnant, newly delivered, newly sexually initiated and menopausal women were prone to crime. Most women, therefore, could become criminally deviant during any portion of their adult lives' (O'Brien 1982: 68).

The female criminal, then, was at the end of the spectrum of an inherently regressive, biologically limited female sexuality. This widespread notion that women were not greatly influenced by socialization but were biologically determined, meant that female criminals were perceived as less receptive to rehabilitation than male criminals whose crimes were perceived, in stark contrast, in terms of social rather than natural deviance (O'Brien 1982: 69). To a large extent, penal institutions were seen as being absolved of any useful role in the rehabilitation of women.

O'Brien's account of the fundamental differences in the social perceptions of female and male criminality reinforces Foucault's identification of the process of hysterization of the female body as a dominant form of social control in the nineteenth century. However, in *The History of Sexuality*, where it is introduced, this concept remains unelaborated and no attempt is made in *Discipline and Punish* to explore how the regulation of the body of the female prisoner intersects with conceptions of female sexuality dominant in other realms. To put it another way, it is necessary to explore how meanings, particularly representations of gender, are mobilized within the operations of power to produce asymmetrical relations amongst subjects. In the analysis of institutional regimes, such as the prison, it is important to show how and why women do not relate to these institutions in the same way as men.

Along with the prison, Foucault also identifies military training as one of the principal sites from which arose techniques for regulating the body, not by external threat or coercion, but by acquired, internalized modes of operation:

> Politics, as a technique of internal peace and order, sought to implement the mechanism of the perfect army, of the disciplined mass, of the docile, useful troop, of the regiment in camp and in the field ... The classical age saw the birth of ... meticulous military and political tactics by which the control of bodies and individual forces was exercised within states (*Foucault 1977a: 168*).

Here too, Foucault's historical analysis does not account for the different ways the female body may be positioned in relation to the generalization of a military technology of the body, to a wider form of social control. With regard to dominant conceptions of masculinity, there is a continuity, on many levels, between the notion of the soldier and that of the citizen/worker. As Nancy Fraser (1987) points out, the concept of citizenship encompasses a strong soldiering aspect, the idea of the citizen as the defender of the polity and protector of those – women, children, the elderly – who allegedly cannot protect themselves. In terms of Foucault's schema, this soldiering aspect of citizenship can be interpreted as a residual trace of the military origins of disciplinary power which invests the male body as a productive and obedient citizen/worker. The soldiering element in citizenship is an indication of how the role is implicitly masculine and it also means that women can occupy the role of citizen only with some conceptual uneasiness; 'this division between male protectors and female protected intro- duces further dissonance into woman's relation to citizenship' (Fraser 1987: 44).

Whilst it is undoubtedly right to criticize Foucault for failing to pursue the implications of his theory of the body and power in relation to the issue of sexual difference, there are, however, theo- retical problems arising from too great an insistence on the specificity of female bodies. There is a danger that, by placing too much emphasis on the different strategies by which women's bodies are disciplined, one ends by positing a separate history of repres- sion for women, thereby, perpetuating an artificial polarization between the experiences of men and women. As a consequence, women are placed outside, or in a position of innocence, *vis-à-vis* the male-defined social realm. For example, at various points in her article, Bartky seems to make the problematic assumption that women are simply passive victims of systems of patriarchal domi- nation. She argues that the disciplinary techniques which invade the female body are 'total', 'perpetual' and 'exhaustive'. At times, women have offered resistance to this system of domination, but resistance has always failed and this very failure further strength- ens the inexorable hold of disciplinary techniques upon the body: 'As women (albeit a small minority of women) begin to realise an unprecedented political, economic, and sexual self-determination, they fall ever more completely under the dominating gaze of pa- triarchy' (Bartky 1988: 82–3). The implicit assumption Bartky makes is that under the 'ensemble of systematically duplicitous practices' which control the female body, there is a 'true' female body, unde- termined by social constraints, that has yet to be expressed. Added to the well-documented difficulties of a notion of liberation de- fined in terms of an 'extra' social essence, Bartky reduces the com- plex ways in which feminine identity has been and is constructed in social relations to a long history of repression in which women have always masochistically complied. Consequently, this reduces the historically realized experiences and desires of women to a case of false consciousness or misrecognition.

An analysis of disciplinary techniques must undoubtedly take account of the distinct ways that the female body is operated upon, but care must be taken not to elide this distinction into an absolute separation or polarization. The development of the female body does not constitute a separate history of an unchanging, constant repression. Rather, just like the category of 'woman' in which it is caught up, the female body is socially and discursively constructed and, therefore, an historically variable construct. It follows from this that the history of the female body is not completely separate from that of the male body. Whilst the body is worked upon by gender constructions, it is also inscribed by other formations: class, race, the system of commodity fetishism. These formations may, to varying degrees, be internally gendered but they also work across gender distinctions, breaking down the absolute polarity between the male and the female body. Thus, to use an obvious example, conceptions of the black body cut across and problematize in a fundamental manner any homogeneous category of woman's body. Similarly, in *Distinction*, Pierre Bourdieu illustrates how the marks of class are inscribed upon the body in a manner as fundamental as those of gender (Bourdieu 1984: 169–225). Thus, in many respects, the female body is worked upon and inscribed by the same institutional mechanisms that inscribe the male body. The sexed body is caught up with the different ways in which the body, as a general category, is conceived in relation to concepts such as the unconscious, society, the person, etc. As Denise Riley puts it:

> If it's taken for granted that the category of women simply refers, over time, to a rather different content, a sort of Women Through the Ages approach, then the full historicity of what is at stake becomes lost. We would miss seeing the alterations in what 'women' are posed against, as well as established by – Nature, Class, Reason, Humanity and other concepts – which by no means form a passive backdrop to changing conceptions of gender (*Riley 1988: 7*).

This is not to deny the differences in the way in which the male and female bodies are constructed, but rather to accept that female bodies are worked upon in socially and historically specific ways, rather than in terms of an eternal, undifferentiated opposition between the sexes. To borrow Winship's terms, the history of the female body is simultaneously included and set apart in the history of the male body (see Winship 1978). As Denise Riley explains, it is necessary to abandon 'the ambition to retrieve women's bodies from their immersions beneath "male categories, values and norms". The body circulates inexorably among the other categories which sometimes arrange it in sexed ranks, sometimes not. For the concept "women's bodies" is opaque, and like "women" it is always in some juxtaposition to "human" and to "men"' (Riley 1988: 107). An analysis of the female body needs to examine, therefore, not just the disciplinary techniques exclusive to the female body – for

example, Foucault's idea of hysterization – but also needs to show
how the history of the female body is caught up with the history
of the male body and how, in turn, both are related to changes
within the social realm. This may seem an obvious point, but some
feminists give the impression that women's history constitutes a
catalogue of separate experiences of oppression which have little
connection to other changes occurring within society (see Riley
1988: 1–17).

Ultimately, then, whilst criticisms about a certain level of gender
insensitivity in Foucault's work are correct, they draw attention to
lacunae rather than major theoretical difficulties with his theory of
the body. Furthermore, these lacunae have, to a large extent, been
filled by subsequent feminist studies of the 'feminine' body which
have employed a Foucauldian approach. I believe, however, that
there are more serious problems, connected to the monolithic,
unidirectional notion of power with which Foucault works and which
has problematic implications for an understanding of the relation
between the body and gender identity. This criticism of the one-
dimensional nature of Foucault's theory of power has been made by
some social theorists (Habermas 1987 and G. Rose 1984) but has not
been developed much by feminists in relation to the question of
gender. These issues will be considered in the following sections.

POWER AND RESISTANCE

In an earlier section, it was established that one of the most innovative aspects of Foucault's theory of power was the insistence
on power as a productive and positive force, rather than as a purely
negative, repressive entity (see Foucault 1978a: 88–98). In relation
to the body, power does not simply repress its unruly forces, rather
it incites, instills and produces effects in the body. There is, therefore, no such thing as the 'natural' or 'pre-social' body; it is impossible to know the body outside of the meaning of its cultural
significations. Such a conception of power problematizes over-
simplified notions of the 'feminine' body – used by both traditionalists and some radical feminists – which tend to equate the
biological capacities of women with their social capabilities.

However, despite Foucault's theoretical assertion that power is
a diffuse, heterogeneous and productive phenomenon, his historical analyses tend to depict power as a centralized, monolithic force
with an inexorable and repressive grip on its subjects. This negative definition of power arises, in part, from the fact that Foucault's

examination of power is one-sided; power relations are only examined from the perspective of how they are installed in institutions and they are not considered from the point of view of those subject to power. Peter Dews has pointed out that Foucault's analysis of the disciplinary techniques within the penal system is skewed towards the official representatives of the institutions – the governors, the architects, etc. – and not towards the voices and bodies of those being controlled. Failure to take into account any 'other' knowledges – such as a prison subculture or customs inherited from the past – which those in control may have encountered and come into conflict with means that Foucault significantly overestimates the effectivity of disciplinary forms of control (see Dews 1987: 188 and CCCS 1981: 15–16).

In reply to this charge of limiting his view of disciplinary power to its 'official' representations, Foucault could refer to his idea of resistance which he sees arising at the points where power relations are at their most rigid and intense. The category of resistance is closely linked, therefore, to the idea of power as productive. For Foucault, repression and resistance are not ontologically distinct, rather repression produces its own resistance: 'there are no relations of power without resistances; the latter are all the more real and effective because they are formed right at the point where relations of power are exercised' (Foucault 1980: 142). In this way, Foucault gets round the problematic tendency to posit resistance as an 'extra-social' force.

From this understanding of resistance, it follows that the sexed body is to be understood not only as the primary target of the techniques of disciplinary power, but also as the point where these techniques are resisted and thwarted. The sexed body may have been 'driven out of hiding and constrained to lead a discursive existence' (Foucault 1978a: 33), but at the same time, 'discourse transmits and produces power; it reinforces it, but also undermines and exposes it, renders it fragile and makes it possible to thwart it' (Foucault 1978a: 101). Thus, on the one hand, the 'perverse implantation' of the nineteenth century – the massive proliferation of discourses on 'deviant' sexualities – served to reinforce social controls in the area of 'perversity' and to legitimate a notion of 'normal' heterosexuality. Yet on the other hand, this very multiplication of controlling discourses created a counter-vocabulary or 'reverse discourse' which could be used by those labelled deviant to establish their own identity and to demand certain rights: 'homosexuality began to speak in its own behalf, to demand that its legitimacy or "naturality" be acknowledged, often in the same vocabulary, using the same categories by which it was medically disqualified' (Foucault 1978a: 101).

Yet despite Foucault's assertions about the nature of resistance, on the whole, this idea remains theoretically undeveloped and, in practice, Foucault's historical studies give the impression that the body presents no material resistance to the operations of power. In *The History of Sexuality*, bodies are 'saturated' with disciplinary techniques, sex is 'administered' by a controlling power that 'wrapped the sexual body in its embrace'. Individuals live 'under the spell' of telling the truth about sex, they cannot resist the 'imperious compulsion' to confess: 'We have . . . become a singularly confessing society . . . One confesses – or is forced to confess . . . The obligation to confess is now relayed through so many different points, is so deeply ingrained in us, that we no longer perceive it as the effect of a power that constrains us' (Foucault 1978a: 59–60). Despite his assertions to the contrary, Foucault in fact produces a vision of power as a unidirectional, dominatory force which individuals are unable to resist. This tendency of Foucault to elide power with domination is apparent in *Discipline and Punish*, where Foucault sees disciplinary methods as producing 'subjected and practised bodies, "docile bodies"' (Foucault 1977a: 138).

Without elaborating how resistance to the insidious workings of modern 'biopower' may be developed from the libidinal forces of the body, the body is, in effect, deprived of any salience or oppositional force. In this respect, there is a tension in Foucault's work between his explicit statements about not wishing to deny the materiality of the body and his failure to show in what way such a materiality manifests itself. The result of this annulment of the materiality of the body is that power 'loses all explanatory content and becomes a ubiquitous metaphysical principle' because it has nothing determinate against which it operates (Dews 1987: 166). For the concept of power to have some critical force, it is necessary to produce a counterfactual which would show how a situation would change if an operation of power were cancelled or resisted. Although the body is the principal site of the operations of power, it poses no such resistance and power becomes a unidirectional monolithic force.

INDIVIDUALS AS DOCILE BODIES

A consequence of Foucault's definition of power exclusively in terms of its disciplinary effects on passive bodies is that other aspects of individuals' existence are effaced. This is to say that Foucault tends to understand subjects as 'docile' bodies, rather than as individuals or persons. However, some critics have rightly argued that the construction of the subject cannot simply be explained through reference to bodily experiences, but must be understood as a complex and often contradictory amalgam of legal, social and psychological constructs (see G. Rose 1984). Foucault emphasizes too heavily the effects of a corporeally-centred disciplinary power at the expense of considering how other forms of power – such as legal definitions of the person – contribute to the construction of the modern individual. As a result, Foucault simplifies the process through which hegemonic social relations are maintained and also effaces the different types of experiences of individuals in modern society. Thus, as we have seen, Foucault argues that the female body was subjected in the nineteenth century to a process of hysterization. By representing the female body as 'thoroughly saturated with sexuality' and inherently pathological, a certain knowledge was established which allowed the regulation of desire and sexual relations with the ultimate aim of discipline and control of family populations.

Although, during the nineteenth century, there was undoubtedly an intensified feminization of the female body, the implication of Foucault's monolithic conception of power and passive account of the body is that the experiences of women were completely circumscribed by this notion of a pathological and hysterical feminine sexuality. What Foucault's account of power does not explain is how, even within the intensified process of the hysterization of female bodies, women did not slip easily and passively into socially prescribed feminine roles. Foucauldian 'biopower' provides no understanding of how the presence of power dynamics within sexuality cannot be equated with 'a simple consolidation or augmentation of a heterosexist or phallogocentric power regime' (Butler 1990a: 31). Although the unity of gender is the effect of a regulatory practice that seeks to render gender identity uniform through a compulsory heterosexuality, this effect of unity is never fully installed. The rigid dualism of masculine/feminine is constantly being disrupted and undermined by gender discontinuities that run through the heterosexual, gay and bisexual communities in which gender does not necessarily follow from sex. For example, the presence of heterosexual conventions within homosexual contexts, such as the ideas of butch and femme sexual styles, cannot be explained as 'chimerical representations of original heterosexual identities. And neither can they be understood as the pernicious insistence of heterosexual constructs within gay sexuality and identity ... The replication of heterosexual constructs in non-heterosexual frames brings into relief the utterly constructed status of the so-called heterosexual original' (Butler 1990a: 31).

THE EXCLUSION OF EXPERIENCE

For feminists, Foucault's emphasis on the body, at the expense of a more rounded notion of individuality, is particularly difficult given the stress that is placed on the re-discovery and revalorization of women's experiences. Thus, without wanting to underestimate the effects of the apparatus of regulatory practices brought to bear on women in the nineteenth century, feminist historians have attempted to show how, within the oppressive constraints that operate around ideas of femininity, there are contradictions and instabilities which, at times, have provided women with a base from which to undermine the very system which constricts them. As Ellen Willis comments:

> Power is not a monolithic system but a system of overlapping contradictions. Women have always struggled against their situation both individually and collectively. They have seized on contradictions in the system – demanding, for example, that the concept of human rights be applied to women – thereby using the discontinuities in the system to mobilise for their own power (*Willis 1988: 118*).

An example of this reassessment of women's historical experiences is Caroll Smith-Rosenberg's study of the power that Victorian expectations of chastity gave women to attack the hypocrisies they saw in their society. The New York Female Moral Reform Society was a group, set up by Christian women in the mid-nineteenth century, whose aims were to tackle the problem of urban prostitution, to close the city's brothels and to confront the double standard and the male sexual licence it condoned. In one respect, these bourgeois women and their campaign can be considered as highly orthodox, conforming to roles of female behaviour prescribed by the two dominant male ideologies of evangelical Protestantism and the Cult of True Womanhood (Smith-Rosenberg 1986: 40). However, there was an ambivalence about the reforming zeal of these women which dislocated the stereotype of devout, obedient and modest femininity. This ambivalence arises from the way in which these women represented the problem of urban prostitution. The situation was construed purely in matriarchal terms; mothers must rescue their fallen daughters from an unbounded and destructive male lust. This representation of the problem of prostitution ran counter to the dominant Victorian view where prostitutes were regarded as fallen women and a threat to social stability. By renaming prostitutes as daughters and victims of a system which legitimized exploitative male desire, the women of the Reform Society were usurping a male perogative of naming and defining a social problem. Furthermore, by challenging the male double standard, women assumed what were regarded as the more material attributes and powers of men. The Society argued that organization, knowledge and determination should replace feminine dependence, docility and silence (Smith-Rosenberg 1986: 45). This aggressive championing of the rights of other women by women over men had the effect of subverting the distinction between public and private and its implied opposition of male and female. The Society's women saw that in order to defend what they called 'True Womanhood', the 'pious woman' had to assert her right to act and to extend her domestic power to public realms. As Rosenberg points out, when the Society's members spoke about 'True Womanhood' this was not a rationalization of a male-constructed class system, but rather a condemnation of that system.

Undoubtedly, Foucault's analysis of the disciplined body provides some important insights into the way in which individuals are controlled in modern society. However, Foucault slips too easily from describing disciplinary power as a *tendency* within modern forms of social control, to positing disciplinary power as a monolithic and inexorable force which saturates all social relations. This is clearly an over-statement of the efficacy of disciplinary power. It also leads to an impoverished understanding of the individual which cannot encompass experiences, such as those related above, which fall outside the realm of the 'docile' body.

RIGHTS

The reduction of individuals to docile bodies not only offers an inadequate account of many women's experiences, but also leads to an underestimation of the significance of the freedoms that women have won in modern society. Modern social relations cannot simply be explained as a manifestation of an all-encompassing 'biopower', but must be understood as the result of an amalgam of different types of power. The lack of differentiation in Foucault's account of power – his failure to conceive of power in any other way than as a constraining form of corporeal control – presents serious limitations in so far as many aspects of experience in modern life remain unexplained. Thus, for example, the development of the prison regime is not considered in relation to legal power and its definitions of the rights of the individual. As Habermas puts in:

> As soon as Foucault takes up the threads of the biopolitical establishment of disciplinary power, he lets drop the threads of the legal organisation of the exercise of power and of the legitimation of the order of domination. Because of this, the ungrounded impression arises that the bourgeois constitutional state is a dysfunctional relic from the period of absolutism' (*Habermas 1987: 290*).

By positing biopower as the fundamental constitutive principle of the social realm, the history of law, the history of knowledge, the history of all social institutions are reduced to simple effects of an all-pervasive biopower (see G. Rose 1984). Thus, in *The History of Sexuality*, Foucault argues that biopower displaces other forms of power, in particular the law, by subsuming it into its own administrative, regulatory functions:

> I do not mean to say that . . . the institutions of justice tend to disappear, but rather that the law operates more and more as a norm, and that the judicial institution is increasingly incorporated into a continuum of apparatuses (medical, administrative, and so on) whose functions are for the most part regulatory. A normalizing society is the historical outcome of a technology of power centred on life. We have entered a phase of juridical regression (*Foucault 1978a: 144*).

There is no theoretical space in Foucault's model for reversing this causal chain and examining the way in which the law may structure and regulate the exercise of power within both penal institutions and society in general. As a result, Foucault underestimates the different types of freedom, legal and otherwise, that have been achieved in modern society. The complicated dialectic characteristic of modern society – that the very means through which (legal) freedom is established are often the means through which freedom is put in jeopardy – is not considered (see Habermas 1987: 291). Legal, social and psychological freedoms are understood, in a one-dimensional fashion, as effects of a ubiquitous form of social control. Whilst not underestimating the discrepancy that often exists between formal and substantive rights, many freedoms have often derived from changes within the law, the most obvious example being the granting of female suffrage. Other legally established rights, such as the possibility for a woman to have an abortion, cannot be dismissed simply as another example of control over the body; rather, it has given women significantly more freedom in the control of their lives.

The extent to which Foucault underestimates the potential of the law to protect as well as limit the freedom of individuals is most clearly illustrated in the notorious stand that he took on the issue of rape in a debate on the reform of criminal law in France. Foucault argued that rape should be decriminalized and treated as an act of violence, like other acts of aggression, rather than as a sexual act. As de Lauretis explains, the logic behind Foucault's stance represents an effort to counter the technology of sex by breaking the link between sexuality and crime. By enfranchising sexual behaviour from legal punishment, the sexual sphere would be freed from intervention by the state (de Lauretis 1987: 36–7). However, what Foucault fails to see is that such a decriminalization of rape would further legitimize the sexual oppression of women in so far as it overlooks that the violence in rape is fundamentally derived from the asymmetrical construction of sexual relations in modern society. As Monique Plaza puts it in a response to Foucault's position: 'rape is sexual essentially because it rests on the very sexual difference between the sexes ... It is social sexing which is latent in rape. If men rape women, it is precisely because they are women in a social sense' (Plaza 1980: 31).

The debate on rape illustrates how Foucault fails to appreciate that, although the law may be far from perfect on this issue, the vulnerability of women in respect to sexual crime is at least recognized and some form of legal redress is offered. In a similar fashion, Foucault underestimates the significance of the psychological freedoms gained by women this century. So as we have seen, in *The History of Sexuality* Foucault argues that since the nineteenth century, the body has been increasingly subjected to surveillance and discursively invested with neurosis; a self-regulating compulsion to confess is thereby produced in the subject. Psychoanalysis is one of the main practices through which the urge to confess is

instilled and through which the production of self-policing individuals is ensured (see Foucault 1978a: 129–31). This account of
the regulatory role of psychoanalysis is, however, tendentious in
its simplification, particularly in regard to those women who have
benefited from a greater understanding of their sexuality and desires. Undoubtedly, the practice of psychoanalysis, in which the
practice of confession is enshrined, is overlaid with oppressive
power relations. However, much psychoanalytic work has meant a
gain in freedom and expressive possibilities for women in regard
to their sexuality: 'In the not too distant past there were commands
of chastity for women, a production of female frigidity, a double
standard for men, the stigmatising of deviant sexual behaviour, as
well as all the kinds of degradation of love life about which Freud
heard in his treatment room' (C. Honegger, quoted in Habermas
1987: 292). By depicting the development of modern power as an
increasingly insidious form of domination and by obscuring any
lifeworld context which may organize and regulate the exercise of
power, Foucault retroactively effaces the specific nature of female
subordination and overestimates the normalizing effects of disciplinary power in industrial society.

CONCLUDING REMARKS

There is no doubt that Foucault's theory of the body has made a
stimulating contribution to feminist analysis of the subordination
of women. Whilst feminists recognize that an idea of the body is
central to explanations of women's oppression, there are theoretical difficulties connected to defining the body. Foucault's thesis
that power relations are constitutive of the social realm, and that
they operate principally through the human body, provides a way
for feminists to show how the construction of gender inequality
from anatomical difference is central to the creation and maintenance of social hierarchies. Genealogical analysis of how different
discursive practices shape the body circumvents the need to posit
an original sexual difference which is represented *a posteriori* in social
practices.

Yet despite the potential of Foucault's theory of the body for
feminist critique, I have also argued that it is limited in crucial
respects. Feminist awareness of these limitations has tended to focus
on the lack of attention given to the gendered character of the
disciplined body. Foucault's failure, albeit unintentional, to con-

sider issues of gender results in the perpetuation of a 'gender blindness' which predominates in the very forms of orthodox social theory which he claims to attack. Whilst the criticism of gender blindness is not without force, I have argued that it is not necessarily the most serious limitation of Foucault's theory of the body. Rather, following criticisms of Foucault's undifferentiated and unidirectional account of power, I argue that a more serious flaw is the definition of individuals as 'docile' bodies which cannot explain many of the experiences of women in modern society and results in an impoverished and over-stable account of the formation of gender identity. The paradox that Foucault's work presents for feminists is that, by placing so much emphasis on the body as an historically specific entity, he finishes by bypassing any notion of individuality and experience. Thus, whereas feminists have recognized the need to show that women are more than passive victims of domination through the rediscovery and revaluation of their experiences and history, Foucault's understanding of individuals as docile bodies has the effect of pushing women back into this position of passivity and silence.

2

From the Body to the Self

THE RETURN OF THE SUBJECT

It is in the two subsequent volumes of *The History of Sexuality* – published just before his death in 1984 – that Foucault initiated a change in theoretical focus from the body to the self. The emergence of a notion of the self into Foucault's work has been interpreted by some critics as representing an abrupt turn-around in his intellectual project. It is argued that the introduction of an idea of the self represents a tacit admission by Foucault that his previous work, which so systematically attacked and undermined the notion of the subject, had been along the wrong lines and had run itself into a theoretical dead end (see O'Farrell 1989). Thus, Luc Ferry and Alain Renaut argue that the 'retraction of his later years' is entirely inconsistent with Foucault's previous work and, as a result, 'profoundly problematical' (Ferry and Renaut 1990: 107–21). Undoubtedly, towards the end of his life Foucault became aware of the limitations of his earlier work and, as a result, developed the idea of practices of the self. However, practices of the self must be understood as a modification of Foucault's previous intellectual concerns rather than as a refutation of them. Indeed, many of his earlier lines of thought clearly inform his new idea.

The notion of techniques of the self derives from a self-critique conducted by Foucault on his earlier account of the links between power and the body. Like many of his critics, Foucault acknowledges that, in his previous work, the emphasis he placed on the effects of power upon the body resulted in an understanding of social agents as passive bodies and in a monolithic and functionalist account of power. In retrospect, Foucault argues that in order to reach an adequate understanding of the modern subject, an analysis of techniques of domination must be counterbalanced with an analysis of techniques of the self:

> If one wants to analyse the genealogy of subject in Western civilization, one has to take into account not only techniques of domination, but also techniques of self. One has to show the interaction between these two types of the self. When I was studying asylums, prisons and so on, I perhaps insisted too much on the techniques of domination. What we call discipline is something really important in this kind of institution. But it is only one aspect of the art of governing people in our societies. Having studied the field of power relations taking domination techniques as a point of departure, I should like, in the years to come, to study power relations, especially in the field of sexuality, starting from the techniques of the self (*Foucault 1985b: 367*).

Foucault's earlier studies of how the subject is constituted as an object of knowledge are to be complemented with an analysis of how the individual comes to understand him/herself as a subject. Techniques or practices of the self is what Foucault calls the process through which the individual reaches such an understanding. Foucault provides a concrete illustration of what he means by practices of the self in his studies of ancient Greek and Roman behaviour, which make up the second and third volumes of *The History of Sexuality*: *The Use of Pleasure* and *The Care of the Self*, respectively. As many commentators have noted, this shift from an examination of the modern attitude to sexuality in the first volume to a study of classical mores is, at first sight, surprising and somewhat esoteric. However, in the introduction to *The Use of Pleasure*, Foucault expalins both the historical and theoretical significance of this shift in focus.

In relation to the historical shift, Foucault explains that in his study of sexuality, he found that a predominant underlying theme was that of the 'desiring subject', which seems to have been inherited into the modern understanding of sexuality from Classical and early Christian thought. Therefore, in order to understand better the formation and experience of sexuality, it was necessary for Foucault to undertake a 'genealogy of the desiring subject':

> With this genealogy the idea was to investigate how individuals were led to practise, on themselves and on others, a hermeneutics

of desire, a hermeneutics of which their sexual behaviour was doubtless the occasion, but certainly not the exclusive domain. Thus, in order to understand how the modern individual could experience himself as a subject of a 'sexuality', it was essential first to determine how, for centuries, Western man had been brought to recognize himself as a subject of desire (*Foucault 1985a*: 5–6).

This genealogy of the desiring subject takes Foucault back to a study of antiquity where he perceives the theme first arising.

Corresponding to a shift in historical focus, Foucault also alters his theoretical approach to the study of the relations between power and the self. For in order to understand how the individual comes to perceive him/herself as a subject of desire, Foucault is unable to proceed in his 'top heavy' analysis of discursive practices. This is a significant shift, for, as was noted in the previous chapter, Foucault's tendency to reconstruct phenomena, such as disciplinary regimes in prisons, from within the official discourses of penal reform resulted in both an overestimation of the efficacy of disciplinary power and also obscured the existence of 'other' conflicting knowledges or discourses. In *The Use of Pleasure*, however, Foucault no longer talks of individuals as docile bodies; instead he seeks a more dynamic understanding of how individuals interpret their experiences:

> ... the games of truth and error through which being is histori-
> cally constituted as experience; that is, as something that can and
> must be thought. What are the games of truth by which man
> proposes to think his own nature when he perceives himself to
> be mad; when he considers himself to be ill; when he conceives
> of himself as a living, speaking, labouring being (*Foucault 1985a*:
> 6–7).

Foucault is led to alter his theoretical perspective from his observation that, from a certain perspective, ancient Greek and early Christian moral injunctions around sexuality appear very similar. Not only did both cultures share injunctions relating to the prohibition of incest, male domination and the subjugation of women, but also they shared similar attitudes and anxieties about sex. Both Greek and Christian cultures expressed fear about the deleterious effects of uncontrolled sexual activity on the health of the individual (Foucault 1985a: 15–17). Both cultures valorized fidelity within marriage as a manifestation of the virtue and inner strength of the partners involved. Although Greek culture was more tolerant of homosexual relations, nevertheless, according to Foucault, one could still discern in certain images in their literature the beginnings of 'intense negative reactions' and 'forms of stigmatisation' which would extend to the Christian period (Foucault 1985a: 19–20). Finally, both cultures privileged an ascetic ideal in which abstention from sexual activities and other pleasures was linked to a 'form of wisdom that brought them into direct contact with some superior element in human nature and gave them access to the very essence of truth' (Foucault 1985a: 20).

However, despite these continuities which operated at the level of themes or injunctions, Foucault claims that at the level of the individual there were significant differences between Classical and Christian moralities. One of these is associated with the degree of freedom of individual behaviour tolerated by both systems. For example, whereas in Christian thought the demands of austerity were compulsory and universal, in pagan thought the demands of austerity were not grounded in a unified, authoritarian moral system, but were more in the nature of a 'supplement' or 'luxury' in relation to the commonly accepted morality. Individuals were allowed much greater freedom in the interpretation and application of the demands of austerity to their own lives:

> It did not speak to men concerning behaviors presumably owing to a few interdictions that were universally recognized . . . It spoke to them concerning precisely those conducts in which they were called upon to exercise their rights, their power, their authority and *their liberty*: in the practice of pleasures that were not frowned upon, in a marital life where no rule or custom prevented the husband from having extramarital sexual relations, in relationships with boys, which . . . were accepted, commonly maintained, and even prized. These themes of sexual austerity should be understood, not as an expression of, or commentary on, deep and essential prohibitions, but as the elaboration and stylisation of an activity in the exercise of its power and the *practice of its liberty* (*Foucault 1985a: 23; my italics*).

In his genealogy of the desiring subject, Foucault brings into play a distinction, which he had not used in his previous work, between morality as a set of imposed rules and prohibitions, and morality as the 'real behaviour of individuals in relation to the rules and values that are recommended to them . . . the manner in which they comply more or less fully with a standard of conduct,

the manner in which they obey or resist an interdiction or prescrip-
tion' (Foucault 1985a: 25). Within this second understanding of
morality, Foucault establishes four different ways of examining
how an individual may respect or disregard a given set of values
or prescriptions. Firstly, Foucault identifies a principle called the
'determination of ethical substance' which refers to the way in
which the individual chooses to focus on a part of the self or mode
of behaviour as the prime material of his/her ethical conduct. Thus,
there may be a general moral rule of conjugal fidelty, but in relation to this rule, the individual may choose to make his/her
behaviour conform only from an external perspective, or s/he may
decide that the essence of fidelity consists in the mastery of one's
internal desires. Secondly, the ethical behaviour of the individual
can be studied in terms of the 'mode of subjection', that is the way
in which an individual establishes his/her relation to a given rule
and recognizes him/herself as obliged to put it into practice. Thus,
one can practise conjugal fidelity because one acknowledges oneself to be a member of a group that accepts it as a principle for
various spiritual or traditional reasons, or one can practise it in
response to an appeal from someone else. Thirdly, Foucault claims
that there are differences in the 'forms of elaboration of ethical
work'. This is to say that sexual austerity may, for example, be
practised through a 'long effort of learning, memorisation and
assimilation', or it can be practised in a 'sudden, all embracing and
definitive renunciation of one's pleasures' (Foucault 1985a: 27).
Finally, Foucault discerns differences in what he calls the 'telos of
the ethical subject', that is by virtue of the place it occupies in a
pattern of conduct. Thus, conjugal fidelity may be implicated within
a schema of moral conduct which aspires to complete mastery of
the self, or it could be part of a moral conduct which advocates a
radical detachment from the world and its material pleasures
(Foucault 1985a: 28).

These different aspects to the formation of one's self as an ethical
subject are incorporated by Foucault under the category of practices
or techniques of the self, or an 'aesthetics of existence'. It is these
different practices, ranging from the concrete process of ordering
one's day-to-day existence to the spiritual significance that one
attaches to one's activities, that Foucault understands as the ways
in which individuals give meaning to their activities and seek to
interpret their experiences:

I am referring to what might be called the 'arts of existence'.
What I mean by the phrase are those intentional and voluntary

actions by which men not only set themselves rules of conduct, but also seek to transform themselves, to change themselves in their singular being, and to make their life into an *œuvre* that carries certain aesthetic values and meets certain stylistic criteria (*Foucault 1985a: 10–11*).

Every era is typified by its own particular arts of existence or practices of the self. However, the relationship between codes of behaviour and forms of 'subjectivization'[1] vary from era to era. Thus, Foucault sees Christianity as a morality that is orientated more towards codes than ethics. This is to say that the emphasis within that morality is upon the individual's conformity to externally imposed codes of behaviour; subjectivization occurs basically 'in a quasi-juridical form, where the ethical subject refers his conduct to a law, or set of laws, to which he must submit at the the risk of commiting offenses that may make him liable to punishment' (Foucault 1985a: 29–30). In contrast to moralities which emphasize codes, Foucault counterposes moralities orientated towards ethics which he sees as exemplified in Classical Greek thought. In this second type of morality, there is a strong dynamic element in so far as there exists a relative autonomy between a system of laws and the individual's ethical behaviour. Rather than conformity towards the law, the emphasis is on the formation of the relationship with the self and on the methods and techniques through which this relationship is worked out. For Foucault, this second type of morality permits a greater element of freedom in individual behaviour in relation to general rules of conduct. The individual is relatively free to interpret the spirit of the law in his/her own style, rather than conform to the exact letter of the law:

> With Christianity, there occurred a slow, gradual shift in relation to the moralities of Antiquity, which were essentially a practice, a style of liberty. Of course, there had also been certain norms of behaviour that governed each individual's behaviour. But the will to be a moral subject and the search for an ethics of existence were, in Antiquity, mainly an attempt to affirm one's liberty and to give one's own life a certain form ... whereas in Christianity, with the religion of the text, the idea of the will of God, the principle of obedience, morality took on increasingly the form of a code of rules ... From Antiquity to Christianity, we pass from a morality that was essentially the search for a personal ethics to a morality as obedience to a system of rules (*Foucault 1988a: 49*).

THE CLASSICAL FORMATION OF THE SELF

It is against the backdrop of these historical and methodological considerations that Foucault conducts his study of the formation of the desiring subject in the Classical era. The central aesthetic theme around which practices of the self revolved was, as it is in Christianity, a notion of austerity or self-mastery. However, unlike Christian austerity, which was based on the renunciation of wordly pleasures and the extirpation of inner desires, ancient Greek ascetic practices had a 'this worldly' end in that sexual austerity was intended to give their lives much more intensity and much more beauty: 'For the Greeks there could not be desire without privation, without the want of the thing desired and without a certain amount of suffering mixed in' (Foucault 1985a: 43). Practices of austerity were not intended to eradicate desire but to augment it through stylization.

The notions of self-mastery or moderation which were central to the Greek idea of daily conduct were centred around two variables: a notion of intensity of practice and a distinction between activity and passivity. Firstly, what differentiated men from one another was not the type of object which they desired, nor the type of sexual practice they prefered, but the intensity with which they carried out their sexual practices (Foucault 1985a: 44–6). Immorality was associated with excess and surplus; the moral person was he who exercised self-restraint and moderation in relation to sexual activity. Related to this distinction between moderation (morality) and excess (immorality) is the second modality based on the idea of role. For the Greeks, the 'aphrodisia' was thought of as an activity involving two actors, each with a clearly defined role and function – the one who performs the activity and the one on whom it is performed. The division between activity and passivity fell mainly between men and women, but there was also a second division between adult free men and a category including women, boys and slaves. The ethical man did not just exercise self-restraint in his sexual conduct, but was the one who assumed the active role (active means penetration). Inversely: 'For a man, excess and passivity were the two main forms of immorality in the practice of the aphrodisia' (Foucault 1985a: 47).

Foucault goes on to elaborate how these two distinctions, between restraint and excess, and activity and passivity, constituted the moral framework within which the Greek notion of the ethical self was situated, and structured the aesthetics of existence in the four main areas of daily life: dietetics, economics (marriage), erotics (boys) and wisdom. In relation to dietetics, sexual pleasure was defined by the Greeks in terms of a certain way of caring for the body based on a distrust of excessive regimes. Sexual conduct was considered in relation to phenomena such as the weather and alimentary prescriptions and was ordered in closest conformity to what the Greeks considered nature demanded. In relation to sex, there was an ambiguous border line between excess and restraint. Excessive indulgence could harm the body, but so too could rigorous restraint.

Similarly, in regard to marriage and the relationship with the wife, the principle which obligated men not to have extramarital liasons was not based on a notion of reciprocal fidelity, but rather on a notion of self-mastery, or what Foucault calls a 'stylisation of dissymmetry'. Women were obliged to be faithful because of their inferior status and because they were under the control of their husbands. Men, however, were faithful only because it was a manifestation of their self-control: 'For the husband, having sexual relations only with his wife was the most elegant way of exercising his control' (Foucault 1985a: 151). Foucault cites the case of Nicocles, King of Cyprus, who is faithful to his wife not out of some heteronomously prescribed sense of duty, but because as a king who commands others, he must also demonstrate that he is in command of himself. Self-control was a public, theatrical display of one's ethical worthiness.

This deliberate stylization of the exercise of power in marriage was connected to the isomorphic relation that was perceived between the household and the state. The free man respects his wife in a similar fashion to the respect he accords his fellow citizens: 'The double obligation to limit sexual activities relates to the stability of the city, to its public morality, to the conditions of good procreation, and not to the reciprocal obligations that attach to a dual relation between husbands and wives' (Foucault 1985a: 170). The obligation of a husband to a wife inheres not in a personal commitment, but rather in a deliberate limitation of power which connected the sexual self to the ethical and political self. Thus, although the potential to tyrannize one's wife and social inferiors was built into the structure of ancient society, the ethical Greek man who adhered to an aesthetics of existence refrained from such behaviour. As Foucault observes, practices of the self were based around a principle of self limitation and were not a universally practised code of behaviour. In the case of the king, his aesthetic and political behaviour were directly linked. If he wants people to accept him, he must have a kind of glory that will survive him and this glory is inseparable from aesthetic value.

Unlike the relationship between husband and wife, which was regulated, to some extent, by the institutional constraints of the *'oikos'*, the principles of regulation in relationships between men had to be drawn from the relation itself. Whereas in the areas of dietetics and marriage, it was the man only who exercised dominating self-restraint, in the relation between men, the male loved object was also supposed to exercise self restraint:

> In economics and dietetics, the voluntary moderation of the man was based mainly on his relation to himself; in erotics, the game was more complicated; it implied self-mastery on the part of the lover; it also implied an ability on the part of the beloved to establish a relation of dominion over himself; and lastly, it implied a relationship between their two moderations, expressed in their deliberate choice of one another (*Foucault 1985a: 203*).

It is with the relationship between men that Foucault detects an element of anxiety arising in the Classical techniques of the self. He calls this uncertainty the 'antinomy of the boy' and it is connected to the crucial distinction between active and passive role playing. The Greeks felt an uneasiness about the fact that, as a loved object, the boy had to occupy a passive role in sexual relations, when later, as a free man, he was to assume an active role. Somehow, the boy had to occupy the role of object of pleasure without acknowledging that he was in that position: 'The relationship that he was expected to establish with himself in order to become a free man, master of himself and capable of prevailing over others, was at variance with a form of relationship in which he would be an object of pleasure for another' (Foucault 1985a: 221).

The problem presented by the antinomy of the boy produced an oscillation in Greek thought on the morality of the love for boys. Whilst in one respect, the sex of the loved object was irrelevant, in another respect, stress was increasingly placed on how love for a boy could not be morally honourable, unless within it were elements which could change it into a socially valuable tie (Foucault 1985a: 225). Foucault argues that this anxiety remained unresolved until it was later taken up in Socratic and Platonic reflections on love which produced a shift in the way in which the love of boys is problematized. Platonic erotics responds to the difficulties that the Greeks found inherent to love between men by shifting the question of love away from the object itself, to an interrogation of the subject

of love and to the relation between love and truth. There is a shift
from the deontological question about what constitutes proper
conduct, to an ontological investigation of the very nature and
origin of love. The problem of the dissymmetrical relation posed
by love between men is bypassed and replaced by a Platonic notion of convergence in true love. In as much as love is drawn to
truth, it is the person who is more in love and, therefore, nearer the
truth who becomes the central figure in the relationship. The master
of truth takes the place of the lover and the love of the master
replaces the previous concern with the status of the boy. Foucault
argues that this shift initiated by Platonic erotics breaks the ground
for the shift into the Christian preoccupation with the self and the
renunciation of desires:

> In a way that may be surprising at first, one sees the formation,
> in Greek culture and in connection with the love of boys, of some
> of the major elements of a sexual ethics that will renounce that
> love by appealing to the above principle: the requirement of a
> symmetry and reciprocity in the love relationship; the necessity
> of a long and arduous struggle with oneself; the gradual purifi-
> cation of a love that is addressed only to being per se, in its truth;
> and man's inquiry into himself as a subject of desire (*Foucault
> 1985a: 245*).

The third volume of *The History of Sexuality: The Care of the Self*
– examines how, by the time of the Roman Empire, this shift away
from the deontological question of pleasure and the aesthetics of
its use, to an ontological inquiry into the desiring subject, has
become more entrenched. This shift prepares the ground for the
Christian obsession with the self which, Foucault argues, reaches
its culmination in the modern compulsion to confess. In Hellenistic
Rome, then, a new way of conceiving the relationship that one
ought to have with one's status, functions and activities emerges.
Classical ethics had established a correspondence with power over
oneself and power over others. However, although Graeco-Roman
ethics still considered these questions of status, there was also an
increasing emphasis on the establishment of a relation with the self
that relied as little as possible on outward signs of respect and
power: 'It is then a matter of forming and recognizing oneself as
the subject of one's own actions, not through a system of signs
denoting power over others, but through a relation that depends
as little as possible on status and its external forms, for this relation
is fulfilled in the sovereignty that one exercises over oneself'
(Foucault 1986: 85).

Foucault documents the effects that this intensification of the relation to the self had on the four realms of the body, marriage, boys and truth. In regard to the body, a close correlation was established between care of the self and medical practice which was expressed through an intense form of attention to the body. It was believed that the ills of the body and soul could communicate with each other and exchange their distresses. As a result, an image arose of the adult body as fragile and threatened and there was an increased anxiety about the sexual act in relation to the ill effects it may have on the body. Positive consequences began to be attributed to sexual abstinence and there was a move towards the 'conjugalisation' of sexual relations. Within marriage, there was an increased austerity in sexual relations which attempted to both limit them and valorize them in relation to a 'procreative finalisation' (Foucault 1986: 166–7). The relationship between husband and wife also altered with the intensification of the relation to the self. The attachment between the two partners was no longer subordinated to the needs of the *oikos* and the technique of male self-government; instead there was a move towards the establishment of a more reciprocal and voluntary union. In this 'stylistics of the individual bond', the conjugal relationship was seen to incorporate love and the respect accorded to both partners was supposed to be equal and mutual. According to Foucault, the intensification of the concern for the self necessarily involved an increased valorization of the other.

Parallel to this intensified privileging of the relation between men and women was a philosophical disinvestment in the love for boys (Foucault 1986: 192). Increasing emphasis was placed on abstention from loving boys and this abstention was no longer connected to a notion of virile self-domination; rather it was linked to the idea of retaining a virginal integrity against the potential deleterious effects of sexual activity on the body and the soul (Foucault 1986: 228–32). In sum, what arose under the Roman Empire was the beginnings of a universal ideal of the subject. Nature and reason became the standards against which the individual's concern for the self was judged. There was an increased sense of the fraility of the self against the standards of truth against which it was assessed. Implicit in this universalization of the sexual subject was an intensification of the code element in morality. The freedom of individual ethical conduct tolerated in ancient Greece was replaced by notions of prohibition and obedience. Although this intensification does not compare with the levels of constraint to be reached in Christian times, nevertheless, a certain threshold in relation to the problematization of the self had been crossed:

One is still far from an experience of sexual pleasure where the latter will be associated with evil, where behaviour will have to submit to the universal form of law, and where the deciphering of desire will be a necessary condition for acceding to a purified existence. Yet one can already see how the question of evil begins to work upon the ancient theme . . . of art and *techne*, and how the question of truth and the principle of self-knowledge evolve within the ascetic practices (*Foucault 1986: 68*).

FROM DOCILE BODIES TO ACTIVE INDIVIDUALS

It has been necessary to outline Foucault's work on Classical techniques of existence at some length both because it is less well known than his earlier writings, and also in order to indicate the changes that the development of an idea of the self initiated in his work. From this description, it is apparent that there is a significant methodological shift in Foucault's understanding of how power relations influence the behaviour of individuals. If he had continued with the type of analysis of power – characteristic of his previous historical studies – from within its own 'official' discourses, then the differences that he identifies between the Classical and Christian attitudes to sexual morality would not have emerged. The differences between the two systems, at the level of the individual's ethical behaviour, would have remained submerged beneath the similarities at the level of moral code.

In the previous chapter, it was shown how there was a discrepancy between Foucault's theoretical understanding of power as a diffuse and productive phenomenon and his concrete studies of power relations which tended to show power as a monolithic, dominating force. However, in his final work, it appears that Foucault seeks to resolve this discrepancy by coming to terms more adequately with the notion that individual behaviour does not reflect, in a straightforward fashion, overarching ideologies and systems of belief. Through the idea that the individual actively fashions his/her own existence through the adoption of various practices, Foucault suggests a more dynamic relationship between social structures and individuals than he allowed in his previous work. In the first volume of *The History of Sexuality*, Foucault suggests such a dynamic relation with the notion of the 'rule of double conditioning'. He uses it to illustrate the point that power relations are diffuse, heterogenous and changeable rather than reducible to one ultimate determining source:

One must conceive of the double conditioning of a strategy by the specificity of possible tactics, and of tactics by the strategic envelope that makes them work. Thus the father in the family is not the 'representative' of the sovereign or the state; and the latter are not projections of the father on a different scale. The family does not duplicate society, just as society does not imitate the family (*Foucault 1978a: 100*).

Here, Foucault rejects the idea that there is any straightforward causal chain between large-scale determining structures and the actions of individuals. The power relations that determine the role of the father in the family are not simply microcosmic reflections of more general, authoritarian systems of government. Rather, each type of authority is determined by its own specific set of social forces and power relations.

Although there is no straightforward causal connection between individual action and social structure, this is not to say that there is a complete discontinuity between the two levels of action. It is possible to perceive how the authority of the father in the family eventually feeds into more global patriarchal systems which devalue women without reducing the former to a reflection of the latter. The family is both a relatively autonomous unit which has its own logic and specific history; at the same time, it has been 'invested and annexed' by more 'global mechanisms of domination' (Foucault 1980: 99). A similar idea of a non-exhaustive mutual determination is expressed in the idea of the 'duality of structure' proposed by other social theorists, notably Bhaskar and Giddens. The idea this concept expresses is that the human agent is neither the origin of social relations nor the passive product of an externally imposed system of social constraint: there is a mutual dependence of structure and agency. The activities of social agents are necessarily situated and constrained, although the determinants of activity are multiple and contradictory and cannot be subsumed under the logic of a single monolithic system. At the same time, however, social structures are constituted by human agency, and also are the very medium of this constitution. The relationship between structure and agency must be grasped as dynamic, not static; existing structures are reproduced by human agents who modify and change these structures to differing degrees as they are shaped by them.[2] As Giddens puts it, 'structures form "personality" and "society" simultaneously, but in neither case exhaustively because of the significance of unintended consequences of action, and because of unacknowledged conditions of action' (Giddens, 1979: 70).

In his earlier studies of disciplinary power, Foucault was unable to develop the idea of the rule of double conditioning beyond the stage of theoretical assertion, because his understanding of individuals, principally in terms of bodies, allowed no space to elaborate an idea of autonomous action. However, with a shift in emphasis from body to self, Foucault is able to attribute a certain degree of autonomy and independence to the way in which individuals act, especially in the ordering of their day to day existence. The development of a more rounded notion of the self arose at the same time as Foucault's rereading of certain liberal theorists, including Hayek, in a seminar series at the Collège de France. In interviews, however, Foucault emphasises that his idea of the self in no way represents a retreat into a notion of a 'sovereign, founding subject' understood to be the origin of all social action:

> I . . . believe that there is no sovereign, founding subject, a universal form of subject to be found everywhere. I am very sceptical of this view of the subject . . . I believe, on the contrary, that the subject is constituted through practices of subjection, or, in a more autonomous way, through practices of liberation, of liberty, as in Antiquity' (*Foucault 1988a: 50*).

Thus, although Foucault understands the type of self-mastery practised by the Greeks as giving access to 'an active freedom', this freedom was always determined, in the final instance, by larger cultural constraints. It was a freedom that was 'indissociable from a structural, instrumental and ontological relation to truth' (Foucault 1985a: 92). The individual might exercise a degree of choice in the way in which he fashioned his existence, but the practices through which self-mastery was achieved were always conditioned and overdetermined by the socio-cultural context. At the same time, although practices of the self are defined by the social context, the way in which the individual is related to these practices is by no means reducible to such a context:

> I am interested . . . in the way in which the subject constitutes himself in an *active fashion*, by the practices of self, these practices are nevertheless not something that the individual invents by himself. They are patterns that he finds in his culture and which are proposed, suggested and imposed on him by his culture, his society and his social group (*Foucault 1988b: 11; my italics*).

The introduction of the notion of the self represents, then, an attempt by Foucault to integrate more thoroughly into his historical studies the theoretical idea of a necessary non-correspondence, but mutually determining relation, between the individual and society. However, it must not be interpreted as a refutation of his earlier attacks on humanist systems of thought and, in particular, its epistemological mainspring, the 'constitutive subject'. Rather, Foucault's conception of the self represents an attempt to attribute a degree of agency and self-determination to the individual without jettisoning his anti-essentialist view of the subject. In the working through of his idea of the self, Foucault attempts to express the concepts of autonomy and subjectivity in such a way as to avoid any suggestion that such freedom takes the form of a recovery of an authentic, 'natural' self (see Dews 1989: 38).

FROM ANTIQUITY TO THE PRESENT

Although the idea of practices of the self represents a significant development in terms of Foucault's previous understanding of the subject, it may, at first, be difficult to discern the relevance that it has for contemporary social theory. For feminist social theorists, in particular, this impression may be confirmed by Foucault's insistence that ancient practices of the self were an exclusively 'virile' ethics that did not address women at all: 'This ethics was not addressed to women; it was not their duties, or obligations, that were recalled, justified or spelled out. It was an ethics for men: an ethics thought, written, and taught by men and addressed to men . . . A male ethics, consequently, in which women figured only as objects' (Foucault 1985a: 22).

It is apparent, however, from various interviews that Foucault regards practices of the self as a suitable analytical category to understand the way in which people act in modern society. As we have seen, Foucault regards the transition from the Classical to Christian eras as initiating a shift from moralities orientated towards ethics to moralities orientated towards codes. With this shift corresponded a decline in the amount of freedom tolerated in the ethical behaviour of individuals and a greater emphasis on obedience and conformity to externally imposed rules. By the nineteenth century and the increase of the grip of disciplinary power on the bodies of individuals, these rules are less externally apparent; rather they have been internalized by individuals and are manifested in the modern compulsion to confess. During the twentieth century, the operations of biopower become more insidious and the control of the body is intensified and directed towards 'an economic exploitation of eroticisation'; 'we find a new mode of investment which presents itself no longer in the form of control by repression but that of control by stimulation. "Get undressed – but be slim, good looking, tanned!"' (Foucault 1980: 57). In his final interviews, however, Foucault appears to have changed his view; he indicates that in contemporary society, there has been a certain relaxation in the modern obsession with the self and the body or, at least, he no longer regards it in purely negative terms: 'I can't help but think that discussion around a whole series of things, even independently of political choices, around certain forms of existence, rules of behaviour, etc., has been profoundly beneficial – the relation with the body, between man and woman, with sexuality' (Foucault 1988a: 49–50).

From this observation, Foucault is led to compare contemporary society with ancient Greek culture in so far as he sees the former at a stage in its evolution that is able to accommodate a similar process of autonomous self-stylization as was tolerated in the Classical era: 'It is important . . . to show how the same advice given by ancient morality can function differently in a contemporary style of morality' (Foucault 1988a: 247). With what Foucault regards as the decline of the 'grand narratives' of religion and politics in the second half of the twentieth century, a space has been opened for the creation of a modern aesthetics of existence: 'If I was interested in antiquity to Christianity it was because, for a whole series of reasons, the idea of a morality as obedience to a code of rules is now disappearing, has already disappeared. And to this absence of morality corresponds, must correspond, the search for an aesthetics of existence' (Foucault 1988a: 49).

The implications of Foucault's statements on the need to establish a contemporary morality based around the autonomous action of the individual will be considered in detail in the following three chapters. What is of significance here are the implications of Foucault's revised understanding of the individual for feminist theory, especially given feminist dissatisfaction with his earlier model of individuals as 'docile' bodies.

FEMINISM, POWER AND DIFFERENCE

The tendency to regard women as powerless and innocent victims of patriarchal social structures hampers many types of feminist analysis. This tendency, however, is increasingly coming under attack from other feminist theorists who perceive the need for a more complex and differentiated analysis of the relations between gender and power in order to account for the potential of women's creativity and agency within social constraints (see de Lauretis 1987; Felski 1989). The problematic assumptions which underlie the notion of women as innocent victims of a male power are well documented and need only be briefly stated here. An insistence on women as passive victims of male oppression oversimplifies the complexities of women's subordination by placing too great a stress both on the universal nature of oppression and the common, undifferentiated enemy of patriarchy. Because of this insistence and a consequent failure to carry through a differentiated analysis of different cultural and historical contexts, areas of women's experience are either not understood in their full complexity, are devalued or remain obscured altogether (see Showstack Sassoon 1987: 19). As the feminist historian Linda Gordon has noted, for many feminists power has become a perjorative term.

The problem of thinking through adequately the question of power is one of the central issues at stake in the recent feminist debate on difference. This debate has revolved around the idea that if a feminist politics is to appeal to women in general, it must be recognized that gender is not the only determining influence on women's lives. The debate was initiated by black feminists who argued that although the oppression of women by men was very general and central to an understanding of the experiences of women, it is not the only form of oppression that exists. Indeed, it is only for a few privileged, white western women that sexism is the main form of oppression. Dominant new-wave feminism, however, takes white women's experiences as the norm and generalizes them in the assumption of a universal and shared oppression between women. Black and other women of ethnic minorities have different histories and experiences in relation to slavery, forced labour, enforced migration, plantation, colonialism, imperialism, etc. (Ramazanoglu 1989: 125–9). Indeed, as Carby (1982) has shown, power relationships between white and black women in Britain have their roots in colonial relationship. It is here, then, that the question of difference can be seen to intersect with the problem of power. For power differences between women can be so great that apparently similar struggles against men can be, in practice, fundamentally different.

The more complex and layered notion of difference that Foucault tries to capture in his idea of practices of the self resonates with the calls, from black and other feminists, for a demotion of the assumed primacy of sexual difference. Although there may be overarching structures which determine individuals' lives, these structures are never manifest in a pure and discernible form. This is because any individual's life is determined by multiple factors which conflict and interlink with each other, producing differential effects. It is also because, against this background of multiple determinants, individuals act upon themselves and order their own lives in numerous and variable ways. Thus, as Foucault notes at the beginning of *The Use of Pleasure*, from a general perspective the Classical and Christian experiences of asceticism appear to be similar. However, at a concrete level these experiences were fundamentally different: Christian asceticism being based on a feminine model of viriginity and a notion of absolute renunciation, the Classical experience being based on a notion of the augmentation of desire and on a masculine model of self-mastery. Just as it is no longer possible to refer to a universal experience of asceticism once these differences are realized, it is no longer possible to think of gender as a globally constant phenomenon. Gender intersects with race, class, ethnicity, etc., to produce different – at times, radically different – experiences of what it is to be a woman or man. Furthermore, the individual's own identification with and investment in different subject positions makes it even more difficult to speak of gender as some kind of unified or bonding experience.

The problem of theorizing power differences between women presents immense difficulties for many types of feminism which rely on some definition of female collectivity. As Henrietta Moore has argued, the problem for feminism is that the concept of difference threatens to deconstruct this isomorphism upon which the theory of feminist politics is based (Moore 1988: 10–11). Moore goes on to argue, however, that it is necessary for these unitary assumptions to be broken down in order for feminism to develop theoretical constructs which can deal with difference, particularly with 'how racial difference is constructed through gender, how racism divides gender identity and experience, and how class is shaped by gender and race' (Moore 1988: 11; see also Adams and Minson 1978).

Anthropology, Moore believes, is in a position to provide a critique of feminism based on the deconstruction of unifying categories about oppression. Anthropologists are in such a position because in their study of different cultures they have had to tackle the problem of difference, especially in relation to the way in which gender is experienced through specific social and historical mediations, e.g. class, race, colonialism, neo-imperialism. Thus feminist anthropologists have shown how certain sets of analytical distinctions such as nature/culture, domestic/public, which are premised on the cross-cultural homogeneity of such categories, are problematic and potentially distorting because they are essentially 'western' concepts. The universal subordination of women cannot be assumed, nor can it be read off straightforwardly from symbolic and cultural representations. Rather, what have to be considered are the questions of what women actually do in a particular society, their access to resources, the amount of economic and political autonomy they have and how these factors are articulated within specific definitions of femininity.

In many different areas of study then – social theory, history, anthropology – feminist theoreticians have been concerned to break down the analysis of women's oppression in terms of a schematic dominator/dominated paradigm. It leads not only to misinterpretation and, therefore, to simplification of the diverse aspects of many women's experience in modern society, but also negates the massive differences of race and class that divide women in favour of an ideal category of a common oppression. The negative relation of women to different social practices is not constant but rather 'a variable and piecemeal affair' (Cameron 1984: 13).

PRACTICES OF THE SELF AND FEMINIST CRITIQUE

In relation to the above issues, Foucault's idea of practices of the self parallels developments in the feminist analysis of women's oppression that seek to avoid positing women as powerless victims of patriarchal structures of domination. This is a significant shift from Foucault's earlier work. Albeit unintended, Foucault's understanding of individuals principally in terms of the operations of power upon the body had the effect of keeping women in the position of passive victims. The process of hysterization, through which the female body was saturated with sexuality, is so total that it is difficult to explain how women were able to act creatively and autonomously in other areas. However, the idea of practices of the self – based on a problematization of any straightforward causal connection between social determinants and individual practices – brings Foucault's work closer to the non-reductive analyses of women's social status proposed by recent feminist theory. Undoubtedly, there are structures of domination, in particular constructions of gender, which ensure the overall subordinate position of women in society. However, in their daily lives many women do not experience themselves as oppressed and, indeed, they exercise an amount of power and influence over other individuals. To be a female social subject is not always to be a woman. As social subjects, women are engendered across a vast number of subject positions, some of which are gendered to a much greater degree than others. To borrow de Lauretis' terms, there is a discrepancy and slippage between 'Woman' as representation and women as historical beings and as the subjects of real relations of which gender is a primary but not the only relation (see de Lauretis 1987: 10). In order to understand this discrepancy, it is necessary to analyse power not just from the perspective of mechanisms of domination, but also from the level of a 'microphysics' of power.

Concurrent with such feminist arguments, Foucault's work on the self suggests a potential analysis of the differentials of power that exist between and amongst women (and men) through the examination of the various techniques of the self which are employed to order their lives and by which they exert influence on other individuals. In an interview given four months before his death, Foucault explains again his theory of power as a positive force. He states that his idea that power is everywhere in modern society does not mean that domination is universal; rather, power relations are the necessary precondition for the establishment of social relations. There are indeed states of domination, characterized by power relations which are asymmetrical and irreversible. However, the nature of normal power relations is that they are unstable and changeable. An element of freedom is inherent to all power relations in the sense that they can only operate between free individuals and are, therefore, unfixed, fluid and reversible:

> One must observe also that there cannot be relations of power unless the subjects are free. If one or the other were completely at the disposition of the other and became his thing, an object on which he can exercise an infinite and unlimited violence, there would not be relations of power. In order to exercise a relation of power, there must be on both sides at least a certain form of liberty (*Foucault 1988b: 12*).

Practices of the self are situated at this level of power relations, at the point where individuals autonomously order their own lives and, in doing so, attempt to influence other individuals.

Foucault attaches his notion of practices of the self to a concept of governmentality. In relation to the state, governmentality is used to explain how the modern state is not a unified apparatus of domination, but is made up of a network of institutions and procedures which employ complex techniques of power to order social relations. The aim of governmentality is not the imposition of laws, but the regulation of the population through various techniques, such as the stimulation of the birthrate or the improvement of the health and longevity of the population. In this respect, governmentality is linked to disciplinary power in so far as it annexes disciplinary techniques in order to achieve its aim of the regulation of populations. Like disciplinary power, governmentality also targets the individual as means with which to maintain social control: 'Interest, both at the level of each individual who goes to make up the population, and also the interest of the population as such, regardless of individual interests and aspirations, this is the new target and the fundamental instrument of the government of population' (Foucault 1979: 18). Yet paradoxically, Foucault also argues that it is through techniques of self-government that individuals can resist this 'government of individualisation'. This notion of the individual's ability to resist power through the very techniques by which he or she is governed will be considered in the following chapters. Here, it is enough to note that self-government implies both the ways through which individuals police themselves, and also the ways in which individuals ensure their freedom:

> I say that governmentality implies the relationship of self to self, which means exactly that, in the idea of governmentality, I am aiming at the totality of practices, by which one can constitute, define, organize, instrumentalize the strategies which individuals in their liberty can have in regard to each other. It is free individuals who try to control, to determine, to delimit the liberty of others and, in order to do that, they dispose of certain instruments to govern others. That rests indeed on freedom, on the relationship of self to self and the relationship to the other (*Foucault 1988b: 19*).

In a similar though unrelated way, feminists anxious to deconstruct the notion that women are uniformly oppressed by a 'patriarchal' state have shown how the welfare state has led to both a new potential unity amongst women and new potential contradications. The institutionalization of women's dual role as wage earners and mothers, and associated social changes such as the use of domestic technology, have contributed to diminishing class differences amongst women. Yet at the same time, the welfare state has led to new differences amongst women: between professional women and unskilled women, between women employed by the state and women as consumers of state services. Thus, in *Women and the State*, Sassoon argues that the state 'has vastly improved women's social and economic position and enabled women to gain more influence as workers and citizens at the same time as the locus of oppression has shifted from private to public' (Showstack Sassoon 1987: 30).

The non-unitary nature of the oppression of women is illustrated by Bennett, Coward and Heys (1980) in an analysis of taxation and welfare practices which demonstrates how there is no consistency across these practices in fixing women in a subject position. Some welfare provisions, such as supplementary benefit, privilege 'mothers', while others, for example taxation, privilege males. They conclude that there is no general 'discrimination against women' in taxation and welfare practices. The relative power of 'woman' depends on particular practices which differently favour 'mothers', 'single women', 'married women', etc. The welfare system is not a uniform ideological state apparatus which discriminates against women in an unvarying fashion, but rather a complex network with equally complex histories (Henriques et al. 1984: 117)

An analysis of the different forms of self-government that women employ – as individuals and specific groups – is essential if their activities as autonomous social subjects are to be fully understood. As Anthony Giddens notes, a common tendency of many types of sociological analysis is to discount an examination of agents' reasons for their actions in order to discover the real stimuli of their activity. Such a perspective, however, implies a derogation of the lay actor by regarding actors as 'cultural dopes' with no worthwhile understanding of their surroudings. Against this, Giddens argues that all social actors, no matter how oppressed, have some degree of penetration of the social forms which oppress them:

> Where partially closed, localised cultures become largely unavailable, as is increasingly the case in advanced capitalism, scepticism about official views of society often is expressed in various forms of 'distancing' – and in humour. Wit is deflationary. Humour is used socially both to attack and to defend against the influence of outside forces that cannot otherwise easily be coped with' (*Giddens 1979: 72*).[3]

Whilst the idiosyncratic perspectives of individual women do not in themselves constitute adequate categories for the analysis of society, it is necessary to take them into account because otherwise there is a danger of ignoring 'the varying degrees of dissent, resistance and struggle for change which have existed among women in different historical and cultural contexts' (Felski 1989: 225). Foucault is never unaware that, in the final analysis, practices of the self are suggested or imposed on the individual by their wider social context. However, he also recognizes that this imposition is never straightforward and that in order to capture the dynamic and positive aspects of power, it is essential to examine 'those *intentional* and *voluntary* actions by which men not only set themselves rules of conduct, but also seek to transform themselves, to change themselves' (Foucault 1985a: 10; my italics).

Many feminist researchers have realized the importance of this shift in analytical perspective for challenging assumptions about the powerlessness of women. Such an assumption is often made about women working in the domestic sphere who are seen to adopt a more caring, instinctive approach to life compared to the rational 'masculine' approach believed to be embodied in professional work. However, Kari Waerness has shown that women in the domestic sphere do not necessarily perceive themselves in such terms, but rather view their domestic functions, in particular the caring for dependents, as a flexible and alternative rationality which often runs counter to the authority of professionals. In other words, women who have traditionally been regarded as the most isolated, oppressed and dependent do not necessarily always understand their situation in such terms, but rather have created an alternative system of positive values through which they interpret their experiences. The problem is, as Waerness points out, to obtain official recognition within a public care system of the practical experience and personal knowledge of many women (Waerness 1987: 35). As Sassoon argues, what this example illustrates is that there is a need in feminism to deconstruct exegetical clichés such as the 'dependence of women' in order to reinterpret their experience in a more complex and more positive light (Showstack Sassoon 1987: 30).

GENDER IDENTITY

At some level, of course, practices of the self are suggested or imposed on the individual by the wider social context and, in this respect, some practices are more imperative, or offer less scope for autonomous choice, than other practices. For example, it is much harder to stylize freely one's identity in the realm of sexuality – given the taboos and injunctions that operate around masculinity and femininity – than it is to stylize one's existence as a political citizen. However, practices of the self suggest a more active notion of how individuals assume their gender identity than was implied in Foucault's earlier work. In the previous chapter, I showed that one of the consequences of Foucault's idea of docile bodies was an impoverished account of the construction of gender identity. Gender is understood as an effect of dominant power relations which is imposed upon the inert bodies of individuals. This static model reifies sexual difference and implies that the assumption of gender identity is unproblematic and total. It also obscures the slippages and multiple experiences which occur between or outside of the polarized options of masculinity and femininity. In contrast to this static model of gender construction, Foucault's later idea of practices of the self implies an understanding of gender as an active and never-completed process of engendering or enculturation.

In an interesting article on the sex/gender distinction, Judith Butler considers the implications of Simone de Beauvoir's statement, 'one is not born, but rather becomes, a woman'. Butler notes that the verb 'become' contains a consequential ambiguity in that it implies that gender identity is both culturally constructed and also, in some senses, constructed by individuals themselves: 'For Beauvoir, to become a woman is a purposive and appropriative set of acts, the gradual acquisition of a skill, a 'project' in Sartrian terms, to assume a culturally established corporeal style and significance' (Butler 1987: 128). The concept that individuals construct their own gender is problematic not only because it undermines the idea that gender is culturally constructed, but also because the notion of choice, on which it relies, implies that an individual can occupy a position outside of gender in order to choose a gender. Thus, a problematic 'disembodied' notion of agency becomes a prerequisite for taking on a gender. Butler argues, however, that Beauvoir's notion of 'becoming' a gender does not mean a movement from a disembodied freedom to cultural embodiment, but rather a move from the natural to the acculturated body. Furthermore, this movement from sex to gender is not a linear process because that implies a presocial body and also a temporally discrete origin to gender, after which it is fixed in form. Rather,

> gender is not traceable to a definable origin because it itself is an originating activity incessantly taking place. No longer

understood as a product of cultural and psychic relations long past, gender is a contemporary way of organising past and future cultural norms, a way of situating oneself in and through those norms, an active style of living one's body in the world (*Butler 1987: 131*).

Choosing one's gender, then, is a process, not wholly conscious but nevertheless accessible to consciousness. It involves the interpretation of a cultural reality which is laden with sanctions, taboos and prescriptions. It is a certain way of existing in one's body which involves the individual's idiosyncratic interpretation of already established corporeal styles. For Beauvoir gender is based on a notion of the body as a 'situation' which has a twofold meaning. The body is both the locus of cultural interpretations, i.e. it is always already caught up and defined within a social context. The body is also the site at which the individual has to take up and actively interpret that set of received interpretations:

> As a field of interpretative possibilities, the body is a locus of the dialectical process of interpreting anew a historical set of interpretations which have already informed corporeal style. The body becomes a peculiar nexus of culture and choice, and 'existing' one's body becomes a personal way of taking up and reinterpreting received gender norms (*Butler 1987: 133–4*).

An advantage of Beauvoir's notion of 'becoming' one's gender is that it infuses the process through which gender is constructed with an emancipatory potential. Gendered identity is not simply stamped on individuals' bodies by inexorable cultural forces, but involves individual participation on a large scale. Obviously, the social constraints on gender compliance and the taboos connected to deviance are so powerful that it is difficult to exist to a socially meaningful extent outside of gender norms. As Butler explains: 'If human existence is always gendered existence, then to stray outside of established gender is in some sense to put one's very existence into question' (Butler 1987: 132).

However, the very idea that the constitution of gender identity involves a process of interpretation attests to the possibility of dislocation of gender norms, to what Butler calls 'the essential freedom at the origin of gender'.

Although Foucault does not claim explicitly to offer a theory of gender identity, it is a more active notion of the acquistion of gender identity, similar to Beauvoir's, that his notion of practices of the self suggests. His study of ancient Greek ethics reveals how masculine identity rested on the individual's active stylization of his bodily existence. Whilst the various corporeal styles accessible to the individual were constrained by cultural taboos around the notions of activity and passivity, moderation and immoderation, the individual was essentially free in his adoption and interpretation of certain practices which would constitute his masculine identity in terms of self-mastery. Unlike the static notion of the body as a *tabula rasa*, which underpins Foucault's earlier works, the body is understood in his later work in a more dynamic fashion as a variable surface or boundary which shapes the individual's stylistics of existence. Moreover, Foucault no longer subsumes the individual under the one-dimensional notion of a docile body, but rather he attributes a degree of agency or self-determination to the individual who is free to determine, within certain constraints, his own stylistics of existence.

By returning to the Greeks, Foucault underscores differences between ancient and modern forms of sexuality, and thereby denaturalizes the contemporary idea that one's sexual identity provides the innermost truth about the individual. For the Greeks, sex was just one of several aesthetic activities. There was no preoccupation with the self as a desiring subject. Individuals were not categorized by the distinction between heterosexuality and homosexuality. Rather, they were simply concerned to stylize their sexual activity in order to maximize their desire and pleasure. By going back to an era in which sex was placed in such a different register from that of the present, Foucault implicitly undermines contemporary assumptions about the universality of sex. By showing that sexuality is not a historical constant, Foucault indicates that there may be other ways of defining ourselves and of experiencing sexual and bodily pleasures. In other words, there is more freedom in the constitution of ourselves as gendered subjects than contemporary ideas about the indissoluble link between sex and sexual identity allows us to believe.

Of course, Foucault is not suggesting that the Greek attitude to sex provides a blueprint for contemporary behaviour: as Mark Poster points out, Foucault does all he can to undermine a nostalgic presentation of Greek sexuality. However, what Foucault's genealogical analysis does achieve is a history 'that undermines the unquestioned legitimacy of the present by offering a re-creation of a different past. The rupture between the past and the present generates the space for critique' (Poster 1986: 209). In this respect, the later volumes of *The History of Sexuality* elaborate on a theme that is briefly raised in the first volume – that of the juxtaposition between *'ars erotica'* and *'scientia sexualis'*. Although in his development of the idea of practices of the self, Foucault does not mention the notion of erotic art as its predecessor, there is, nevertheless, a striking similarity between Foucault's description of the aesthetics of existence and an *ars erotica*:

> In the erotic art, truth is drawn from pleasure itself, understood as a practice and accumulated as experience; pleasure is not considered in relation to an absolute law of the permitted and the forbidden, nor by reference to a criterion of utility, but first and foremost in relation to itself; it is experienced as pleasure, evaluated in terms of its intensity, its specific quality, its duration, its reverberations in the body and the soul (*Foucault 1978a: 57*).

Foucault compares *ars erotica* with the Western idea of *scientia sexualis* – the idea that knowledge of our sexual desires constitutes an objective truth about our selves – not in order to privilege the former over the latter. Rather, Foucault makes the comparison to indicate, as he does in the final two volumes of *The History of Sexuality*, that there have existed, and probably continue to exist, other ways of experiencing our bodies and desires beyond a regulatory heterosexuality and obsession with the self.

STYLE AND HISTORICAL METHOD

Whilst Foucault's idea of practices of the self overcomes some of the problems of his earlier idea of individuals as bodies, it is not, however, without its limitations. The following three chapters will consider in detail some of the theoretical limitations and problematic implications of practices of the self. I consider here one particular problem, which is that Foucault's stress on practices of the self as primarily an aesthetics of existence tends to gloss over the question of the priority of different practices of the self. This is to say, by reducing the varying techniques of the self to the same effective level of self 'stylisation', Foucault does not distinguish sufficiently enough between practices that are merely 'suggested' to the individual and practices that are more or less 'imposed' in so far as they are heavily laden with cultural sanctions and taboos. It is important to make this kind of distinction if we are to assess to what degree individuals act autonomously and in an innovative fashion, or to what degree they merely reproduce dominant social structures and inequalities. Foucault's failure to distinguish between the varying priorities of different techniques of the self is a problem in relation to his treatment of gender as one of these techniques. On the one hand, I have argued that Foucault's study of the different attitude to sexuality held by the ancients opens up a point of critique of the modern belief in sex as the truth of the self. Despite this, however, I believe that the idea of aesthetics or style is not an entirely adequate category within which to understand aspects of the formation of gender identity.

It is important, of course, not to be anachronistic in the criticism of Foucault's approach to gender. The danger of reading our own criteria, divisions and understanding of sexuality back into Greek culture is precisely what Foucault warns against when he deconstructs the similarity of code in western morality in order to highlight differences at the level of an ethics of historical behaviour. With this error in mind, however, there are, nonetheless, discernible tensions and ambiguities in Foucault's treatment of gender as style. These tensions can be perceived both at the level of an empirical historical study, and also at the level at which Foucault indicates that practices of the self can be used as an analytical tool in contemporary social critique.

With regard to the question of historical method, Mark Poster has argued that there is a considerable slackening in the rigour with which Foucault applies his theoretical approach in the final volumes of *The History of Sexuality*. In the introduction to *The Use of Pleasure*, Foucault describes his method as both genealogical and archaeological. Genealogical analysis permits the historical study of the formation of the desiring subject; archaeological analysis examines the conditions which make it possible to utter certain statements in a given discourse:

> The archaeological dimension of the analysis made it possible to examine the forms themselves; its genealogical dimension enabled me to analyze their formation out of the practices and the modifications undergone by the latter. There was the problematization of madness and illness arising out of social and medical practices, and defining a certain pattern of 'normalization'; a problematization of life, language, and labour in discursive practices that conformed to certain 'epistemic' rules; and a problematization of crime and criminal behaviour emerging from certain punitive practices conforming to a 'disciplinary' model. And now I would like to show how, in classical antiquity, sexual activity

and pleasures were problematized through practices of the self, bringing into play the criteria of an 'aesthetics of existence' (*Foucault 1985a: 11–12*).

This method of examining texts sets aside the intentions of the authorial subject, and instead explores how statements are possible. By working within the texts themselves, Foucault analyses the text as a discourse, as an objective field of positions or statements. It is called archaeology because the analysis is conducted at a level beneath the consciousness of the author. Thus, in the first volume of *The History of Sexuality*, Foucault's archaeological analysis of psychoanalytic texts uncovers the disciplinary strategy of the confession, although the explicit intention of these texts is the treatment of psychic disorder. Similarly, in *Discipline and Punish*, although penal reformers like Bentham sought to find humanitarian methods by which to rehabilitate criminals, Foucault uncovers a network of disciplinary techniques centred on the body. As Poster puts it: 'In this method [archaeology], everything hinges on the ability of the critic to go beyond the intentional level of the discourse to locate a system of problematics that are at once outside the text and within it, and once elaborated reveal a new level of significance in the text' (Poster 1986: 217).

However, despite the announcements that Foucault makes about his methodology, Poster argues that he abandons the objectivist level of reading statements in the text, and instead relies too heavily on the intentional level of meaning, direct arguments and explicit phrases. To illustrate Foucault's abandonment of objectivist critique in favour of traditional recitation, Poster points to the uncritical manner in which Foucault draws on Musonius to back up his assertion that during the Hellenistic Roman era, there was an intensification of the marriage tie at the expense of the love of boys. Whilst detailed descriptions of Musonius' texts do not conflict with what Foucault contends, the archaeological level of analysis is never reached (Poster 1986: 217–18).

Poster's criticisms of Foucault's uncritical approach to his historical sources can be used to indicate the shortcomings of Foucault's treatment of the issue of gender. When Foucault asserts that Greek practices of the self were based on an 'ejaculatory schema' which 'was not addressed to women', he appears, once again, to rely too heavily on an acceptance of the intentional level of meaning in his historical sources. If women did not figure in ethics of the self, then, adopting an archaeological perspective, it would be pertinent to ask what were the conditions that made it possible for a discourse to address only men. Foucault considers this problem fleetingly when he condemns the tyrannical structure of ancient society, based on slave labour and the subjugation of women. However, he does not take this level of analysis any further.

It is not enough simply to acknowledge that the freedom of an elite was guaranteed by the subjugation of the masses. Rather, it should be asked, given the fact that the practice of an aesthetics of existence was dependent on the maintenance of a strict social hierarchy, to what extent can the stylization of the self really be called a 'practice of liberty' or a freedom? Thus, some feminist historians have shown how the images of women in Greek litera- ture and philosophy consistently fluctuate between idealization or depreciation. Both types of representation, however, are interrelated and can be linked to patriarchal anxieties about the necessity of con- trolling female sexuality in order to maintain a social system based on the exchange of women. As Marilyn Arthur points out, the Greeks were highly aware of their '*polis*' and '*oikos*' as a structure which embodied certain rational and universally valid principles. The idealized stereotype of the mother is based as much on the notion of a potentially destructive feminine sexuality as the stereo- type of the whore. However, in the case of the mother this threat has been subordinated to the regulatory agency of the family structure, an expression of masculine rationality (see Arthur 1984; Peradotto and Sullivan 1984).

Foucault registers these ambivalences in Classical representations of women: at one point, he argues that women merely figure as objects in the 'virile' ethics; at another point, women are expected to exercise the same form of self-mastery as men (Foucault 1985a: 22, 82–3, 129). However, he does not attempt to analyse their sig- nificance. Such a level of analysis would not necessarily under- mine the changes outlined by Foucault in the history of sex, but what it would highlight is the inadequacy of the term aesthetics, or style, to differentiate between varying techniques in terms of im- portance. Thus, given that the future of Greek society depends on the maintenance of the *oikos*, the stylization of existence in the realm of marriage necessarily admits less free or autonomous behaviour than, say, the stylization of one's daily regimen. Not all practices of the self are simply an exercise in aesthetics; some are more cru- cially linked than others to the maintenance of social hierarchies.

It is not necessary to turn to other historical sources to examine the shortcomings of Foucault's treatment of gender, for at points, Foucault's argument undoes itself. In a certain respect, Foucault appears to sidestep quite legitimately the issue of gender with his

assertion that for the Greeks, the principal sexual opposition was
not that between masculinity and femininity but between passivity
and activity: 'for the Greeks it was the opposition between activity
and passivity that was essential, pervading the domain of sexual
behaviours and that of moral attitudes as well' (Foucault 1985a:
85). With such an assertion, Foucault neatly sidesteps an examination of the gendered nature of practices of the self. However,
some commentators, such as Maria Daraki, have maintained that
this is a misrepresentation of Greek culture and that on close examination, it breaks down. To illustrate his contention that the
Greek male felt greater anxiety about occupying the passive, rather
than the feminine, role in any social or sexual relationship, Foucault states that a man wearing makeup would be reprehensible to
the Greeks not because of his effeminate appearance, but because
the makeup signifies an inclination towards occupying more passive
social roles:

> On seeing a boy who was too dressed up, Diogenes would get
> annoyed, but he allowed for the fact that such a feminine ap-
> pearance could just as well betray a taste for women as for men.
> In the eyes of the Greeks what constituted ethical negativity par
> excellence was clearly not the loving of both sexes ... it con-
> sisted in being passive in regard to the pleasures (*Foucault 1985a:
> 85–6*).

Whilst not wanting to underestimate the extent to which the Greeks
had a different attitude towards relations between men, Foucault's
separation of femininity from passivity and the consequent
privileging of the latter as the main dynamic force behind Greek
ethics is problematic. This separation and privileging is an artificial
manoeuvre in that the idea of passivity cannot be totally separated
from that of femininity because both occupy a similar position in
a series of structurally analogous binaries. Both femininity and
passivity are indissolubly linked. Indeed, at points the artificial
separation Foucault tries to maintain between femininity and passivity breaks down and the two categories are shown to be imbri-
cated in each other:

> That moderation is given an essentially masculine structure has
> another consequence ... *immoderation derives from a passivity that
> relates it to femininity*. To be immoderate was to be in a state of
> nonresistance with regard to the force of pleasures, and in a
> position of weakness and submission; it meant being incapable

of that virile stance with respect to oneself that enabled one to be stronger than oneself. In this sense, the man of pleasures and desires, the man of nonmastery . . . or self indulgence . . . was *a man who could be called feminine*, but more essentially with respect to himself than with respect to others (*Foucault 1985a: 84–5; my italics*).

In this light, the passage from Diogenes that Foucault cites to back up his argument can be read equally as an expression of the fear of appearing feminine as well as appearing passive. This alternative reading is supported by feminist research into ancient Greek society which shows how Greek conceptions of masculinity were inextricably caught up with a fear of the feminine. Maria Daraki points out that the Greeks regarded over-indulgence in the sexual realm as feminizing. This contrasts with Foucault's claim that the principal fear of the ethical Greek was the adoption of a passive, rather than a feminine role. Against this, Daraki demonstrates that even were he to occupy an active role, the sexually indulgent man was still regarded as effeminate. At the heart of masculine identity, then, there was a constant struggle against what was regarded by the Greeks as the 'woman within' (Daraki 1986: 102). This further reinforces a point that has been made by many feminists: that throughout Western history, various conceptions of sexuality, however diverse among themselves, have been based on 'the perennial contrast of "male" to "female" sexuality' (Bland 1981: 56; see also de Lauretis 1987: 14). In other words, female and male sexuality has been invariably defined in contrast and in relation to each other. For Foucault to assert that women did not figure in the 'exclusive domination of the virile model' is to remain at a basic level of analysis, given that the 'plenitude' of masculinity only gains its significance in relation to the 'lack' of femininity. This blindspot of Foucault is more remarkable given that most of his previous works – most notably *Madness and Civilization* – have been dedicated to demonstrating how domination is achieved through the constitution of a marginalized and inferior 'other'.

STYLE AS AN ANALYTICAL CATEGORY

The shortcomings in Foucault's historical study of practices of the self point to similar inadequacies if the concept were used as a tool for contemporary social critique, as Foucault suggests. The problem remains that without considerable elaboration, the idea of style or aesthetics as the predominant term in practices of the self fails to explain clearly the relation between particular practices and its socio-cultural determinants. Once again, this is particularly a problem in relation to the treatment of gender.

Embedded in the idea of a stylization of the self is a notion of choice. Practices of the self are 'intentional and voluntary actions' by which individuals seek to understand and transform themselves in an active fashion. What this notion of aesthetic choice does not tackle very well, in relation to gender and sexuality, is the involuntary and biological dimensions to sexuality. In saying this, it is important not to forget Foucault's insights into the socially constructed nature of sexuality arising from his critique of the modern belief of sexuality as the most intractable element in our selves. Bearing this in mind, however, there are nevertheless certain desires and biological phenomena which cannot be overcome or transformed simply through a conscious act of self-stylization. This is not to say that there are certain bodily impulses and desires which can never be reconceptualized. But it draws attention to the fact that in order to change certain aspects of sexuality, there must be a detailed examination of the network of deeply entrenched cultural norms in which our bodies are embedded. The concepts of stylization and aesthetics are not appropriate categories with which to tackle the issues involved. For example, a notion of aesthetics of the self does not make clear why it is that certain practices, which involve the taking up of subject and object positions, are not equally available to men and women. As Wendy Holloway says, 'it's virtually impossible for women to put themselves in the position of subjects in the male sexual drive discourse when it comes to practices such as bottom pinching or wolf-whistling' (Holloway 1984: 236).

The inadequacy of the idea of aesthetics to tackle certain aspects of the formation of individuals as sexual subjects can be linked to Foucault's failure, throughout all three volumes of *The History of Sexuality*, to tackle the emotional or affective side of sexual relations. Mark Poster suggests that this 'relative and remarkable absence of discussion about the affective nuances of sexual relations' is related to Foucault's aversion to Freudian discourse, preoccupied as it is with questions of conscious and unconsicous feelings (Poster 1986: 214). Despite this aversion to psychoanalysis, it is still clear, however, that the notion of an aesthetics of existence is too rational or intentional a category to capture some of the affective, involuntary aspects of sexuality. Aesthetics does not, for example, provide an explanation of how individuals invest in certain discursive positions in a not necessarily conscious or rational way. In this regard, the notion of 'investment' suggested by Wendy Holloway to explain the semi-conscious manner in which individuals adopt different subject positions is more useful:

> By claiming that people have investments . . . in taking up certain positions in discourses, and consequently in relation to each other, I mean that there will be some satisfaction or pay off or reward . . . for that person. The satisfaction may well be in contradiction to other resultant feelings. It is not necessarily conscious or rational. But there is a reason (*Holloway 1984: 238*).

The notion of investment helps to explain the kinds of 'reward' women obtain from placing themselves in positions which are commonly regarded as subordinate. Thus, quoting a study by Angela McRobbie on adolescent, working-class girls and their ambition to 'attract and keep a man', Holloway argues that commonly accepted practices of femininity take it for granted that there is status and power attached to attracting and possessing men. Thus, what is often perceived as the subordination of women to male demands and desires, is not necessarily experienced as such by those women, but rather as an expression of their power. The idea of investment not only explains why women historically have made different investments, taking up different positions in relation to gender identity and sexual practice – celibacy, monogamy, non-monogamy, lesbianism, heterosexuality, feminism, etc. – but also it explains how 'other major dimensions of social difference, such as class, race and age, intersect with gender to favour or disfavour certain positions' (Holloway 1984: 239).

CONCLUDING REMARKS

In this chapter I have shown how Foucault's elaboration of a notion of the self in his final work represents a significant shift in his theoretical interests. This shift must not be interpreted, however, as a rejection of his earlier work. Rather, it must be seen as an elaboration of themes that were present in his earlier work but were never fully developed. Foucault himself remarks on the efforts and risks involved in trying to 'alter one's way of looking at things, to change the boundaries of what one knows' (1985a: 11). Thus Foucault's study of practices or technologies of the self can be seen as rounding out or complementing his previous studies of

various technologies of domination. Although Foucault still believes that power constitutes individual subjects, he no longer
locates it exclusively in external and impersonal mechanisms and
institutions. Rather, a more specific and diffuse idea emerges of
individuals actively constructing their day-to-day existences in a
relatively autonomous fashion.

I went on to show how this notion of the self overcomes some
of the theoretical difficulties – identified in the first chapter – of
Foucault's earlier equation of individuals with their bodies. I argued that this shift from bodies to selves opens up new potential
points of convergence between Foucault's work and feminist theory.
In particular, Foucault's idea that individuals exert a degree of
autonomy in shaping their immediate conditions of existence
accords with a recent feminist concern to explain how, despite
large scale gender inequalities, women are not just passive dupes
of patriarchal structures of domination. At the same time however,
I pointed out certain points of theoretical ambiguity in the idea of
practices of the self that would need to be worked through thoroughly if feminists are to make use of this element of Foucault's
thought. I argued that Foucault's privileging of the aesthetic nature
of practices of the self presents particular difficulties. These difficulties are not so much associated with an aesthetic elitism, as
some commentators have suggested, but rather with the way in
which the notion of aesthetics glosses over differences in priority
between varying practices of the self. This is particularly a problem
for the analysis of practices of the self associated with gender. By
reducing all practices of the self to the level of self-stylization,
Foucault does not elaborate sufficiently on the socio-cultural determinants which may impose some practices, more than others, upon
the individual. Although Foucault is right to reject the idea that
gender identity is definitively imposed on individuals by external
forces, at the same time, his notion of style significantly underestimates the force of the cultural norms that come into play in the
formation of individuals' gender identity.

Despite these limitations, the idea of practices of the self represents, nonetheless, an interesting and significant shift for feminists interested in Foucault's work. In this chapter, I have focused
mainly on the implications of Foucault's idea of the self as a descriptive category for social analysis. In the following three chapters,
I will examine the notion of practices of the self in more depth; in
particular, I will focus on the way in which Foucault links it to an
idea of a contemporary ethics.

3

Ethics of the Self

INTRODUCTION

Foucault has frequently been called an anti-Enlightenment thinker. Such charges are based on readings of his earlier work where he devotes himself to a deconstruction of the notions of the constitutive and rational subject. For many critics, particularly those on the left, what is unacceptable about Foucault's one-dimensional account of the subject as a 'docile' body, is the denial of the individual's capacity for rational and autonomous thought. In short, Foucault denies individuals the capability of overcoming the limitations and inequalities of the society in which they live and, by implication, he refuses the possibility of progressive social change. The attacks on Foucault's rejection of some of the central political ideals of the Enlightenment have been fierce. His work has been charged with distilling an 'Elixir of Pure Negation' (Merquior 1985: 159). Richard Rorty has accused him of adopting an unrepentant and highly irresponsible 'anarchic Nietzscheanism' (Rorty, quoted in O'Farrell 1989: 114), and Ian Wright has described the Foucauldian method of thought as a 'counsel of despair' which entirely abandons 'dreams of progress' and the possibility of 'meaning in history' (Wright 1986: 16).

However, whilst these charges have some force with respect to Foucault's earlier work, they need to be reassessed in relation to Foucault's work on the self. For one of the interesting features of the idea of practices of the self is that Foucault does not use it simply as a descriptive tool for the analysis of techniques of subjectification; rather, he also places it at the basis of what he calls

a 'modern ethics' of the self. Furthermore, this modern ethics of the
self is infused with an emancipatory potential which Foucault links
to the individual's capacity for self-determination and autonomy.
The introduction of a notion of ethics with an emancipatory impulse
signals, therefore, a significant shift for an 'anti-Enlightenment'
thinker. Indeed, Foucault himself saw his last work as following a
tradition of Enlightenment thought rather than running counter to
it.

The following three chapters will consider the implications of
this shift in Foucault's thought. In this chapter, I have three principal
aims. Firstly, through a close reading of his work I will outline the
move that Foucault makes from practices to ethics of the self. Secondly, I will draw out in what ways Foucault perceives a connection between his work and a tradition of Enlightenment thought.
Finally, I will consider the implications of a Foucauldian ethics on
feminist critiques of orthodox moral theory. On the one hand,
feminists have presented a powerful critique of basic moral concepts, such as rationality and impartiality, by undermining their
claims to value neutrality and showing them to be generalizations
of historically specific, dominant values. On the other hand, some
subsequent feminist attempts to formulate alternative ethics that
incorporate a respect for specificity (the 'other') and those values
which have been excluded by traditional moral thought, are problematic in that they tend to be based upon an ahistorical idea of the
mother borrowed from object relations theory. I argue that
Foucault's formulation of an ethics around a non-essentialist conception of identity, and around a reworking of the Enlightenment
concept of autonomy, indicates a way of overcoming some of the
difficulties in certain existing 'feminine' ethics. I conclude that,
ultimately, Foucault's ethics of the self offers to feminists the challenge of thinking through the differences within sexual difference.

ETHICS OF THE SELF

In the previous chapter, we have seen how the introduction of the
category of practices of the self overcomes the theoretical impasse
of Foucault's earlier work, which does not explain how social agents
operate as autonomous individuals. My discussion concentrated
on practices of the self as a descriptive tool for social analysis and
how it implied a more sophisticated understanding of the relationship between the individual agent and social structures than

has previously been exhibited in Foucault's work. Practices of the self, however, does not just remain a descriptive analytical category for Foucault. By examining these practices, he introduces them into a process of ethical reflection understood not in terms of a meta-ethics but at the concrete level of historical practices.

As we have seen, for Foucault, the central difference between Christian and pagan ethics is the degree of freedom accorded to the individual in determining the actual form that his/her ethical practices should take. Foucault explains the difference in terms of a distinction between a morality turned towards ethics and a morality turned towards codes. What is of interest is that Foucault perceives in these ancient practices a potential model for an ethics of existence for the modern individual. He is not naïve enough to believe that Greek ethics can be simply transported into contemporary society as a blueprint for behaviour. Indeed, he is adamant that it is not possible to 'find the solution of a problem in the solution of another problem raised at another moment by other people' (Foucault 1984b: 343). Nevertheless, he believes that contemporary society has reached such a degree of scepticism about large-scale systems of belief that it must seek a more individual or localized basis for a modern morality. In this respect, Foucault is of the opinion that we can learn something from the moral perceptions of the Greeks: 'And if I was interested in Antiquity it was because, for a whole series of reasons, the idea of a morality as obedience to a code of rules is now disappearing, has already disappeared. And to this absence of morality corresponds, must correspond, the search for an aesthetics of existence' (Foucault 1988a: 49).

What Foucault values most highly in the ancient ethics of existence is the degree of autonomy exercised by the individual in relation to the more general social and moral codes. In many of his earlier works – *Madness and Civilization, Discipline and Punish* and the first volume of *The History of Sexuality* – Foucault's objection to contemporary society is the way in which the tendency to embed social norms and rights in what are misperceived as the rational and objective structures of the law and science lead to the individual being caught up within a normalizing web of law and medicine. What Foucault rejects about Christian ascetics, indeed about Christianity as a whole, is that it is ultimately heteronomous in as much as it requires the subordination of the individual's moral conduct to an externally contrived set of principles. The pressure to conform obliterates the autonomy of the individual. For Foucault, modern secular ethics are more insidious because they are no longer grounded in religion, but in the 'so called scientific knowledge of what the self is, what desire is, what the unconscious is'. Modern power operates not by ignoring individuals, but by claiming to have arrived at the 'truth' of the individual and, thereby, limiting individuality to a 'set of very specific patterns' (Foucault 1982: 214):

> This form of power applies itself to immediate everyday life which categorizes the individual, marks him by his own individuality, attaches him to his own identity, imposes a law of truth on him which he must recognize and which others have to recognize in him. It is a form of power which makes individuals subjects. There are two meanings of the word *subject*: subject to someone else by control and dependence, and tied to his own identity by a conscience or self-knowledge. Both meanings suggest a form of power which subjugates and makes subject to (*Foucault 1982: 212*).

The normalizing tendencies of modern technologies of power are obscured behind the screen of individualization. The endless examination of one's inner self, which Foucault sees as a dominant characteristic of modern society, does not lead to greater self-knowledge, but rather is the result of a forgotten coercion. The obvious example of this is Foucault's famous attack on psychoanalysis.

In contrast, Foucault regards ancient Greek ethics as free from such normalizing pressures. Although they operate around certain central moral imperatives, the privileged moment within these ethics is what Foucault calls a 'certain practice of liberty', whereby the ancient Greek is free to establish a relation with himself, idiosyncratically to stylize his existence in order to maximize the pleasure, beauty and power obtainable from life. It is this principle of an autonomous aesthetics of the self that Foucault presents as an antidote to the normalizing tendencies of modern society. One of the most pressing political struggles for modern individuals, he argues, is the 'struggle against the forms of subjection', that is, against the regulated forms of identity and sexuality that are tolerated in contemporary society:

> The political, ethical, social, philosophical problem of our days is not to try to liberate the individual from the state, and from the state's institutions, but to liberate us both from the state and from the type of individualization which is linked to the state. We have to promote new forms of subjectivity through the refusal of this kind of individuality which has been imposed on us for several decades (*Foucault 1982: 216*).

This passage illustrates how the notion of autonomy is not, for Foucault, a purely descriptive category; it is also connected to a notion of political resistance or opposition in so far as he sees that there are modes of individual behaviour that can counter the homogenizing tendencies of modern life. In the first volume of *The History of Sexuality*, Foucault's conception of power works against the possibility of any form of resistance to modern forms of disciplinary domination. The argument here is that every counter-power already moves within the horizon of the power against which it struggles. As soon as it is victorious, this counter-power is transformed into a power complex that provokes a new counter-power (see Habermas 1987: 281). Thus for Foucault, the liberating power of psychoanalysis as a therapeutic practice is illusory since, in effect, it serves to implicate individuals even deeper in the network of disciplinary power by instilling in them the urge to confess. In psychoanalysis, confession is not extracted from the subject under analysis; rather, the urge to confess becomes so deeply embedded in the modern subject that it is no longer perceived as coerced, but is regarded as an act of self-liberation. Under the illusion of leading to greater self-knowledge, the disclosure of one's inner self and unconscious desires leads to a more efficient regulation and normalization of sexuality through the production of self-policing subjects (see Foucault 1978a: 60).

By dissolving the link between consciousness, self-reflection and freedom, Foucault effectively closes off an explanation of how individuals may act in an autonomous fashion and, in turn, how such autonomous actions may lead to progressive social change. The confessing subject is both the instrument and effect of domination. However, with the notion of practices of the self, Foucault proposes a way out of this inevitable cycle where resistance is transformed into domination, through a process which involves the adoption of an attitude of self critique and the exploration of new modes of subjectivity.

On the whole, Foucault expands very little on his theory of a modern ethics of the self in order to explain what it is about certain practices that make them resistant to incorporation into dominant conceptions of individuality. His most sustained consideration of a modern ethics occurs in the article 'What is Enlightenment?' (1984a), where he draws upon a mixture of the work of Kant and Baudelaire. The title 'What is Enlightenment?' is borrowed from a minor article of Kant's where he defines the Enlightenment as a break from traditional systems of thought and as a heightened critical awareness of today as difference in history. Although generally considered to be one of Kant's marginal texts, Foucault argues that 'What is Enlightenment?' is of great significance because it is the first time that a philosopher has considered his work not as a quest for universal values, but in terms of the specific historical moment at which he is writing. Indeed, in a recent essay, Habermas points out the extent to which Foucault's reading of Kant as the first philosopher to articulate a critical consciousness of the present runs against standard interpretations of Kant as the philosopher of universal moral tendencies (Habermas 1989: 174). For Foucault then, Kant's text represents the first time that critical reflection on the present as different from yesterday appears as a motive for a particular philosophical task: 'it seems to me that with this text on the *Aufklarung* we see philosophy . . . problematizing its own discursive contemporaneity' (Foucault 1988a: 88). To use other terms, 'What is Enlightenment?' is seen to inaugurate the first philosophical consideration of modernity. As Habermas puts it, 'Foucault discovers in Kant the first philosopher to take aim like an archer at the heart of a present that is concentrated in the significance of the contemporary moment' (Habermas 1989: 177).

It is Kant's treatment of the Enlightenment as an attitude of critical self-awareness that Foucault regards as relevant to the formation of a modern ethics of the self. The work of Baudelaire is drawn upon to indicate what direction and what form this critical self-awareness should take. It is not the work of Baudelaire the poet that is of interest to Foucault, but the figure of Baudelaire the dandy who makes of 'his body, his behaviour, his feelings and his passions, his very existence, a work of art'. As the paradigmatic modern individual, the dandy is 'the man who tries to invent himself' (1984a: 41). To be modern is, for Foucault, to take oneself as an 'object of complex and difficult elaboration' like a work of art. What interests Foucault in this idea of an ascetic reinvention of the self are the moments when art passes over into the sphere of life. Foucault places great stress on Baudelaire's pan-aestheticism, where art no longer occupies its own private niche, but where it gives birth to lifeforms directly:

> What strikes me is the fact that in our society, art has become something which is related only to objects and not to individuals, or to life. That art is something which is specialized or which is done by experts who are artists. But couldn't everyone's life become a work of art? . . . From the idea that the self is not given to us, I think that there is only one practical consequence: we have to create ourselves as a work of art . . . we should not have

to refer the creative activity of somebody to the kind of relation he has to himself, but should relate the kind of relation one has to oneself to a creative activity (*Foucault 1984b: 350–1*).

An essential feature of the constitution of oneself as a work of art is that it entails a limit attitude. One rejects established patterns of individualization through the interrogation of what are thought to be universal, necessary forms of identity in order to show the place that the contingent and the historically specific occupy within them. For the individual, freedom from normalizing forms of individuality consists of an exploration of the limits of subjectivity. By interrogating what are held to be necessary boundaries to identity or the limits of subjectivity, the possibility of transgressing these boundaries is established, and therefore the potential of creating new types of subjective experience is opened up (Foucault 1984a: 46). In so far as this exploration reveals new areas for analysis and for self-formation, the critical attitude of modernity is also an experimental one (Foucault 1984a: 46–7). The question to be explored is how can the 'growth of capabilities be disconnected from the intensification of power relations?' (Foucault 1984a: 48)

It is important to note that Foucault sees this exploration of the self not as a liberation of a true or essential inner nature, but rather as an obligation, on the part of the individual, to face the endless task of reinventing him or herself. 'Modern man' he says, 'is not the man who goes off to discover himself, his secrets and his hidden truth; he is the man who tries to invent himself. This modernity does not 'liberate man in his own being'; it compels him to face the task of producing himself' (Foucault 1984a: 42).

It is this distinction, between the uncovering of oneself and the reinvention of oneself, that is central to understanding what Foucault means when he says that practices of the self follow a tradition of Enlightenment thought rather than running counter to it. What Foucault rejects about Enlightenment thought is the linking of moral codes to a global perspective which is generally a notion of universal reason. Following a traditional Weberian argument, Foucault regards discourses of universal reason as indissolubly linked to the rationalization of society of which, as we know, he has a purely negative view: 'The relationship between rationalisation and excesses of political power is evident. And we should not need to wait for bureaucracy or concentration camps to recognise the existence of such relations' (Foucault 1982: 210).

For Foucault, therefore, the freedom of the individual from oppressive aspects of modern society cannot be contingent upon any

metanarrative of justice, rationality or whatever. One such metanarrative that Foucault rejects is the discourse of humanism which,
he argues, bolsters a certain, fixed conception of human nature.
It is Foucault's rejection of humanist values which have led critics
to label him an anti-Enlightenment thinker. Foucault argues,
however, that the Enlightenment is not coextensive with humanism. Rather, the two are in a state of tension because one fosters
static conceptions of human nature, whilst the other encourages a
process of critical self-awareness and self-overcoming (Foucault
1984a: 44). It is this second element of Enlightenment thought –
'the principle of a critique and a permanent creation of ourselves
in our autonomy' – that Foucault attempts to salvage whilst rejecting
the humanist theme of a fixed human nature which lends itself to
modern practices of the normalization and the homogenization of
individuality.

Although he may reject the Enlightenment belief in a universal
rationality, what Foucault retains from the Enlightenment is the
notion of autonomy which is regarded as essential to a state of
positive liberty, defined as the individual being able to exercise his
critical judgement free from the influence of dominant beliefs and
desires. For Enlightenment thinkers, this notion of autonomy is
bound up with a theory of rationality, or a fully integrated subjectivity. Foucault, however, rejects the notion that there is any
founding, and universal form of rationality. Rather, he argues that
there are multiple, historically specific forms of rationality: 'I do
not believe in a kind of founding act whereby reason, in its essence, was discovered or established . . . I think, in fact, that reason
is self created, which is why I have tried to analyse forms of rationality: different foundations, different creations, different modifica-
tions in which rationalities engender one another, oppose and
pursue one another' (Foucault 1983: 202). This does not mean that
we cannot use our reason to criticize other 'rational' practices. On
the contrary, Foucault intends to unhitch a principle of autonomous critique from such overarching notions of rationality, whilst
preserving, at the level of the individual, some notion of transcendence in the sense of being able to go beyond the limits that
have been imposed on us. A Foucauldian ethics of the self is not
based upon adherence to externally imposed moral obligations,
but rather upon an ethic of who we are said to be, and what,
therefore, it is possible for us to become. John Rajchman sees
Foucault's ethics as furthering the modern ethical tradition, initiated by Sartre, which revolves around the question of a 'modern
praxis': 'A modern practical philosophy . . . is the philosophy for a

practice in which what one is capable of being is not rooted in prior knowledge of who one is. Its principle is freedom, but a freedom which does not follow from any postulation of our nature of essence' (Rajchman 1985: 166–7).

Having outlined Foucault's theory of an ethics of the self, I would now like to consider potential points of convergence between his work and the feminist critique of rationality.

FEMINIST CRITIQUE OF RATIONALITY

It is the goal of trying to preserve a notion of transcendence – in terms of overcoming the limitations of present social conditions – whilst, at the same time, disconnecting it from a theory of universal reason that, I think, makes Foucault's idea of practices of the self of interest for feminists. A potential point of convergence can be established between Foucault's critique of metanarratives and the feminist rejection of what are understood to be the phallocentric concepts of universal reason and autonomy.

The feminist critique of the concept of universal reason is wide ranging and, for the purposes of argument, I will only briefly outline its main features.[1] The critique is prompted by a sense of the historical connections between rationalist ideas and the belief in a hierarchical opposition of 'mind' and 'nature'. This opposition is, in turn, associated with a contempt for the embodied condition which is seen as essentially a feminine condition. By uncovering this chain of associations, feminist researchers have shown that supposedly objective, impartial standards, such as universal reason and autonomy, are, in fact, historically situated and contingent terms, often extrapolations of masculine characteristics and values that serve to legitimize and reproduce a dominantly masculine culture. From this perspective, the Enlightenment rhetoric of autonomy and objectivity creates and perpetuates a male definition of reality which is based on the devaluation of femininity and everything which, by analogy, is associated with it: emotions, desires, materiality, etc. Although the counter-argument would be that the term 'man' is generic in that it incorporates both the experiences of men and women, Spender shows how a simple example proves this to be false: the statement 'man has difficulty in childbirth' is nonsense (Spender, quoted in Hekman 1990: 33). As a consequence of this disregard of the gendered perspective, feminists have called into question the dominant philosophical project of

seeking objectivity in the guise of a 'God's eye view' which tran-
scends any situation or perspective (see Fraser and Nicholson 1988;
Harding and Hintikka 1983).

Although feminists agree that rationality has been defined in
masculine terms, they do not agree on a single response to this
issue. Some feminists argue that it is possible to accept the Enlightenment definition of rationality and merely broaden it to in-
clude the perspective of women. Others argue that feminists should
accept Enlightenment definitions of the rational/irrational dichotomy since they accurately portray the true nature of relations
between men and women. However, feminists should revalorize
the feminine side of the dichotomy. Finally, some feminists argue
that we should abandon altogether Enlightenment rationality and
its false dichotomies of subject/object, rational/irrational. This leads
to two counter-strategies. Either feminists can reformulate an alternative and distinct feminine knowledge, e.g. the French feminist
strategy of *'écriture feminine'*. Or as in 'postmodern' feminism, they
can aim to rid themselves of the gendered connotations of
knowledge altogether. There is no space here to consider all these
feminist responses, not only because they are so varied, but also
because they are situated across a wide range of academic disciplines, and therefore they discuss different specific issues (see
Hekman 1990: 39–61). Here, I will focus on the feminist critique of
moral theory and what has been the influential formulation of an
alternative 'mothering' ethics.

Following on from the critique of the notion of a universal rationality, feminists have sought to develop alternative systems of ethics
and ways of understanding social relations which incorporate a
gendered perspective. Just as rationality must not be defined in
terms of an implicitly male notion of universality, so morality must
not be based on notions of rights and formal reasoning – what
Gilligan calls the 'justice perspective' – which, once again, privilege
a male point of view. Ethics can no longer be grounded in a cat-
egorical imperative or in a respect for an abstract moral law. Rather,
a feminist ethics is based on a responsiveness to others and a respect
for the particular which leads to moral concerns connected to
providing care, preventing harm and maintaining relationships. In
order to clarify what such a feminist ethics would look like in contrast
to an abstract, masculine ethics, feminist philosophers have drawn
quite extensively on the notion of 'mothering theory' outlined by
Nancy Chodorow in *The Reproduction of Mothering* (1978). Setting
herself to explain the internal, psychological dynamics which lead
many women to willingly reproduce social patterns associated with

female inferiority, Chodorow posits the cross-cultural activity of
mothering as the primary object of investigation. She questions why
it is that mothering is reproduced over time as a female-associated
activity and how it is that the experience of mothering produces a
new generation of women with the psychological inclination to
mother whilst men are not so inclined. Her solution lies in the fact
of gender identity: female mothering produces women whose deep
sense of self is relational and men whose deep sense of self is based
on separation and autonomy.

The difficulty with mothering theory is that, whilst it claims to be
grounded in a concern for the particular and the 'concrete other', it
surreptitiously reintroduces some of the essentialist and ahistorical
features of the very metanarratives that feminists are questioning.
Mothering theories are essentialist in so far as they are based on
certain assumptions about the nature of human beings and the
conditions of social life. They are ahistorical in so far as their methodology is unmediated by cultural or historical considerations, and
therefore they function 'de facto as permanent, neutral matrices for
inquiry' (Fraser and Nicholson 1988: 382). These problems will now
be considered in more detail.

'FEMININE ETHICS' AND MOTHERING THEORY

Some of the most influential recent work on feminist moral theory
is that of Carole Gilligan on particularist ethics. Gilligan attempts
to replace what she regards as masculine definitions of moral
maturity in terms of abstract notions such as 'justice and rights'
('the generalised other') with an idea of ethics based more on caring and interpersonal relations. This alternative system of ethics is
derived from what she has observed to be the particular characteristics of women's moral judgements, which are more contextual
and more immersed in the details of relationships and narratives
(the 'particular other'). Once these characteristics are seen not as
deficiencies, but as essential components of adult moral reasoning,
then what is regarded, from an abstract 'male' perspective, as
women's moral confusion of judgement becomes a sign of their
strength. Moral deficiency becomes moral maturity in as much as
the self recognizes itself as immersed in a network of relationships
with others (see Benhabib 1987).

From one perspective, Gilligan's work has a powerful anti-
foundationalist thrust in that it challenges the way in which formal

moral systems have persistently effaced and devalued women's lives and experiences under false, univocal claims to universality. However, as Fraser and Nicholson have noted, Gilligan's position is ambiguous in so far as her challenge involves the construction of an alternative universal model of feminine moral development. The problem is that Gilligan's counter-model is open to the same charge of false generalization which she leveled at Kohlberg. Although she claims to be speaking 'a' different voice, Gilligan does not specify 'which women, under which specific historical circumstances have spoken with the voice in question' (Fraser and Nicholson 1988: 388). Thus Gilligan generalizes a particular feminine perspective to the exclusion of other perspectives such as class, sexual orientation, race and ethnicity.

This generalization of a particular feminine perspective to represent the universal results in an ahistorical and acultural definition of feminine moral identity which many feminists see as leading Gilligan's work back into an undesirable essentialism. Gilligan draws heavily upon Chodorow's theory of gender identity which attributes fixed, cross-cultural characteristics to masculine and feminine identities. As we have seen, Chodorow argues that mothering is a basic cross-cultural activity which produces a feminine identity whose sense of self is relational and a masculine identity whose sense of self is based on autonomy and separation from others. This particular model of development is known as 'object relations theory'. Drawing upon this argument, Gilligan claims that the experience of mothering is central to understanding the more caring and empathetic moral standpoint of women. Whilst many feminists have found in Chodorow's theory a cogent account of the psychic differences between men and women, it nevertheless has problematic foundations in ahistorical and essentialist assumptions. Thus, in respect to Gilligan's appropriation of Chodorow's theory, Kate Soper contends that Gilligan's argument – that it is purely because of their nurturing experience that women acquire this particularist ethical perspective – implies that there would be a moral duty to confine them to a mothering role as a way of guaranteeing the presence in society of these 'female', caring capacities (see Soper 1989: 102). Moreover, scepticism has been expressed about the idea that there exists an invariant and monolithic distinction between male and female identity. Virginia Held notes that Gilligan's 'dual culture interpretation' of the difference between masculine and feminine moral reasoning would have been warranted if she had conducted her research in a prototypically patriarchal society. In contemporary Western culture, however, there is such extensive contact between men and women that it is difficult to believe that the feminine and masculine realms constitute separate cultural spheres (Held 1987: 146).

There are many other difficulties connected to the essentialist underpinnings of Gilligan's feminine ethics. One particular problem which should be noted here is connected to the idea of a fixed gender identity. As Fraser and Nicholson have pointed out, it is premised on the idea that 'everyone has a deep sense of self which is constituted in early childhood through interaction with one's primary parent and which remains relatively constant thereafter' (Fraser and Nicholson 1988: 385). This gendered deep sense of self continues through adult life and cuts across divisions of class, race, ethnicity, etc. This sense of self is derived from mothering conceived of as an ahistorical, cross-cultural constant, rather than as a culturally determined activity. Also, it is based on only one of the many activities that women do. Whilst not wanting to deny the importance of the experience of mothering, there is no reason why it, of all forms of social interaction, should be taken as paradigmatic of human relations in general. Relations between mothers and children can be just as oppressive as any other social relation and when this is the case, relations between equals, who can decide whether to enter into agreements, may seem comparatively more desirable (see Held 1987; Soper 1990).

The criticism that object relations theorists such as Chodorow and Gilligan produce an ahistorical and over-stable conception of the subject, is made not just by historical materialists, but also from a different perspective by post-Lacanian theorists. Jacqueline Rose, for example, argues that object relations theorists fail to account for the unconscious and for the radical discontinuities which characterize the psyche prior to the formation of the ego and a distinct and separate sense of self. By claiming that certain kinds of identifications are primary, object relations theorists make the relational life of the infant primary to psychic development itself, conflating the psyche with the ego and relegating the unconscious to a less significant role. Lacanian theorists insist on the unconscious as a source of discontinuous and chaotic drives which renders the ego a perpetually unstable phenomenon, resting upon a primary repression of unconscious drives which return to undermine the ostensible unity of the ego (see J. Rose 1986: 90).

Feminist anthropologists offer a critique of the tendency of feminist object relations theorists to give the role of mother – understood as an emotional nurturer – a central place in their ahistorical, acultural definition of 'woman'. Recently feminist anthropologists have

pointed out that, in fact, it is only in Western societies that the notions of 'woman' and 'mother' overlap in such a way as to lead to
dominant definitions of woman which are crucially dependent on
the concept of mother. It is not simply a question of cultural diversity
in the way in which women perform their roles as mothers. Rather,
it is a matter of how the category of woman is linked in each culture
to certain attributes of motherhood such as maternal love, nurturance,
fertility, etc. (see Moore 1988: 25–30). In *Philosophy and Feminist
Thinking*, Jean Grimshaw notes that the idea of woman as emotional
nurturer was foreign to the Greeks (Grimshaw 1986: 63). In another
context, Ruth Bleir cites anthropological research to contest the idea
that there 'is such a simple entity as women's status' throughout
history. She argues that in some societies women's productive activities and social relations determine the relations of reproduction.
For example, !Kung women, nomadic gatherers in the Kalahari
desert, nurse their babies for three years in order to control the
spacing between births and thereby accommodate childbearing to
the demands of their productive activities. This contradicts standard
views that see reproduction as the primary determining factor on
women's social activity and also exposes the ethnocentric limitations
of many feminist theories of mothering (Bleir 1984). Thus, despite
its claims to value heterogeneity, mothering theory does not develop
the methodological tools to deal with difference related to class,
race, ethnic and other cultural variants.

  Whilst there is undoubtedly a need to develop an ethics that
takes account of the more emotional and interpersonal aspects of
human existence, it is nevertheless imperative to avoid naturalizing these aspects by arguing that they somehow derive from
woman's biological function of reproduction. Even feminists, who
are aware of the theoretical problems arising from an essentialist
position, have difficulty in formulating an alternative feminist
ethics which does not naturalize aspects of women's socially-
defined nurturing roles.

  The tendency amongst some feminist theorists to naturalize the
female mothering capacity and to place a highly culturally specific
notion of mothering at the core of feminine identity results in the
naturalization of a series of analogous terms. One such set of terms
are the related concepts of autonomy and dependence. Object relations theorists relate autonomy to the male child's split from the
mother to identify with the father, and hence, autonomy is naturalized as an aggressive drive inherent to masculine identity. Similarly, the fact that in an Oedipal account of gender identity, girls
do not undergo such a split from the mother, is taken as explanatory

of the 'natural' feminine inclination to acknowledge dependency by empathizing and caring for an other. However, by naturalizing the concepts of autonomy and dependence through their association with a reified account of identity formation, feminists have relinquished the opportunity of being able to reconstruct, in non-naturalistic terms, an image of autonomy as a quality of a humanizing social existence. It is this challenge of reconstructing the notion of autonomy so as to uncover its emancipatory potential that Foucault is concerned with in his ethics of the self. The failure of feminists to take up this challenge and to consider the use that Foucault's work might provide in overcoming present limitations in feminist ethics are considered next.

AUTONOMY AND DEPENDENCE

An example of this persistence in naturalizing the concepts of autonomy and dependence, whilst paradoxically being aware of the dangers of adopting an essentializing approach to the issue of a feminist ethics, is provided in the work of Jessica Benjamin. In an article written in 1982, 'Shame and Sexual Politics', Benjamin talks of a dilemma in feminist politics, between the need for women to enter into traditional fields of male power in order to transform them ('transcendence'), and the need for women to stamp the field of politics with the experiences of their suffering and powerlessness in order to dissolve traditional political practices altogether ('immanence'). She argues that the only way to resolve this dilemma is to break down the patriarchal logic which artificially polarizes the distinction between transcendence and immanence, or between the desire for autonomy and the recognition of one's dependence on others:

> But if the divergence between male and female values has been created by men ... then so has the split between transcendence and immanence, between giving and risking life. Contrary to appearance, dependence and independence are not opposed – nor is one side dispensable ... our politics must find a form of transcendence which does not repudiate immanence, the ties that give and maintain life (*Benjamin 1982: 153*).

According to Benjamin, if feminists were to overcome the transcendence/immanence dichotomy this would imply a 'profound break with the history of revolutions in our modern western world'

(Benjamin 1982: 154). Revolutions, she states, imply the risking of life and transcendence in two interrelated ways. Firstly, there is the risk of physical death in the confrontation with the material forces that one aims to defy. Secondly, there is the risk of symbolic or psychological death in the sense that the physical and emotional ties which make life familiar, which, according to Benjamin, 'protect us from naked self exposure', are ruptured. Whilst this rupturing of the familiar is a traumatic and destabilizing process, it is necessary if new forms of social interaction are to be established. Moreover, there is no way to engage in a material power struggle without psychological and symbolic risk. Benjamin claims, however, that all past revolutions have attempted to rationalize their goals in the sense that they have made their politics purely material, economic or physical. The threat of symbolic instability is too threatening for a male political rationale, and this means that as long as the risk of psychological death is repressed, politics remains reformist rather than truly revolutionary.

In certain respects, there is a congruence of aims between Benjamin's argument for the necessity of breaking down the dichotomized relation between freedom and dependence through an interrogation of one's accepted desires and needs, and Foucault's insistence that it is only through a reinvention of the self that the subject can experience a degree of autonomy and self-determination. The element of radical self-interrogation at the heart of Foucault's ethics – what he calls the 'transfiguring play of freedom with reality' – incorporates the idea of a destabilization of the self similar to the 'psychological death' which Benjamin sees as essential for the transformation of rationalized, orthodox political practices. For Foucault, it is not possible nowadays for ethics to be grounded in universal moral imperatives or impersonal systems of belief, given the modern disenchantment with large-scale metanarratives such as religion or politics. Rather, ethics must be a 'practical critique', conducted at the level of the individual and taking the form of a radical self-criticism: 'Criticism is no longer going to be practised in the search for formal structures with universal value, but rather as a historical investigation into the events that have led us to constitute ourselves and to recognise ourselves as subjects of what we are doing, thinking, saying' (Foucault 1984a: 45–6). For both Benjamin and Foucault, the transformation to a more radical form of political practice is not possible without a risking of the self. In other words, a radical personal politics is still absolutely central to the success of any kind of political change at the more general level of the ordering of social relations.

At the same time, the transformation is not one-way; the incorporation of identity politics into orthodox forms of political practice not only transforms the latter, but also draws the self out from its field of immanence. Issues related to identity, which are generally deemed to be 'private', are politicized and opened up as sites of transformation. Ethics of the self is not a cult of authenticity, but rather an endless task of self-production: 'Modern man . . . is not the man who goes off to discover himself, his secrets and his hidden truth; he is the man who tries to invent himself. This modernity does not "liberate man in his own being"; it compels him to face the task of producing himself' (Foucault 1984a: 42).

The linking of self-transformation with wider political transformation that is essential to a modern ethics is prefigured in Foucault's study of ancient practices of the self. In Greece the individual flourished, but at the same time this individuality was always subordinated to the demands of the Greek *polis*. The individual exercised self-mastery in sexual relations, not only to increase his desire and pleasure, but also to prove that he was a good citizen and worthy, as a free man, to rule others: 'The individual's attitude towards himself, the way in which he ensured his own freedom with regard to himself, and the form of supremacy he maintained over himself were a contributing element to the well-being and good order of the city' (Foucault 1985a: 79). What Foucault's study of Greek ethics brings to the fore is the artificiality of the modern counterposition of the rights of the individual to the rights of the group; as if, nowadays, 'a society which could satisfy the rights of all and the rights of each were unthinkable' (Daraki 1986: 95). Foucault's insistence on the intertwinement of self-construction with social change challenges this assumption and maintains that one cannot be realized without the other.

This incorporation of the personal into the political realm contrasts with theories of feminine ethics which regard the incorporation of feminine values into the patriarchal realm of politics in a unidirectional fashion, as transforming for the latter, but not for the former. From this perspective, feminine values represent a site of authenticity and truth and the political signifies a realm of uniform patriarchal oppression. However, if everything that is political is patriarchal, then patriarchy ceases to retain any distinctive meaning and 'we are deprived of any means of discriminating between cultural modes which serve the maintenance of patriarchy and cultural modes which tend to subvert it' (Soper 1990: 15). In contrast, Foucault's ethics of the self is based on a complex interchange between the process of self-transformation and that of political transformation. This dialectic implies a way of understanding forms of feminist practice as activities that are multiply determined, rather than as an authentic self-expression of an autonomous, 'feminine' subject.

In theory, then, both Benjamin's and Foucault's conceptions of a radical exploration of the self are opposed to invariant concepts of identity, in particular the idealized notion of the mother upon which much feminist work on alternative ethics is based. Yet despite Benjamin's assertion that feminists can only overcome the artificial polarity of autonomy and dependence through a radical inter- rogation of everything that is familiar and stable about the self, she slips back into a naturalization of the role of the mother, and therefore back into the received feminist understanding of autonomy as an aggressive, masculine drive to be rejected *per se*.

This slippage, from the deconstruction of the autonomy/de- pendence binary to its reinscription, is exemplified in Benjamin's engagement with the work of Horkheimer, in particular his sociol- ogy of the family. To summarize, Horkheimer regards the family in early bourgeois society as having a definite productive and pro- gressive function which has been eroded in late capitalist society. In the early bourgeois family, the respect and reverence which was accorded to the father in a tightly structured domestic context served to instil into the other members of the family an obedience and respect for authority. The family became an agency for society in so far as it 'rationalized the irrationality of power' and shaped individuals to conform with the demands of the social system. Combined with this legitimizing role, the authority of the father has a progressive function in as much as the internalization of paternal authority by the other members of the family contributes to the formation of a strong ego capable of independence of thought and action. Horkheimer is aware of the oppressed condition of women in the early bourgeois family, and in his theory it is prin- cipally the male child who internalizes the father's demands, thereby assuming notions of inner discipline, individual responsibility and independence. However, even in the self-sacrificing devotion of the mother in the early capitalist family, Horkheimer perceives a progressive potential in so far as the relations of solidarity and intimacy that centred on the mother figure provided a safe haven from the calculating instrumental relations of the market place.

In contrast to the significance of the family in early bourgeois society, the importance of the family in late capitalist society has been eroded. Authority is no longer invested in the figure of the father, but in impersonal and external institutions. As a result of this loss of paternal authority, children no longer internalize paternal authority, and therefore lose the capacity for autonomous critical thought and independent action. For Horkheimer, late capitalist society is characterized by a retreat to conformism.

Benjamin's response to Horkheimer's work is twofold. Firstly, she totally rejects the link Horkheimer establishes between the internalization of paternal authority and the formation of an independent conscience. She argues that this association 'promotes the undialectical and individualistic proposition that freedom consists of isolation' (Benjamin 1978: 51). In other words, it does nothing to break down the patriarchal assumption that 'masculine identity . . . assumes the denial of the need for the other to be the route to independence' (Benjamin 1978: 51). Because Horkheimer sees freedom as a matter of the assumption of individual responsibility by an independent social actor, his idea of emancipation precludes any theory of solidarity and community with others. By denying the possibility of a maternal nurturance which also encourages autonomy, Horkheimer perpetuates a phallocentric strategy which opposes autonomy to dependence, transcendence to immanence.

Secondly, the only part of Horkheimer's analysis that Benjamin wishes to salvage is his account of the role of maternal love, which is counterposed to that of paternal authority in the early bourgeois society. Following on from this, she argues that maternal nurturance is not antipathetic to the growth of autonomy, but rather necessarily implies it: 'what is nurturance if not the pleasure in the other's growth?' (Benjamin 1978: 51). It is the task of feminists to articulate freedom in relation to this maternal bond, rather than in opposition to it. The 'mother-bond' is the starting point of freedom because it combines the desire for autonomy with the need for dependence. The uncontingent love of the mother-bond allows one to be

> known and accepted for who you are, as well as who you can become. To oppose freedom to it is to place freedom in the context of the conditional and the earned, into the Paternal world of reward and punishment, instead of into a world beyond good and evil. To discover freedom beyond this bond, not in opposition to it, is the promise of sisterhood (*Benjamin 1982: 158*).

Horkheimer's theory is clearly not without problems in its treatment of gender, yet Benjamin's appeal to a nurturant maternal love ultimately only repeats the terms of the antinomy that it hopes to mediate. Rather than breaking down traditional conceptions of the nurturing mother, Benjamin 'calls upon a merely traditional, unnegotiated relationship' and ends up with an account of compatibility between a nurturing mother-love and encouragement to individuation, rather than a mediation of the terms autonomy and dependence (Johnson 1988: 28). Benjamin does not succeed in recovering a notion of autonomy for feminism; instead she reinscribes the idea that autonomy is a version of the masculine desire for domination and sentimentalizes the feminist desire for sisterhood and solidarity.

THE RECONSTRUCTION OF AUTONOMY

Given that the Enlightenment construction of freedom as the autonomy of the rational ego is said to entail a repressive gender politics, it appears inappropriate to the formulation of the emancipatory hopes of the feminist movement. However, what feminists have not engaged with is the extent to which the logic of domination discovered in the Enlightenment image of freedom represents a deformation of its origins in an essentially emancipatory project. In *The Philosophy of the Enlightenment*, Ernst Cassirer describes the emancipatory kernel of the Enlightenment project thus: 'Man is not simply subject to the necessity of nature; he can and should style his destiny as a free agent' (Cassirer 1955: 9). Using the classic Weberian distinction between an instrumental and substantive rationality, it is possible to argue, as Horkheimer does, that these emancipatory aims become blocked and deformed when instrumental reason becomes the dominant mode around which society is organized. The object of feminist critique, then, has been this deformed image of freedom and autonomy, which has led feminists, in reaction, to formulate alternative ethics grounded in naturalized ideas of dependency and 'mother-love'. What most feminists have failed to do is to attempt to reconstruct, in non-naturalistic terms, an image of autonomy as a quality of a humanizing social existence.

In a recent collection of essays, *Women and Moral Theory* (Kittay and Meyers 1987), various authors have attempted to shift feminist moral theory away from a feminine ethics, and in relation to this, some have tried to reformulate the relation between feminism and autonomy. Thomas Hill, for example, argues that Gilligan's critique of autonomy, as an ideal peculiar to a dominant group which serves to reinforce established patterns of oppression, is undoubtedly correct in many points. However, he goes on to argue that this

particular feminist critique is too undifferentiated and results in
a blanket rejection of the concept of autonomy. As a result, feminists overlook many fundamental elements implied in the notion
of autonomy which are important for moral theory and are compatible with the concept of compassion and the recognition of one's
dependencies. Hill identifies three specific points embedded in
the concept of autonomy which should be salvaged by feminists: i) autonomy as impartiality in the review and justification
of moral principles and values, ii) autonomy as a right to make
certain personal decisions and iii) autonomy as a goal for personal
development.

In relation to the first point, Hill argues that Kant's thesis that
the individual must strive to remain impartial in the review and
justification of moral principles is still fundamental to the establishment of any form of contemporary ethics. According to Hill,
Kant often elides the idea of impartiality in the legislation of moral
choices with the idea that in his/her daily life the individual should
strive to act on impartial principles, freeing him/herself from
particular attachments and ignoring distinguishing features of individuals and specific situations. For Hill, it is essential to distinguish between these two definitions of impartiality: whilst the latter
is problematic in that it may contradict moral imperatives to be
compassionate, the former does not necessarily conflict with the
demand for compassion. Impartiality in determining moral principles does not exclude compassion, but it is essential if we are to
transcend a morality based solely by reference to our own needs
and wants or by reference to those of other individuals identified
essentially by relation to ourselves.

In relation to the second point on autonomy and rights, Hill
argues that individuals should respect each other's freedom to
deliberate and act on their moral problems. As he describes it, 'it
is a right to make otherwise morally permissible decisions about
matters deeply affecting one's own life without interference by controlling threats or bribes, manipulations, and willful distortion of
relevant information' (Hill 1987: 134). This right of autonomy is, of
course, not uncircumscribed, it does not simply imply a moral
attitude of *laissez-faire*; people's decisions about their own lives
should be consistent with 'other basic moral principles including
recognition of comparable liberties for others'. It does not imply
that a self-sufficient independence and separation from others
are goals worth pursuing. Nor does it express a faith in rational
decision-making as intrinsically valuable. However, individuals
should be at least granted the opportunity to make choices without

interference from others on grounds that they are non-rational or
unwise.

Finally, Hill argues that the idea of autonomy should be understood as a goal of self-development. By this, Hill means that individuals should be self-governing in the sense that their responses
to problems are not dictated by neurotic impulses and prejudices
of which they are unaware: 'Ideally autonomous, or self govern-
ing, moral agents would respond to the real facts of the situation
they face, not to a perception distorted by morally irrelevant needs
and prejudices' (Hill 1987: 137).

I have given detailed attention to Hill's arguments because it
seems to me that his reworking of the idea of autonomy crystal-
lizes some of the main elements in Foucault's reworking of the
notion of autonomy in ethics of the self. Both Foucault and Hill
reject the side of Kant's definition of autonomy which emphasizes
the need for the individual to act on abstract, impartial moral principles regardless of the network of relations and dependencies
in which s/he may be caught up. However, unlike some feminists
who, having criticized this aspect of the concept of autonomy then
reject the concept altogether, both thinkers attempt to retain an
original emancipatory aim of the Enlightenment notion of autonomy. For Kant, autonomy and enlightenment consisted, in part,
in the 'mature' use of reason; it was 'the moment when humanity
is going to put its own reason to use, without subjecting itself to
any authority' (Foucault 1984a: 38). And it is this notion of the
mature and autonomous use of reason that Foucault salvages:

> it seems to me that a meaning can be attributed to that critical
> interrogation on the present and on ourselves which Kant for-
> mulated by reflecting on the Enlightenment . . . the critical ontol-
> ogy of ourselves . . . has to be conceived as an attitude, an ethos,
> a philosophical life in which the critique of what we are is at one
> and the same time an historical analysis of the limits that are
> imposed on us and an experiment with the possibility of going
> beyond them (*Foucault 1984a: 49–50*).

Foucault seeks to redefine the concept of autonomy so as to reconcile
the critical interrogation of the socio-cultural and emotional determinants of an individual's situation with a capacity for critical
independence or self-governance. For Hill the aim of this autonomy
is for the individual to achieve a positive state of liberty through
the development of a critical understanding of the motivations of
his/her thoughts and actions. This contrasts with negative concep-

tions of autonomy according to which freedom appears merely as the absence of constraining or inhibiting relations. For Foucault, the aim of this autonomy is not to achieve a state of impersonal moral transcendence, but rather to refuse to submit to the 'government of individualisation' by constantly interrogating what seems to be the natural and inevitable in one's own identity:

> We must try to proceed with the analysis of ourselves as beings who are historically determined, to a certain extent, by the Enlightenment. Such an analysis implies a series of historical inquiries that are as precise as possible; and these inquiries will not be oriented retrospectively toward the 'essential kernel of rationality' that can be found in the Enlightenment . . . they will be oriented toward the 'contemporary limits of the necessary,' that is, toward what is not or is no longer indispensable for the constitution of ourselves as autonomous subjects (*Foucault 1984a: 43*).

DECONSTRUCTION OF NEED

Foucault's notion of autonomy as an attitude of permanent critique contrasts with the naturalized notions of autonomy and dependence underlying many theories of feminine ethics. Ultimately, Benjamin fails to sucessfully rearticulate the relation between autonomy and dependence because she naturalizes these categories, rather than analysing them as culturally determined concepts. This tendency to naturalization is connected to an uncritical treatment of the notion of need, which is understood as a pre-social category that determines the nature of one's identity. In other words, identity is mimetically or causally linked to one's basic needs, which are always sexually determined. Masculine identity is based on an aggressive drive for autonomy and self-assertion which is related to a separation from the mother. Feminine identity revolves around the basic need to care for others which is explained through the dynamics of the mother and female child dyad. Gender is seen as reflecting a biological sex and pre-social needs. Thus despite her declared intention, Benjamin finishes by opposing autonomy to dependence because she presents the desire for the security of intimate kin relations and solidarity as innate human needs unmediated by any cultural experience. Concepts such as a self-denying 'natural' mother-love remain entirely unproblematized. By displacing the political and discursive origin of gender identity

onto an essentialized core, Benjamin precludes an analysis of the
political constitution of the gendered subject and its fabricated
notions about the ineffable interiority of its sex or of its true identity.

What Benjamin and other feminists have not taken on board is
a point that Foucault makes in *Discipline and Punish*, that 'need is
also a political instrument meticulously prepared, calculated and
used' (Foucault 1977a: 26). What Foucault proposes in his idea of
an ethics of the self is that one does not attempt to discover one's
hidden needs, but rather one attempts to self-consciously deconstruct what are perceived as needs in order to discover new
areas of experience. Some feminists, such as Nancy Fraser, have
recognized the necessity to critically unpack the concept of need.
Following Foucault, Fraser argues that the idea of need has no
fixed biological, sexual or emotional reference point. This is illustrated in the way in which 'needs talk' functions as a central argumentative strategy in different and opposing political claims.
Need, she argues, has not always been central to Western political
culture; it is, in fact, peculiar to late capitalist political discourses
(Fraser 1989: 162). Fraser argues that in order to bring into view the
'contextual and contested' nature of needs claims,[2] it is necessary
to adopt an analytical approach which focuses not on needs but on
discourses of needs. In other words, a politics of need interpretation.

According to Fraser, needs talk is crucial to oppositional discourses because it constitutes a central moment in the self constitution of new collective agents or social movements. However, it is
equally crucial that feminists recognize that the needs they articulate in order to define a new space for women are not uncontested,
univocal or 'natural'. The naturalization of need is also a strategy
employed by dominant groups to deradicalize demands put forward by marginalized and radical individuals and groups. These
discourses of 'reprivatisation' operate by absorbing elements of
oppositional discourses and thereby depoliticizing them. Thus,
discourses of reprivatization seek to contain issues that have only
recently become an issue of public debate, such as gay and lesbian
rights or wife battering, by returning them to the private realm,
and hence depoliticizing them. Thus, it is argued that wife battering is not a legitimate subject of political or legal discourse but a
domestic or religious matter. An obvious example of such a strategy is the discourse of Thatcherism (Fraser 1989: 171–3).

What makes discourses of reprivatization so powerful is the way
in which they blend the old with the new. Thus they do not simply
counterpose traditional values to what are seen as deviant, profligate
discourses of need, but rather they rearticulate oppositional needs

discourses, and thereby empty them of their radical content: 'Because reprivatisation discourses respond to competing, oppositional interpretations, they are internally dialogized, incorporating references to the alternatives they resist, even while rejecting them' (Fraser 1989: 172). Fraser gives an example of the 'pro-family' discourses of the social New Right which, although explicitly anti-feminist, incorporate, in a depoliticized form, feminist-inspired motifs implying women's right to sexual pleasure and to emotional support from their husbands.

Fraser's example highlights why it is crucial for feminists to construct an alternative ethics which is not based on a naturalized understanding of need and a correspondingly fixed definition of identity. In critiques of radical feminism, other feminists have long pointed out that the assertion of a feminine essence relies on the same argumentative strategy – the assertion of a natural sexuality – employed by hegemonic discourses which legitimize gender inequality. One problem worth noting here is that ultimately, the naturalization of the need for a mother-bond, an image shared by radical feminists and traditionalists alike, is that it hypostatizes the 'patriarchal present' as the best arrangement within which to cope with what are understood as our elementary needs. As Johnson puts it, 'Ultimately, it would appear that the abdication by feminist theory from the task of proposing a critical perspective on the authenticity of our felt needs and demands means that it necessarily remains locked into a legitimation of present social relations as offering the most appropriate management of needs spawned by it' (Johnson 1988: 29).

FROM NEED TO IDENTITY

In order to construct alternatives to the government of sexuality, therefore, it appears that radical feminists must relinquish the notion that there is a truth to sexual identity in the form of fundamental, invariant needs. For Foucault, a literature or writing of 'femininity' would not involve the problem of truth – uncovering a true identity; rather, it would be a practical, ethical issue of exploring the potential of new identities. In relation to gay literature, Foucault argues that there is such explicit description of sexual acts because it comes from a sexual life of anonymous and fleeting sexual encounters which have no relation to the heterosexual realm of courtship and romance. Homosexuality is the product of interdiction and it concentrates, therefore, on 'the most heated moment' rather than on an anticipation of conquest (Foucault 1988a: 293–8). To analyse gay literature in terms of a relation between an inherently homosexual desire and linguistic representations, he argues, would be like analysing moneylending in terms of an inherently Jewish kind of desire.

Similarly, although he does not deal with feminism directly, it follows that for Foucault, the exploration of a 'feminine' writing or ethics should not be based on an uncovering of an essential link between a feminine desire and its representation, but rather it should involve the construction of an 'etho-poetics' of the feminine (see Rajchman 1985: 180). In relation to this move away from the assertion of fixed identity towards the exploration of the unknown, Foucault's work concurs with recent feminist theory on this issue. Judith Butler, for example, argues that drag – by playing on the link between the anatomy of the performer and the gender that is being performed – simultaneously reveals both the imitative structure of gender itself and its contingent or culturally determined nature. Through its denaturalization of the link between sex and gender, Butler argues that gender parody or drag is a potentially powerful political strategy through which to break down hegemonic sexual identities and to explore 'a fluidity of identities that suggests openness to resignification and recontextualisation' (Butler 1990b: 338). This shift from the construction of alternative conceptions of femininity – which still remains in the artificial logic of sexual polarities – to 'a proliferation of gender style', does not signify for Butler the failure of feminism but rather a positive challenge for any future feminist politics (Butler 1990b: 339). Such a rethinking of feminist politics is echoed in Foucault's own assessment of the achievements of feminism. As he sees it, 'the real strength of the women's liberation movement is not that of having laid claim to the specificity of their sexuality and the rights pertaining to it, but that they have actually departed from the discourse conducted under the apparatuses of sexuality' (Foucault 1980: 220).

Foucault's emphasis on the self, then, is not based on the privileging and implicit mystification of one particular social role. In this respect, it is as if feminist mothering theorists fail to extend the full implications of their critique of orthodox systems of thought to their own position. On the one hand, they reveal that the naturalization of specific dominant values underlies the claims to universality of many types of abstract thought. Yet on the other hand, they fail to 'denaturalize' the assumptions on which they base an alternative ethics. The mother-child dynamic is set up as the ulti-mate paradigm of the 'natural' caring relationship, and therefore as the ultimate paradigm of all social relations. The mother-child dyad is not seen as a particular social and cultural construct, nor is any consideration given to the fact that an ethics of caring may not be an appropriate approach to all forms of social interaction. Rather than taking mother-monopolized child rearing as a invari-ant phenomenon, a genealogical approach would seek to under-stand mothering as an historically specific experience, an effect of various expert discourses, including mothering theory itself.

Such a critique of feminist mothering ethics does not amount to an outright rejection. Rather, Foucault's work on ethics should remind some feminists that one cannot assume that an emancipa-tory potential is exclusive to any one social position. For Foucault, power works through a myriad of social relations, and therefore an ethics of resistance must also be diffuse and varied. For similar reasons, many feminists are now arguing against the priority ac-corded to the maternal perspective in some feminine ethics. Vir-ginia Held, for example, argues that whilst it is appropriate to use a caring perspective to undermine the case that all particular moral rules can be derived from a few fundamental principles, a caring ethic cannot be the only basis for an alternative morality, but rather must be part of a pluralistic ethics or a 'moral division of labour' (Held 1987: 120; see also Ruddick 1987).

Foucault would not discount the possibility of the values of compassion and sharing embodied in mothering theory contribut-ing to an ethics of the self. However, these values would have no priority over other kinds of experience; rather, they would form part of an ethical plurality. As Jana Sawicki points out, there is a similarity between Foucault's work and that of mothering theorists in that they both employ a relational model of identity. A Foucauldian, therefore, would not exclude mothering theory alto-gether, but simply deny it a theoretical privilege, highlighting in-stead the many other relationships through which individuals are produced (see Sawicki 1988b: 174). In one of his final interviews, Foucault remarks, 'My point is not that everything is bad, but that everything is dangerous' (Foucault 1984b: 343). Here, Foucault guards against privileging any one form of identity as inherently radical through an insistence on an understanding of personal identity as constituted by a myriad of social relationships and practices in which the individual is engaged. These relationship may be contradictory and unstable, and therefore the identity is fragmented and dynamic, always open to change and contestation.

DIFFERENCE

An advantage of an ethics based on such a relational idea of identity is that it encourages us to think of difference as a political resource and also encourages us to think of difference in terms of its construction through the social realm. It has been argued by Sawicki that Foucault's theory of identity as relational, and therefore open-ended, provides the basis for a theory of resistance based on a politics of difference. In such a politics, the aim is not to overcome differences in order to achieve a political unity; rather, it is seen as a resource in so far as it multiplies the points of resistance to the myriad of relations of inequality and domination that constitute the social field. Moreover, a stress on difference does not necessarily imply irreconcilable antagonisms between different social groups because, as Sawicki puts it, 'if we redefine our differences, discover new ways of understanding ourselves and each other, then our differences are less likely to be used against us' (Sawicki 1988a: 24).

The point that Sawicki makes about difference as a resource is important because there is a tendency amongst some feminists and left-wing critics to understand difference in an purely negative way. Difference is defined as a process of fragmentation and separation which erodes the basis for a common political struggle. Although Foucault's ethics of the self prioritizes difference as an antidote to those dogmatic and totalizing discourses which attempt to silence difference, he does not suggest that an ethics of the self supplants other forms of political struggle, such as the construction of cohesive, oppositional group identities. He realizes that by focusing exclusively on the self, there may be a danger of bordering on an atomized, and therefore politically regressive, individualism. Rather, an ethics of the self, based on the assertion of individual difference, is understood to be one strategy – perhaps the most personal and basic – amongst many strategies of resistance. Ultimately, the struggle for one's own identity links up with other more collective struggles against the government of individualization:

> [There] are struggles which question the status of the individual: on the one hand they assert the right to be different and they underline everything which makes individuals truly individual. On the other hand, they attack everything which separates the individual, breaks his links with others, splits up community

life, forces the individual back on himself and ties him to his own identity in a constraining way. These struggles are not exactly for or against the 'individual', but rather they are struggles against the 'government of individualisation' (*Foucault 1982: 211–12*).

Foucault's linking of the individual struggle with more collective forms of action arises from his awareness that there are large-scale systems of domination and exploitation which cannot be countered adequately merely through a refusal, at the level of the individual, of the government of individualization. Ethics of the self represents only one form of resistance. Coalitions are not ruled out, but a relational understanding of identity reminds us that any common struggle is a democratic and provisional one, subject to recreation and renegotiation (see Laclau and Mouffe 1985: 185).

The difficulty with the emphasis placed on the role of the mother by some feminists – that is, the prioritization of an essentialized form of identity – is that, albeit unintended, it disregards the claims and experiences of other oppressed minorities. Richard Sennett describes this as 'destructive Gemeinschaft', by which he refers to a destructive sense of community in which conflict is experienced as a zero-sum contest for personal legitimacy, that is the right to have one's feelings. According to Sennett, individuals involved in such conflicts may become more preoccupied with asserting their own identities than with other political goals, such as establishing solidarities with other groups. Such identity politics can become self-defeating in so far as they may lead to internal struggles over who really belongs to the community: 'Powerlessness comes from the very attempts to define a collective identity instead of defining the common interests of a diverse group of people' (Sennett quoted in Sawicki 1988a: 187; see also Sennett 1980).

Foucault's insistence on the relational nature of identities, whether at the level of the individual or the group, emphasizes the need for a radical politics to move away from the preservation of identity or its imposition on others and to move toward the exploration of types of coalition between various groups with the ultimate aim of ending social injustice. As Sawicki puts it, 'theoretical pluralism makes possible the expansion of social ontology, a redefinition and redescription of experience from the perspectives of those who are more often simply objects of theory' (Sawicki 1988a: 188). This idea of a form of political resistance which moves beyond the assertion of identity is considered in the final section.

DIFFERENCE AND SEXUAL DIFFERENCE

Some feminists would argue that practices of the self does not provide an appropriate basis for a feminist ethics because it displaces
questions of gender to such an extent that it erodes the basis of any
kind of collective feminist politics. Moreover, it can be argued that
Foucault's preoccupation with experimental subject positions is
suspicious in as much as it is the expression of a privileged, white,
male perspective which has already had an Enlightenment and is
now willing to subject that legacy to critical scrutiny. The stress
placed on the unstable and decentred nature of identity is considered repressive because it denies marginalized groups, who have
never experienced any kind of Enlightenment, the space in which
to construct a coherent identity for themselves and thereby initiate
a politics of resistance. As Nancy Harstock has asked, 'why is it
that just at the moment when so many of us who have been silenced
begin to demand the right to name ourselves, to act as subjects
rather than objects of history, that just then the concept of
subjecthood becomes problematic?' (Harstock 1990: 163)

Such criticisms have been made not only of Foucault's work, but
also of poststructuralist and postmodernist theories in general.[3]
These criticisms are important and will be considered in the next
chapter in relation to the debate between feminism and postmodernism. However, here I suggest that it is more fruitful not
simply to accuse Foucault of a straightforward 'gender blindness'
in his ethics of the self, but rather to invert the problem and ask
how his work presents a challenge to feminists to think of an ethics
which does not rest on a fixed or naturalized notion of 'woman'.

Feminists have only very recently begun to take up this challenge, prompted both by the implications of the work of theorists
like Foucault, and also by the critique of Western feminism by
black and other feminists.[4] One such response has been made by
Judith Butler, who argues that it is necessary for feminists to radically rethink the ontological constructions of identity in order to
reformulate a representational politics that might revive feminism
on other grounds. This rethinking is necessary because by conforming to a requirement of representational politics that feminism
articulates a stable subject, feminism exposes itself to charges of
misrepresentation. As Butler explains:

> The premature insistence on a stable subject of feminism, under-
> stood as a seamless category of women, inevitably generates

multiple refusals to accept the category. These domains of exclusion reveal the coercive and regulatory consequences of that construction, even when the construction has been elaborated for emancipatory purposes. Indeed, the fragmentation within feminism and the paradoxical opposition to feminism from 'women' whom feminism claims to represent suggest the necessary limits of identity politics (*Butler 1990a: 4*).

An identity politics based on a seamless notion of 'woman' is not only exclusionary in relation to an understanding of the differences of power and resources between women, but it is also normative in so far as it presents reified, heterosexual relations as the main grounding for feminist politics. This is because, to a large extent, the category of woman is stabilized and unifed through what Butler calls a 'heterosexual matrix' (Butler 1990a: 5).

According to Butler, an understanding of identity as an effect leads to possibilities of agency that are foreclosed by positions that take identity categories as fixed or foundational. For an identity to be an effect means that it is neither fully determined, nor completely artificial and arbitrary. The body forms the surface of gender identity in the sense that gender is the repeated stylization of the body, 'a set of repeated acts within a highly rigid regulatory frame that congeal over time to produce the appearance of substance, of a natural sort of being' (Butler 1990a: 33). The task of feminists is to carry out a political genealogy of gender ontologies in order to expose the contingent acts that create the appearance of a naturalistic necessity.

Butler envisages the type of politics to emerge from this genealogical deconstruction of the notion of identity as an 'anti-foundational coalition politics'. She argues that some efforts have already been made to formulate a coalitional politics, but they have invariably slipped into asserting an ideal form for coalitional structures in advance, and thus close off unforeseen possibilities in the self-shaping dynamics of coalition. An insistence in advance on coalitional unity as a goal assumes that solidarity, whatever its price, is a prerequisite for political action. For Butler, this insistence on unity in advance is one of the causes of the increasingly bitter fragmentation amongst activists. Unity sets up an exclusionary norm of solidarity at the level of identity that rules out the disruption of borders of identity concepts. In contrast, a genuinely anti-foundational coalitional politics accepts contradiction and fragmentation as part of the process of democratization, and acts within these tensions. Without the expectation of unity, provisional unities might emerge in the context of concrete actions that have purposes other than the articulation of identity. When agreed upon identities or agreed upon dialogic structures, through which already established identities are communicated, no longer constitute the theme or subject of politics, then identities can come into being and dissolve depending on the concrete practices that constitute them.

In a similar fashion, Foucault refuses to predict what should be the outcome of an ethics of the self. Such predictions would inevitably close off unforseen areas of exploration in the 'critical ontology of ourselves'. The role of the intellectual in this exploration is not to outline goals or specify truths to be sought after, but 'to question over and over again what is postulated as self-evident, to disturb people's mental habits' and in this way to 'participate in the formation of a political will' (Foucault 1988a: 265). The role of the intellectual is to open up, rather than narrow down, areas for 'the undefined work of freedom' (Foucault 1984a: 46). As Paul Veyne puts it, the originality of Foucault's thought is that 'he does not convert our finitude into the foundation for new certainties' (quoted in O'Farrell 1989: 129).

A deconstruction of identity, then, need not necessarily mean a deconstruction of feminist politics. Rather, for feminists like Butler, such a deconstruction entails the challenge of redefining feminist politics outside of the binary of sexual difference upon which, up until now, it has been based. The displacement of a primary, fundamental gender identity holds the promise of complex and generative subject positions and coalitional strategies that neither presuppose nor fix their constitutive subjects in place. Butler argues that this does not result in a form of atomized and individualistic politics which celebrates difference *qua* difference. Rather, it is a case of redescribing

> those possibilities that already exist, but which exist in cultural domains designated unintelligible and impossible. If identities were no longer fixed as the premises of a political syllogism, and politics no longer understood as a set of practices derived from the alleged interests that belong to a set of already made subjects, a new configuration of politics would surely emerge from the ruins of the old (*Butler 1990a: 149*).

CONCLUDING REMARKS

In this chapter, I have shown how Foucault's work on ethics, the self and autonomy presents the challenge to feminists of thinking through the problem of the differences that exist within sexual difference. In many respects, his work serves as a corrective to some of the essentializing tendencies of theories of 'feminine' ethics. During the 1970s the anti-essentialist thrust of Foucault's earlier work was employed by socialist feminists to refute some of the arguments of radical feminists. However, I believe that the issue of anti-essentialism is still relevant to the feminist debates of the 1990s. In the revised introduction to *Women's Oppression Today*, Michèle Barrett has noted that feminism nowadays is increasingly publicly identified with writers such as Carol Gilligan, Adrienne Rich and the 'new French' feminists, who all stress the distinctive social and psychic existence of women and, as a result, emphasize the question of the absolute and monolithic differences between men and women. The effect of this emphasis on gender difference has been to displace some of the negotiations with the issues of men, class and ethnicity initially posed by socialist feminists but increasingly taken up by black and third world feminists. Implicitly, Foucault's work on identity serves to recentre some of the issues involved in these important displaced debates on difference.

In particular, Foucault's reworking of the Enlightenment notion of autonomy challenges feminists to shift tactics from an insistence on a distinct and cohesive 'feminine' identity to a consideration of what women might become if they intervene in the processes that shape their lives. This idea of woman as an active social agent capable of instituting radical change at the micro-political level undermines a feminist politics based on withdrawal from what are seem as invariably oppressive social structures. This latter approach reproduces a classical split between the individual and the social formation, based on the assumption that it is possible to shed what is seen as a false consciousness, imposed and maintained from the outside, and to speak an authentic truth. In contrast, Foucault's ethics of active intervention opens a space for feminists to understand and intervene in the processes through which meaning is produced, disseminated and transformed in relation to the changing configurations of modern power and domination.

4

The Problem of Justification

INTRODUCTION

In the previous chapter, I argued that Foucault's work on ethics
of the self presents the challenge to feminists of thinking through
the issue of the differences within sexual difference. Addressing
the question of feminist ethics, I presented the case that Foucault's reworking of the Enlightenment notion of autonomy
served as a corrective to some of the essentializing tendencies of
theories of 'feminine' ethics, in particular the assumption that
women have a distinct social and pyschic existence, and therefore that they have separate moral values. Against this theoretical
separatism, Foucault's work indicates a way of considering what
women might become if they intervene in the processes that shape
their lives and, as a result, the potential that may arise for the
construction of new types of identity outside of the label of
femininity.

In this chapter, the implications of Foucault's theory of ethics of
the self for feminist critique are considered in relation to the issue
of normativity and the legitimation of political action. Inevitably,
my consideration of such issues will touch upon the current debate
on postmodernity, and in particular upon the way in which it
has problematized 'metanarratives' of justification. The stress that
Foucault places on difference and the particular in his theory of
ethics of the self has lead some commentators to label him a postmodern theorist. One of my central arguments in this chapter is
that, although there are certain similarities between his work and

postmodern theory, Foucault's work differs in several fundamental respects. Unlike postmodern theorists, Foucault is unwilling to reject completely certain concepts derived from Enlightenment thought, such as autonomy, domination and self-determination, in the name of an undifferentiated celebration of plurality. Rather, Foucault recognizes the importance of these concepts for formulating effective strategies of social transformation and political resistance and he therefore seeks to redefine them in relation to his ethics of individual praxis.

Foucault's reworking of Enlightenment thought and the differences that this establishes between his work and the work of thinkers such as Baudrillard and Lyotard, who are more usually associated with postmodernism, is considered in relation to feminist critique and the current debate about the possibility of formulating a 'postmodern feminism'. I argue that although there is a need for feminist theory to develop analytical tools to deal more adequately with the category of difference, in the final analysis the idea of a postmodern feminism is unviable. This is because at some basic level, feminist critique necessarily rests on normative judgements about what constitutes legitimate and non-legitimate forms of action in relation to the political goal of overcoming the subordination of women. Feminists cannot afford to sacrifice such validity judgements for the more relativist position of performative or local justification espoused by postmodern theorists.

I go on to argue that scepticism about the possibility of a postmodern feminism does not imply a retreat to the totalizing ideals of the Enlightenment as the normative basis for a contemporary feminist critique. Some feminists are now arguing that there is a third way between the metanarratives of modernism and the pluralism of postmodern theory, and that it must be articulated by marginalized groups who hitherto have had little say in the definition of types of politically engaged critique. I argue that Foucault's work on ethics of the self gestures towards that third way, but that on close scrutiny, it is riddled with confusion in respect to its normative underpinnings. Whilst Foucault appears to make use of some of the central concepts of Enlightenment and humanist thought, he constantly retreats from making any definitive statement about the normative basis of his ethics. This use of the rhetoric of political engagement without grounding it in a coherent normative standpoint results in a series of contradictions that run through Foucault's work and make it problematic for feminists who seek to reconcile the idea of difference within an explicit normative and political framework.

VARIATIONS OF THE POSTMODERN

Although postmodernism has emerged as one of the key concepts of the last decade, it is fair to say that there exists no single, accepted definition of the postmodern condition. The commitment to heterogeneity, fragmentation and difference has been applied to a series of conflicting cultural projects, and because of this some commentators have made a powerful case that the term is a redundant neologism which obfuscates more than it elucidates.[1] According to Hassan, the term postmodernism has 'shifted from awkward neologism to derelict cliche' without ever attaining to the dignity of concept' (Hassan 1985: 119). Despite many philosophical problems, however, it cannot be denied that there are certain historical and socio-institutional effects of postmodernism and that the political implications of these effects have to be addressed.

Put in schematic terms, the debate about postmodernism can be seen to fall into three realms. Firstly, there is the aesthetic debate over modernism and postmodernism which originated in architecture and spread to the areas of dance, theatre, painting, film and music (see Husseyn 1986: 179–221). Here, postmodernism challenges and assumes the critical function that once characterized modernism before its 'incorporation into the lucrative art market and its elevation into the new orthodoxy' (Boyne and Rattansi 1990: 10). Through an eclectic mixing of styles and codes, postmodernism challenges the distinctions between high and mass culture, between artist and consumer, upon which modernist art is predicated. Furthermore, whereas modernist art rests on a relatively unproblematic notion of representation, postmodern art feeds off a 'crisis in representation' (see Boyne and Rattansi 1990; Harvey 1989; Lash 1990). Although modernism questions modes of representation such as realism as being inadequate vehicles in which to capture the complexities of existence in modern society, it still retains the belief that abstract art can reveal the truth or essence of modern social relations. In contrast, postmodernism problematizes the relation between representation and reality to such an extent that no discourse or aesthetic form can be said to reveal the truth of contemporary existence and this leads to the acceptance of a plurality of perspectives and playfulness of styles. Given feminist criticisms of the elitist and masculinist tendencies within modernist art, there has been a fruitful crossover between feminist art and postmodern aesthetics (see Husseyn 1986; Owens 1983; Pollock 1982).

The second area of debate around the postmodern has focused on the philosophical and cultural concepts of modernity and post-modernity. Here, one of the central issues is whether it is possible and desirable to formulate and justify strategies of social action and change with reference to universal notions of rationality and mo-rality. In other words, the debate centres around the extent to which the Enlightenment metanarratives of rationality and justice are valid in respect to the justification of action in contemporary society. The terms of the debate have been set out by Lyotard and Habermas. On the one hand, Lyotard argues that the metanarratives of mo-dernity are redundant in modern society and that their decline heralds a postmodern era in which a greater freedom and diversity of action is tolerated: 'Postmodern knowledge is not simply a tool of the authorities; it refines our sensitivity to differences and re-inforces our ability to tolerate the incommensurable. It's principle is not the expert's homology, but the inventor's paralogy' (Lyotard 1984: xxv). Against this, Habermas argues that the project of mo-dernity is still to be completed. All those who reject universal and rational systems of justification for programmes of progressive social change are 'conservatives' in that they simply reaffirm the regressive tendencies towards fragmentation, isolation and superficiality which characterize contemporary society (Habermas 1983: 11–12).

The third area of debate is concerned with the economic, polit-ical and institutional character of postmodern society. Here the issue is whether contemporary society can be defined as entering a postmodern stage characterized, amongst other things, by 'post-Fordist' patterns of production and consumption, the decline in the dominance of traditional manufacturing and the associated waning of traditional class politics. Against this, proponents of modernity, such as Jameson, argue that theorists of postmodernity overestimate the significance of the technological and industrial changes in the last ten years. Large-scale dynamics, such as structural social in-equalities, the increasing domination of multinationals and the continuing drive for profit, all indicate that rather than entering a new postmodern era, we are simply witnessing the unfurling of some of the contradictions of late capitalist society (Harvey 1989; Jameson 1983).

This typology, like any other, is a simplification, but it serves to underscore the diversity and range of the postmodern debate. Feminists have intervened in all areas of the debate. The particular aspect of the postmodern that is relevant to this consideration of feminist critique is the philosophical debate about questions of legitimation and justification.

THE CASE FOR A POSTMODERN FEMINISM

One of the most influential arguments for a postmodern feminism is presented by Nancy Fraser and Linda Nicholson in their article 'Social Criticism without Philosophy: An Encounter between Feminism and Postmodernism' (see also Flax 1990). Fraser and Nicholson argue that because both feminist and postmodernist thought have developed out of a criticism of institutionalized philosophy, and have tried to rethink the relation between philosophy and social criticism, there is a certain area of convergence between the two. In particular, each perspective suggests some important criticisms of the other.

Firstly, a postmodernist scepticism of 'grand narratives' reveals some 'disabling vestiges of essentialism' embedded in concepts such as gender identity and universal oppression, which are still central to much feminist theory (see chapters 2 and 3). Despite the recent debate around the concept of difference, Fraser and Nicholson argue that feminist scholarship is still 'insufficiently attentive to the *theoretical* prerequisites of dealing with diversity, despite widespread commitment to accepting it politically' (Fraser and Nicholson 1988: 389).

From the opposite perspective, Fraser and Nicholson argue that feminism as a form of social critique helps overcome the nihilistic tendencies of the postmodern critique of philosophy which arise when it is generalized to a form of social criticism. The anti-foundationalist critique of philosophy initiated by postmodern theorists often leads to the argument that since philosophy can no longer credibly ground social criticism, criticism itself must be local, *ad hoc* and untheoretical. However, according to Fraser and Nicholson this elliptical leap from the illegitimacy of philosophy to the illegitimacy of social criticism is spurious and must be rejected by feminists. The refusal of the possibility of any kind of legitimate analysis of pervasive relations of dominance and subordination radically undermines the feminist critique of the subordination of women: 'a phenomenon as pervasive and multi-faceted as male dominance simply cannot be adequately grasped with the meager critical resources to which they would limit us' (Fraser and Nicholson 1988: 380). One possible soultion to the relativist and anti-theoretical implications of postmodern theory is, according to Fraser and Nicholson, that a postmodern social theory must not begin with a reflection on the condition of philosophy, but must start from an analysis of the nature of the social object which is to be criticized, e.g. social relations between men and women. Effective criticism of such a phenomenon requires an array of different theoretical approaches not encompassed in the 'philosophical' strand of postmodernism. At the same time, this theoretical 'bricolage' is seen to overcome the problem of totalization or the ascription of correct answers to one particular theoretical paradigm.

If feminism can be used to restore an explicitly political emphasis to postmodern theory and postmodern theory can correct some of the essentializing tendencies of feminist criticism, what then would a postmodern feminism look like? Fraser and Nicholson attempt to outline the form that this eclectic theoretical approach would take. On the whole, however, they do not succeed in articulating a postmodern feminism in anything other than the most brief and general terms. Certain characteristics of a postmodern feminism are outlined: it would be a) theoretical but with an historical stress; b) non-universalist – its mode of analysis would be comparative rather than universalizing; c) it would dispense with the idea of a subject of history. Unitary notions of woman and feminine identity would be replaced with more complex and pluralistic constructions of social identity. However, these characteristics remain at the level of assertion and are not elaborated on in detail: 'In general, postmodern-feminist theory would be pragmatic and fallibilistic . . . this theory would look more like a tapestry composed of threads of many different hues than one woven in a single colour' (Fraser and Nicholson 1988: 391).

Furthermore, Fraser and Nicholson claim, rather contradictorily, that postmodern feminism would integrate large-scale social theory with a simultaneous refusal of universalizing categories. The analysis of sexual inequality 'requires at minimum large narratives about changes in social organization' (Fraser and Nicholson 1988: 380–1), whilst at the same time 'postmodern-feminist theory would be nonuniversalist' (Fraser and Nicholson 1988: 390–1). However, as we have seen, the principal characteristic of the postmodern critique of modernity is a suspicion towards 'grand narrative' – that is, totalizing forms of social analysis and universal systems of justification. It is precisely this aspect of postmodernity that Fraser and Nicholson regard as opening feminism up to difference, and yet, at the same time, they appear to want to retain 'at minimum large narratives about change in social organisation and ideology'. If, as feminists, they recognize that a postmodern microanalysis is not an adequate tool alone for analysing the social situation of women, then what exactly is it about their theory that can be called postmodern? Their hesitations about whether to reject or retain large-scale social theory can be read as a manifestation of an un-ease about the normative underpinnings of feminist theory which do not necessarily mesh that easily with a postmodern privileging of the local and contextual. For although Fraser and Nicholson claim to want to adopt a 'pragmatic and fallibilistic approach', they uneasily skirt around the issue of the normative basis of feminism as critique. As Felski puts it: 'Clearly, not all the assumptions of feminism are equally as fallible and open to refutation – it would be hard to imagine a feminist theory which did not espouse as a bottom line a belief in women's subordination and their right to equality and autonomy' (Felski 1989: 231–2).

Fraser and Nicholson's article is valuable in so far as it outlines some of the central issues involved in the encounter between feminism and postmodernism. However, I would argue that the ambivalences in their discussion of a postmodern feminism is symptomatic of unacknowledged difficulties and aporia which arise from the attempt to link together two distinct, and in many re-spects conflicting modes of thought. Both feminism and postmodernism may have developed out of a contestation with traditional systems of thought, but it does not necessarily follow that the two ways of thinking seamlessly overlap or correspond. Indeed, the urge to establish a correspondence between them may be, as Gayatri Spivak puts it, 'worth no more than the satisifaction of coherence' (Spivak 1990: 34). It seems to me that to a certain extent, the debate about feminism and postmodernism is the most recent version of a certain type of contemporary debate that at-tempts to synthesize different forms of thought. Past variations on this theme have been the debates about Marxism and post-structuralism, feminism and Marxism and deconstruction and Marxism. These debates can and have yielded interesting insights. However, there is a danger that the specific and often conflicting nature of a given theory may be assumed under an identity logic which is preoccupied with the establishment of coherencies and the overcoming of contradictions.

It seems, then, that the convergence between feminist critique and postmodernist thought needs to be approached with caution and with attention to the specificities of argument, rather than through the establishment of general similarities. The concerns for difference and sexual difference may overlap but they are not necessarily homologous (see Barrett 1987). The postmodern cri-tique of metanarratives may be a useful device with which to oppose the vestiges of essentialism and overgeneralization that remain in certain types of feminist theory. However, as an analytical approach to be adopted wholesale into feminist critique, postmodern theory may be of more limited value. I now consider the arguments put forward by feminists who are doubtful about the theoretical promise of the postmodern project.

THE FEMINIST CASE AGAINST POSTMODERNISM

Whilst recognizing the need to overcome any vestiges of essentialism and aculturalism that still hamper feminist theory, many feminists are more sceptical than Fraser and Nicholson about the potential for an alignment between feminist and postmodernist theory. This scepticism is based on an anxiety about what the postmodern rejection of metanarratives implies for feminist theory and politics. Feminist politics is, at a fundamental level, posited on modernist metanarrative of personal emancipation. Similarly, feminist theory rests on general categories and abstractions such as gender, class, race, in order to produce a compelling analysis of social inequality. As we have seen in previous chapters, it is important that by using such general categories, feminism does not fall back into simplified, dualistic interpretations of social power relations along the lines of male power/female submission. Although gender may inflect most of the experiences in individuals' lives, it is never manifest in an entirely unmediated form. Individuals' lives are determined by a multiplicity of influences that cannot be easily categorized and cut across each other to form complex power relations. Nevertheless, this complexity of experience does not imply the redundancy of general theoretical categories such as gender. For, without such abstractions, valuable social critique, which aims both to identify and overcome large-scale forms of oppression, could not function. It is for these reasons, then, that many feminists quite correctly believe that their current project of developing theoretical tools better able to deal with difference cannot be elided with a postmodern rejection of metanarratives.

It is with such issues in mind that the feminist philosopher Susan Bordo expresses reservations about the possibility of a postmodern feminism. She argues that the 'programmatic appropriation' of poststructuralist and postmodernist work by feminists is problematic in so far as it shifts the focus of feminist concerns about the representation of cultural diversity from practical contexts to questions of adequate theory. This theoretical stress has the effect of diverting feminists from attending to the professional and institutional mechanisms through which the politics of exclusion operate

in intellectual communities. It also deprives feminists of the analytical tools for critique of those communities and the heirarchical,
dualistic power structures that sustain them.

Although Bordo sees the feminist debate over difference arising
out of 'concrete experiences of exclusion', she argues that the theoretical turn the debate has taken around questions of gender identity and difference is inappropriate to feminist concerns. Moreover,
it reproduces a type of academic discourse which feminists should
be breaking down rather than perpetuating. According to Bordo,
feminism has been drawn into the 'race for theory' (Bordo 1990: 138;
also Christian 1988). Bordo stresses that she is not retreating into an
anti-academicism. On the whole, she concurs with the demand for
more adequate approaches to identity which arise from the insight
that gender forms only one axis in the complex and historically
specific process of the construction of identity. She questions,
however, the conversion of this insight into the relational nature of
identity to the 'authoritative insight' and from there, 'into a privileged critical framework', a 'neutral matrix . . . legislating the appropriate terms of all intellectual efforts, capable of determining
who is going astray and who is on the right track' (Bordo 1990: 139).

There are two aspects to this theoretical presciptivism. Firstly,
somewhat ironically, the difference perspective which arises out of
criticisms of gender generalization, itself falls back on generalization in its insistence that the only correct perspective on race, class
and gender is the affirmation of difference. Whilst postmodernists
argue against transcendence, Bordo argues that at an unacknowledged level, the desire for transcendence remains: 'The historical
specifics of the modernist, Cartesian version have simply been
replaced with a new postmodern configuration of detachment, a
new imagination of disembodiment: a dream of being everywhere'
(Bordo 1990: 143). Feminists need to guard against the supposition
that if we employ the right method we can avoid ethnocentrism
and false universalizations. No matter how local the focus of attention, some perspectives will always be excluded.

Secondly, Bordo acknowledges that generalizations about gender
can obscure and exclude attention to the specific and contextual.
However, too relentless a focus on heterogeneity can obscure the
transhistorical, hierarchical patterns of white, male privilege that
inform the Western intellectual tradition. Although gender never
exhibits itself in a pure form in the context of lives that are shaped
by a multiplicity of influences, that does not mean that abstractions
or generalizations about gender are methodologically illicit or 'per-
niciously homogenising of difference'. It is always possible to find

an item of difference which can shatter generalizations about gender. However, if one disallows any kind of generalization about society, then one is left with an unworkable particularism where 'what remains is a universe composed entirely of counterexamples, in which the way men and women see the world is purely as *particular* individuals, shaped by the unique configurations that form that particularity' (Bordo 1990: 151).

Ultimately, what is slightly ironic about this particular debate on postmodernism is that while Bordo directly opposes the arguments put forward by Fraser and Nicholson about the desirability of formulating a postmodern feminism, both sides are in agreement at a basic level. This is to say that both acknowledge that feminist theory must learn to deal with the differences that cut across sexual difference in a more sophisticated manner, but at the same time, both recognize that feminism cannot afford to relinquish certain large-scale theoretical perspectives. The disagreement centres not so much on general theoretical approach but on the specific interpretation of the term 'postmodern'. Perhaps part of this ambivalence and confusion can be traced back to the undifferentiated way it is used in Lyotard's work – which is generally taken to be the seminal postmodern reference point – to encompass all different types of generalized perspective: 'The grand narrative has lost its credibility, *regardless* of what mode of unification it uses, *regardless* of whether it is a speculative narrative or a narrative of emancipation' (Lyotard 1984: 37; my italics).

Against Lyotard's uncritical and, somewhat ironically, overgeneralized use of the phrase 'grand narrative', it may be more productive, as Douglas Kellner suggests, to differentiate between different types of narrative. Kellner proposes distinctions between 'master narratives' that attempt to subsume every specific viewpoint under one totalizing theory, and 'grand narratives' which attempt to chart the history and development of, for example, capital, patriarchy or the colonial subject (Kellner 1988: 253). Within grand narratives, it may be possible to distinguish between 'metanarratives' which tell a story about the foundation of knowledge, and macro-social theory that attempts to conceptualize and interpret a complex diversity of phenomena. A further distinction could be between 'synchronic' narratives that examine society at a given point in history, and 'diachronic' narratives that analyse historical change. As Kellner remarks, such distinctions make clear the extent to which Lyotard 'tends to lump all "grand narratives" together and thus does violence to the diversity of theoretical narratives in our culture' (Kellner 1988: 253).

For feminists, then, it is not so much a question of being modern or postmodern, of being for or against metanarratives; rather, it is a case of establishing which narratives blunt sensitivity to difference and which narratives are essential to examine and challenge large-scale gender inequality. Before I elaborate on the differences between Foucault's work and postmodern thought, I want to consider in more detail the arguments made by feminists who recognize that if feminist theory is to develop it is necessary to transcend the schematized terms of the modern/postmodern debate.

BETWEEN ENLIGHTENMENT AND POSTMODERN RATIONALITIES

If many feminists remain sceptical of the prospect of a postmodern feminism and even those, who are more optimistic about the possibility of a convergence, flounder when it comes to specifying what a postmodern feminism would look like, what then is the answer? Difficulties with formulating the project of a postmodern feminism do not necessarily mean an uncritical return to an Enlightenment form of rationality as a basis for a contemporary feminist critique and politics.

In *Critique, Norm and Utopia*, Selya Benhabib argues that there are two necessary moments in any form of critique. Firstly, there is the *explanatory-diagnostic* analysis in which a given 'social crisis' is examined. Secondly, there is the *anticipatory-utopian* moment of critique which articulates the normative groundings of the critique. According to Benhabib, critique becomes mere criticism if this second utopian element is missing. The standpoint of the critic should transcend the present and juxtapose to the existent what 'ought to be or what could have been had the past not been betrayed' (Benhabib 1986: 180). Critique, then, is a mode of explicit 'criteriological' inquiry.

For feminist theory to fulfil this dual definition it must, firstly, develop an explanatory-diagnostic analysis of women's oppression across history, culture and societies and, secondly, articulate an anticipatory-utopian critique of the norms and values of our current society and culture 'such as to project new modes of togetherness, of relating to ourselves and our nature in the future' (Benhabib 1987: 81). Whereas the first aspect of feminist critique requires critical/social scientific research, the second aspect is primarily normative and philosophical; 'it involves the clarification of moral and political principles, both at the metaethical level, with respect to their logic of justification and at the substantive, normative level, with reference to their concrete content' (Benhabib 1987: 81).

This framework is useful to understand better what is at stake for feminists in the modern/postmodern debate. As we have already seen, in terms of social criticism or the first, analytical moment of critique, the postmodern insistence on the local precludes systematic analysis of large-scale levels of oppression, such as general aspects to the subordination of women. However, underlying this is a deeper anxiety related to the second, normative moment of critique, whereby the postmodern rejection of legitimation through meta-narrative undermines the ethical grounds from which feminists can call for an end to sexual inequality. Kate Soper explains that the danger for feminists in adopting a postmodern approach is that an exclusive stress on difference may deprive a feminist ethic of the grounds for calling for any kind of social norms, moral codes or legal rulings at all. The overstressing of the particular leads to an equivalence of all biases and particularities and reduces the femin-ist ethic to just one of many equally valid viewpoints. The fear of neglecting difference implies that one cannot make the sort of comparisons or judgements that are essential to legislation or to a more equal social distribution of goods, resources and oppor-tunities. As Soper puts it, this extreme sort of 'difference' feminism, if taken to its ultimate conclusion, 'must condone an anarchist and wholly de-regulated economic and social policy, and . . . we must ask again whether this – with its obvious neo-rightist overtones – is what feminists are wanting' (Soper 1989: 109–10).

In a similar vein, Sandra Harding presents several reasons for feminists to retain large-scale epistemologies or 'justificatory strategies'. Firstly, feminists need to develop their own epistemol-ogy if they are to present powerful alternatives to the traditional discourses of objectivism and 'interpretationism'.[2] Objectivism – commonly associated with scientific discourses, but present in all disciplines – insists that knowledge can be acquired only through dispassionate, disinterested, value-free objective inquiry procedures and that research guided by feminist concerns does not meet such standards. From this perspective, feminist research is devalued as too partial and committed. From the interpretationist perspective, feminists have a right to their beliefs in the subordination of women, but it is only one belief, which is no more legitimate than any other. This position corresponds to the postmodern emphasis on difference, what Lyotard calls 'the heteromorphous nature of language games' (Lyotard 1984: 66). The problem with this relativist position is that it 'functions to justify the silencing of women/ feminists no less than its objectivist twin by refusing to recognise existing power relations of male dominance and the dynamics that ensure intimate relations between partial and perverse beliefs and social power' (Harding 1990: 88).

Feminists need to develop epistemologies not only to convincingly refute these two perspectives and to justify the position of women as subjects of knowledge, but also to satisfy a need for coherent feminist justificatory strategies to guide feminist theory, research and politics. According to Harding, feminists need theories of knowledge to justify their claims to others when traditional grounds for claims to knowledge are not available. Furthermore, feminists need these theories of knowledge to understand differences that exist amongst women. Such differences are not simply cultural variations, but, as we have seen in the second chapter, can be differences related to structures of domination. Without some general understanding of how relations of social inequality are maintained, differences between women cannot be adequately understood. This final point, that difference can only be understood within a general theoretical perspective and justificatory strategy, is important and will be dealt with more fully in the next chapter.

If the lack of normative grounding is what underlies feminists' objections to the postmodern project, at the same time most feminists recognize that it is not possible to retreat into an Enlightenment notion of rationality in order to ground their critique. As Benhabib argues, it is necessary to recognize that the universalistic rational theories which underlie much Enlightenment thought are problematic in so far as the universalism they are based on is defined 'surreptitiously' by identifying the experiences of a specific group of subjects as the paradigmatic case of the human as such. 'These subjects are invariably white, male adults who are propertied or at least professional' (Benhabib 1987: 81). The universal rationality of the Enlightenment is then a regulative ideal which denies difference and the reality of one's embodied existence and, in this respect, it is unacceptable for feminists.

In regard to this, the feminist criticisms during the 1970s of rationality as a masculinist construct, still have critical relevance despite their essentialist implications. However, what distinguishes some feminist thinking in the late 1980s and 1990s is the realization that the Enlightenment notion of a normative ideal cannot be abandoned altogether. In whatever direction feminist alternatives to Enlightenment projects may develop, it is not clear how they could completely take leave of certain Enlightenment assumptions, in particular the belief in the desirability of social progress and the idea that 'improved theories about ourselves and the world around us will contribute to that progress' (Harding 1990: 99). In an article (Lovibond 1989) which presents the case for a feminist reappraisal of some of the Enlightenment's central values, Sabina Lovibond argues that the postmodern celebration of pleasure 'sometimes wins a trick by appealing to the role of immediate feeling in subverting psychic order'. Furthermore, Lovibond contests that if feminists disown altogether the 'impulse to enlighten', they will be unable to articulate a way in which these possibilities, suggested by postmodern theorists, can be made a political reality. Whilst postmodern theorists are unable, or do not want to distinguish between pernicious and oppressive aspects of modern culture and genuinely progressive elements, feminists must retain some notion of 'false consciousness' if they are to be able to transcend many of the regressive aspects of a 'woman-hating culture'. As Lovibond puts it:

> Subjectivity can be as fluid as you please, but this insight – once decoupled from the feminist ambition to *reconstruct* sensibility in the interest of women – will no longer be of any specifically political interest. Its political significance lies in the implication that contrary to appearances (to the nightmarish uniformity, give or take routine variations in 'style', of the cultural representation of gender), we can remake ourselves as better – more autonomous, less pathetic – people (*Lovibond 1989: 27–8*).

Lovibond concludes that given this goal to strive for a form of enlightened freedom, feminism should continue to perceive itself as a component of Enlightenment modernism, rather than as one more 'exciting feature . . . in a postmodern social landscape' (Lovibond 1989: 28).

We can see that amongst feminists who are sceptical of a postmodern solution to the dilemma of a normative grounding for a contemporary feminism, there is a certain consensus of opinion. Enlightenment values are problematic in so far as they implicitly rely on and legitimize a privileged, male pespective. Yet on the whole, if feminism is to retain a moral force to its declaration that the subordination of women is unjust, then some form of legislative rationality which enables distinctions between progressive and oppressive actions must be retained.

Having outlined some of the issues that lie at the heart of the feminist debate on postmodernism, I will now examine how Foucault's work can be related to this debate.

FOUCAULT AS A POSTMODERN

In so far as it is associated with postmodernism, Foucault's work has been deemed problematic by feminists who remain sceptical of the potential for a fruitful convergence between feminist theory and the postmodernist emphasis of difference. It must be noted, however, that the tendency to categorize Foucault as a postmodern thinker is not specific to feminism but is a current critical trend. David Hoy claims that Foucault was a 'consistent postmodern in that he would never have called himself a postmodern' (Hoy 1988: 30). Susan Hekman argues that Foucault's work embodies the 'very essence of postmodernism', whilst at the same time acknowledging that Foucault rejected such labels (Hekman 1990: 17–18). Scott Lash states that despite the fact that Foucault 'to my knowledge never used the term postmodern', his aesthetic is 'distinctly recognisable as a postmodern aesthetic' (Lash 1985: 8).

The feminist case against Foucault as a postmodern thinker is expressed very forcefully by Nancy Harstock. She argues that despite its anti-foundational claims, postmodernist theory rests on a desire for universality; the desire for totality is replaced with an equally totalizing desire for contextualism, pluralism and heterogeneity. However, as a form of social analysis postmodernism gives little guidance as to how systematic inequalities and oppression are perpetuated in society. Harstock regards Foucault's work as epitomizing the difficulties inherent in a postmodern approach to social analysis. Harstock claims that despite Foucault's obvious sympathies for subjugated and marginalized groups, his analysis of power is limited because it fails to articulate an adequate theory of resistance. For Foucault, resistance is always a localized phenomenon which, as soon as it gains official recognition, becomes caught up in a network of controlling power relations. Foucault does not show how marginalized groups may seize power in order to ensure the transformation of social relations. As a result,

> despite his stated aims of producing an account of power which will enable and facilitate resistance and opposition, [he] instead adopts the position of what he has termed official knowledge with regard to the knowledge of the dominated and reinforces the relations of domination in our society by insisting that those

of us who have been marginalised remain at the margins' (*Harstock 1990: 168*).

This criticism about the political limitations of Foucault's theory of resistance has been made by other commentators. Harstock, however, attributes these limitations to the specifically postmodern thrust of Foucault's theory. His theory that power is diffuse throughout all social relations results in the evanescence of power, thus replicating a postmodern celebration of heterogeneity. The theoretical evanescence of power conflicts with the feminist need to reconstruct theory in order to develop a politics of social trans- formation, and results in a politics of disavowal and apathy: 'Foucault refuses both the ground of foundationalism and the "ungrounded hope" endorsed by liberals such as Rorty, he stands on no ground at all and thus fails to give any reasons for resist- ance' (Harstock 1990: 170).

Along with Benhabib, Harstock recognizes the fundamental re- liance of feminist critique on certain moral and political imperat- ives and claims. The moral force underlying feminist theory – the belief that all forms of social oppression are unjust – is sufficient to justify forms of large-scale social analysis: 'if we are to construct a new society we need to be assured that some systematic know- ledge about our world and ourselves is possible' (Harstock 1990: 171). Thus the feminist reconstruction of theory should not be seen as simply a retreat into another totalizing and falsely universal discourse. To think in this way, she argues, is to be imprisoned within the 'alternatives imposed by Enlightenment thought and postmodernism'. It is not simply a question of adopting the per- spective of the transcendental and disembodied voice of 'reason', or abandoning the goal of accurate and systematic knowledge of the world in favour of an immersion in multiplicity and the con- crete. Other ways of thinking exist and need to be developed by 'hitherto marginalised voices'. Moreover, according to Harstock, a history of marginalization will 'work against creating a totalising discourse' (Harstock 1990: 171).

Whilst I agree with aspects of Harstock's reading of Foucault, I disagree with her conclusion that Foucault retreats into a postmodern politics of 'disavowal and apathy'. There are certainly problems with the normative grounding of Foucault's idea of an ethics of the self, and these will be considered later. But nevertheless, Foucault is clearly engaged in a similar project as Harstock: the constructive reworking – rather than postmodern rejection – of the legacy of Enlightenment thought. Harstock's conclusion is based on an unsympathetic and inadequate reading of his work; she does not take into account any of his later works and interviews which, of all his writings, probably deal most closely with questions of modernity, autonomy and resistance. Secondly, as has been made clear in the previous chapter, Foucault does not retreat into a postmodern politics of apathy. Rather, he is explicitly concerned to think through a politics of resistance grounded not in universal imperatives but in a notion of individual autonomy. Finally, Harstock disregards the fact that Foucault reaches a similar conclusion to her in so far as he argues for the development of a form of social analysis which avoids the polarized options posed by the Enlightenment (modernity)/postmodernity debate, or what he regards as the 'blackmail of the Enlightenment':

> But that does not mean that one has to be 'for' or 'against' the Enlightenment. It even means precisely that one has to refuse everything that might present itself in the form of a simplistic and authoritarian alternative: you either accept the Enlightenment and remain within the tradition of its rationalism (this is considered a positive term by some and used by others, on the contrary, as a reproach); or else, you criticise the Enlightenment and then try to escape from its principles of rationality (which may be seen once again as good or bad) (*Foucault 1984a: 43*).

Indeed, it is ironic that Harstock claims to want to proceed beyond such polarized forms of thinking and then proceeds to reenact them in her simplified reading of Foucault as a postmodern.

In the following sections, I examine Foucault's attempts to work out an analytical approach which avoids the polarized options of the modern/postmodern debate. On the one hand, Foucault's grounding of an ethics of the self in a theory of individual practice denotes an attention to specificity and difference which is similar to a postmodern approach. Yet on the other hand, as I showed in the previous chapter, his retention of some notion of the 'autonomous self' and 'self determination' indicates his intention to rework, rather than reject, central Enlightenment values. I argue that it is such an intention which establishes important differences between his work and postmodern theory.

IDENTITY, SELF AND ACTION

In terms of his own understanding of the relation between his work and the postmodern debate, it is simply misleading to position Foucault within a 'postmodern' trend of thought. Foucault states quite clearly that his work does not address the problem of postmodernity, and indeed he finds the dualistic terms of the debate irrelevant to his concerns: 'Rather than seeking to distinguish the modern era from the "premodern" or "postmodern", I think it would be more useful to try to find out how the attitude of modernity, ever since its formation, has found itself struggling with attitudes of "countermodernity"' (Foucault 1984a: 39). Elsewhere, Foucault explicitly situates his work in a tradition of thought on modernity: 'one may opt for a critical thought that will take the form of an ontology of ourselves, an ontology of the present; it is this form of philosophy that, from Hegel, through Nietzsche and Max Weber, to the Frankfurt School, has founded a form of reflection in which I have tried to work' (Foucault 1988a: 95). Furthermore, throughout his interviews Foucault frequently expresses dislike of the style of polemical debate adopted in the modern/ postmodern controversy, finding it counterproductive to constructive argument (Foucault 1984d: 381–2).

However, even if Foucault's own statements on the modern/ postmodern polemic are disregarded, there are substantial differences between his final work on ethics of the self and the work of thinkers like Baudrillard and Lyotard, who are commonly regarded as theorists of the postmodern (see Kellner 1988).[3] One fundamental distinction revolves around Foucault's treatment of identity through the idea of genealogy, and the postmodern treatment of identity as schizophrenia or as a permanent state of dissolution.

Although Foucault's genealogy of the self is based on the recognition that identity is not fixed but can be broken down and transgressed at many points, it remains crucially different from the subject in dispersion which is the nodal point of postmodern theories on the matter. For the postmodern theorists, most notably Baudrillard, the notions of subject and object, reflexivity and autonomy which characterize the modern understanding of the subject, are obsolete. The stress on plurality *per se*, rather than on the exploration of the interface between the actual and the potential, leads postmodern theorists to posit schizophrenia as the basic model of identity. Drawing on Lacan's definition of schizophrenia as the breakdown of the relationship between signifiers, postmodern theorists generalize this model to the basis of all identity (see Jameson 1983: 118). For Lacan, the experience of temporality – past, present, memory of continuous identity over months and years – is an effect of language: 'It is because language has a past and future, because the sentence moves in time, that we can have what seems a concrete or lucid experience of time' (Jameson 1983: 119). Because of the breakdown in language, the schizophrenic does not have such an experience of temporality, and therefore lives in the perpetual present where distinct moments have no connection with each other. Moreover, the schizophrenic 'does not know personal identity in our sense, since our feeling of identity depends on our sense of the persistence of the "I" or the "me" over time' (Jameson 1983: 119).

It is this idea of the incoherent schizophrenic identity which has been appropriated by postmodernists as a general explanation of the nature of subjectivity in the chaos of contemporary society. It is also this idea which lies at the base of the postmodern category of plurality or heterogenity. Given the fragmented and unstable nature of identity as it is constituted in modern society, the post-modern individual is unable to produce a strategy, or utopian alternative, to transcend the chaos of everyday life. Nihilism replaces the exploration of meaning: 'If being nihilist is to privilege this point of inertia . . . then I am a nihilist. If being nihilist is to be obsessed with the mode of disappearance, and no longer with the mode of production, then I am nihilist' (Baudrillard 1984: 39). Instead, the solution is to wallow in the intensity of the present, to liberate desire in a glorification of the present. Hence, Baudrillard's description of the schizo:

The schizo is bereft of every scene, open to eveything in spite of himself, living in the greatest confusion . . . What characterizes him is less the loss of the real . . . but, very much to the contrary, the absolute proximity, the total instantaneity of things, the feeling of no defense, no retreat. It is the end of interiority and intimacy, the overexposure and transparence of the world which traverses him without obstacle. He can no longer produce the limits of his own being, can no longer play nor stage himself' (Baudrillard 1983: 133).

In contrast, for Foucault, although the individual must break down established subject positions in order to discover hitherto unexplored potentiality in the realm of identity, this does not constitute an abandonment of the self to flux, dissipation and frag-mentation. Rather, it represents a coherent, systematatic exploration or genealogy of the self:

The theoretical and practical experience that we have of our limits and of the possibility of moving beyond them is always limited and determined; thus we are always in the position of beginning again. But that does not mean that no work can be done except in disorder and contingency. The work in question has its generality, its systematicity, its homogeneity, and its stakes (*Foucault 1984a: 47*).

For Foucault, then, the exploration of the self always takes place in the space of coherent identity. This coherence is necessary if Foucault is to link an ethics of the self with a strategy for liberation. For if one understands difference exclusively in terms of the fragmented and contradictory aspects of the individual's experience in society, then it is not possible to formulate a strategy for liberation because one has no tools to explain how the individual acts in a relatively stable and unified way. As Hall puts it: 'The politics of infinite dispersal is the politics of no action at all' (Hall 1987: 45).[4] Moreover, one has no way of explaining how the limits of the actual can be systematically investigated in order to open up the realm of the potential, i.e. progressive social transformation. It seems then, that in his notion of an ethics of the self, Foucault recognizes that the closure that occurs around the notion of the self is arbitrary or fictional, but at the same time, this closure is necessary to enable the individual to act in an effective fashion.

TRUTH AND FREE SPEECH

Whilst Foucault shares with postmodern theorists the rejection of metanarratives as a form of legitimation for the idea of an ethics of the self, what distinguishes his work is the use of a certain notion of 'truth'. The emergence of a notion of truth is surprising given Foucault's insistence in his earlier work that the production of knowledge is always closely linked to the operations of dominant power relations. In *Discipline and Punish* and *The History of Sexuality*, Foucault understands truth as a concept dependent on power, and by doing so, he dissolves the relation between truth and any kind of freedom or resistance on the part of the individual.

In his later work, Foucault introduces a notion of games of truth which resembles Lyotard's notion of language games. Foucault argues that we must relinquish the idea that there is any absolute form of truth. Rather, we must envisage 'different truths and different ways of saying it', or what he calls 'games of truth'. With respect to those who govern society or are in positions of authority,

Foucault still retains his earlier notion of 'truth' as an illusion or a discursive ruse which masks the operations of social control. This view is made clear in his discussions of the relations between intellectuals and political parties. Speaking of the Socialist government in France, Foucault expresses disillusionment with the way in which politicians in power expect sympathetic intellectuals to provide justifications for policies rather than critically examining political actions (Foucault 1989: 306–7). In this respect, Foucault follows an established tradition of thought which insists on the autonomy of the intellectual in the face of the manipulation and distortion of language by professional politicians.

However, what distinguishes Foucault's later from his earlier work is the idea that dominant power structures no longer have the monopoly in defining 'truth'. This change is signalled by the introduction of a notion of 'free speech' (*parrhesia*') which Foucault defines as a practice rather than as a legal right and as a practice of the governed rather than of the governors. Foucault conceives of free speech as a form of political obligation on the part of those who are governed to demand, 'in the name of knowledge', from those who rule 'a certain truth as to final aims, the general choice of its tactics, and on a certain number of particular points, of its program' (Foucault 1989: 314). Truth is understood as the alternative or non-offical knowledge accrued by individuals who exercise their power of free speech; their power to question and challenge the actions of those in authority. Foucault still understands truth as a relative concept but it is now open to contestation from 'below', i.e. through the construction of 'alternative truths' by individuals and marginalized and oppositional groups.

It is worth noting that to an extent, Foucault's idea of *'parrhesia'*, or an oppositional practice of free speech, ressembles his earlier notion of 'disqualified' or 'subjugated knowledges'. By this, Foucault means the discourses and experiences of subordinate and marginalized groups which, by never being fully articulated, have been denied official status. Examples of such subjugated discourses are the knowledge of those who undergo psychiatric treatment, of homosexuals, of women, of children, etc. It is the task of genealogical history to carry out a 'tactical reversal' of these discourses, to activate them into a resistant counterpower (Foucault 1980: 81–4). However, as some commentators have pointed out, this appeal to disqualified knowledges is problematic because they appear to be invested with a cognitive privilege over the dominant possessors of the system in a way that resembles a Lukacsian romanticization of a particular class interest. As Habermas points out, this privileging of working-class consciousness is understandable in terms of the Marxist philosophy of history that Lukacs worked within. However, since in Foucault's earlier work every form of knowledge is an effect of power, then disqualified knowledges have no more claim to revolutionary status than any other discourse. Moreover, since every counterpower moves within the horizon of the power it fights, then' it is transformed, as soon as it is victorious, into a power complex that provokes a new counterpower' (Habermas 1987: 281; also Dews 1987: 190–1).

With the later notion of *parrhesia*, however, Foucault attempts to overcome this problem of having to attribute an authentic status to disqualified knowledges in order to establish a critical point beyond the indissoluble unity of power/knowledge regimes. The oppositional truths articulated from below have no greater claim to 'reality' than official truths, but they have a resistant or progressive function in so far as they hinder the 'domination of truth' by those who govern. In other words, the exercise of free speech is not oppositional *per se*, but has a strategically resistant value. Oppositional truths destablize the concept of an absolute truth by indicating that there are other truths yet to be developed, multiple games of truth yet to be played:

> What caused all Western culture to begin to turn around this obligation of truth, which has taken on a variety of different forms? Things being what they are, nothing has, up to the present, proved that we could define a strategy exterior to it. It is indeed in this field of obligation to truth that we sometimes can avoid in one way or another the effects of a domination, linked to structures of truth or to institutions charged with truth. To say these things very schematically, we can find many examples: there has been an ecology movement . . . which has often been, in one sense, in hostile relationship with science or at least with a technology guaranteed in terms of truth. But in fact, ecology also spoke a language of truth. It was in the name of knowledge concerning nature, the equilibrium of the processes of living things, and so forth, that one could level the criticism. We escaped then a domination of truth, not by playing a game that was a complete stranger to the game of truth, but in playing it otherwise or in playing another game, another set, other trumps in the game of truth (*Foucault 1988b: 15*).

Truth then, for Foucault, is a philosophically problematic concept; nevertheless, if conceived in a non-foundational and fluid fashion, it is a concept through which effective strategies of resistance can be successfully articulated. It is in the interstices of power that truth is undone through the proliferation of alternative games of truth by those who are governed. It is this line of argument which resembles one of Derrida's arguments around the concept of displacement. Derrida argues that whilst it is necessary to question the problematic 'metaphysics of presence' which underpin Western philosophy, it is not possible to step beyond such modes of thought, since there is no absolute exterior to language (Derrida 1981: 24). Instead, the critic must be content to utilize a strategy of displacement, that is, by destabilizing concepts from within through the deconstruction of oppositions, the dissolution of hierarchies, etc. In a similar fashion, Foucault recognizes that for an oppositional discourse to be effective it can strategically deploy the notion of truth in order to break down the monolith of 'official' or received truths, and thereby open up a fluid space where alternative truths – other ways of living and of conceiving of the world – can be articulated.

Foucault's idea of resistant truths is linked not only to the idea of free speech, but also to the introduction of the concept of autonomy into his work. As long as Foucault conceived of subjects as 'docile bodies', incapable of presenting any form of resistance to the mechanisms of power, 'truth' was understood simply as an illusory and controlling effect of an insidious biopower. However, with the introduction of the idea of practices of the self and the ascription of a certain degree of autonomy to the subject in the ordering of his/her everyday life, there arises the corresponding idea that truth is no longer a monolith exclusively defined by a dominant power formation. Rather, truth is a category which is open to contestation through the construction of alternative truths, and therefore alternative realities, by 'free individuals':

> You can observe, insofar as the multiple games of truth are concerned, that what has always characterized our society, since the time of the Greeks, is the fact that we do not have a complete and peremptory definition of the games of truth which would be allowed, to the exclusion of all others. There is always a possibility, in a given game of truth, to discover something else and to more or less change such and such a rule and sometimes even the totality of the game of truth. No doubt that is what has given the West, in relationship to other societies, possibilities of development that we find nowhere else. Who says the truth? Individuals who are free, who arrive at a certain agreement and who

find themselves thrust into a certain network of practices of power and constraining institutions (*Foucault 1988b: 17*).

THE PROBLEM OF NORMATIVITY

In so far as he attempts to deconstruct metanarratives of truth in favour of a plurality of games of truth, Foucault adopts a position similar to some postmodern thinkers, particularly Lyotard. In *The Postmodern Condition*, Lyotard argues that as a result of the decline of the grand narratives of legitimation of the nineteenth century, contempory social relations have dissolved into a plurality of language games:

> The social subject itself seems to dissolve in this dissemination of language games. The social bond is linguistic but is not woven with a single thread. It is a fabric formed by the intersection of at least two (and in reality an indeterminate number) of language games obeying different rules ... This is what the postmodern world is all about. Most people have lost the nostalgia for the lost narrative. It in no way follows that they are reduced to barbarity. What saves them from it is their knowledge that legitimation can only spring from their own linguistic practice and communicational interaction' (*Lyotard 1984: 40–1*).

Lyotard describes the language games which constitute the social bond as a 'pragmatics' which emphasizes the performative as opposed to the denotative uses of language. By this he means that the primary aim of language games is not their referential function, or their validity, but rather the effectivity of a particular language game upon its recipient. The first principle of Lyotard's language games is 'to speak is to fight, in the sense of playing, and speech acts fall within the domain of a general agonistics' (Lyotard 1984: 10). The question of legitimation is unimportant or redundant in a postmodern era. Every move in a language game produces its own legitimation and 'all we can do is gaze in wonderment at the diversity of discursive species' (Lyotard 1984: 26). These postmodern language games yield a 'polytheism of values' and a politics of justice beyond consensus, characterized by Lyotard as the temporary contract.

The problem with this shift from questions of validity as a regulating force of language games to an emphasis on rhetorics or performativity is, as Selya Benhabib points out, that it enables Lyotard to avoid making distinctions between validity and force, reasoned belief and manipulated opinion:

> For Lyotard, the primary use of speech is perlocutionary. The use of speech to affect and influence the hearer, for whatever purposes, is the paradigm. But then the agonistics of language can no longer distinguish between manipulative and non-manipulative uses of speech. The consequence of this position is that not truth alone, but all claims to validity are at best pious wishes, at worst illusions fabricated to deceive' (*Benhabib 1990: 116*).

Like Lyotard, Foucault sidesteps the issue of determining the validity of actions with the notion of strategically deployed games of truth. According to the Foucauldian definition of truth, feminist discourses would have a contestant and radical status in so far as they could be strategically deployed to block the imposition of certain 'masculinist' or 'patriarchal' truths. The problem with this position is that many feminists would claim that the legitimation of feminist discourse through reference to its local or strategic use fundamentally undermines its revolutionary impact. Feminism calls for the complete transformation of all social relations and this call is based on the insight that all realms of society are, to some extent, gendered and that the unequal relations of power that this gendering creates is morally wrong. The feminist call for social transformation is legitimized, in a large part, by an appeal to moral and political justice. Foucault's notion of truth disallows such normative assumptions and would limit feminist discourse to merely a strategic value. As Lovibond puts it:

> I think we have reason to be wary, not only of the unqualified Nietzschean vision of an end to legitimation, but also of the suggestion that it would somehow be 'better' if legitimation exercises were carried out in a self-consciously parochial spirit. For if feminism aspires to be something more than a reformist movement, then it is bound sooner or later to find itself calling the parish boundaries into question (*Lovibond 1989: 22*).

Yet at same time, what distinguishes Foucault's work from the Lyotardian theory of language games is that the notion of games of truth is developed within an Enlightenment discourse of political values. Unlike Lyotard, Foucault's notion of games of truth

relies on concepts such as the notion of autonomous political practice of the individual, free speech and the overcoming of dominations of truth by institutions and other power blocs. In other words,
at an unarticulated level Foucault clearly makes value judgements
about what constitutes progressive political behaviour and what
constitutes an abuse of power or domination of truth, yet he fails
to make these assumptions explicit. It seems that Foucault cannot
fully shrug off the normative implications of the Enlightenment
concepts within which he works. Furthermore, his own belief in
engaged political practice hinders a complete rejection of the legacy
of the Enlightenment belief in progressive social change.

To return to Benhabib's definition of critique: if critique is to
become more than criticism, it is vital that it combines its diag-
nostic analysis of society with an anticipatory or utopian element
which articulates the normative groundings of the critique. Criticism of the present should always be juxtaposed with a notion of
what ought to be, and no matter how non-prescriptive this 'ought'
is, it rests on some kind of normative assumptions, for example,
what constitutes the legitimate and illegitimate uses of power. It is
clear that Foucault's idea of ethics of the self contains a utopian
moment in so far as he envisages a way of resisting the government
of individualization and a way of working towards new forms of
self-expression. Yet he persistently refuses to make explicit the
normative assumptions that his theory of a resistant ethics of the
self is based upon. To put it in other terms, Foucault employs a
vocabulary of political engagement, using concepts such as free
speech, truth and ethics, yet the normative implications of these
concepts that shore up his rhetoric of post-humanist ethics remain
unexamined. To borrow a phrase of Gillian Rose, Foucault employs
'an unexamined conceptuality without the labour of the concept'
(G. Rose 1988: 368).

NORMATIVE CONFUSION IN FOUCAULT'S EARLIER WORK

This point about the lack of normative grounding to Foucault's
criticism of modern society has frequently been made by commentators, in particular in relation to *Discipline and Punish* and the first
volume of *The History of Sexuality*. In *The Philosophical Discourse of
Modernity*, Habermas argues that Foucault's method slips into a
disabling relativism. By claiming that questions of validity are not

relevant to his mode of analysis because truth is simply the effect of a given regime of power, Foucault undermines the foundations upon which his own argument is based. This is similar to a point that Habermas raises in relation to Adorno and Horkheimer's *Dialectic of the Enlightenment*, in which the critique of rationality is so total that it undermines the position from which their own critique is addressed: 'if the truth claims that Foucault raises for his genealogy of knowledge were in fact illusory and amounted to no more than the effects that this theory is capable of releasing within the circle of its adherents, then the entire undertaking of a critical unmasking of the human sciences would lose its point' (Habermas 1987: 279). Following his own logic, Foucault's claim that a genea-logical historiography is superior to more orthodox forms of his-torical analysis because it avoids the error of hermeneuticism, is simply undermined as yet another effect of a specific power/knowledge regime.

Habermas also argues that despite claims to the contrary, Foucault does not avoid the very 'cryptonormativism' – the covert intro-duction of normative values and judgements into forms of analysis which claim to be value free – that he alleges is pervasive in the human sciences. Foucault is openly suspicious of attempts to for-mulate a positive basis for critique. Normative theories are, ac-cording to him, normalizing.[5] However, as Habermas points out, the tone of disapprobation that Foucault adopts when discussing modern disciplinary techniques, and his exhortations to resist es-tablished patterns of individualization through the exploration of the body and its pleasures, implies that Foucault is working with some kind of normative notion. As Habermas puts it:

> If one tries to glean the standards implicitly appealed to in his indictments of disciplinary power, one encounters familiar determinations from the normativisitic language games that he has explicitly rejected. The asymmetric relationship between powerholders and those subject to power, as well as the reifying effect of technologies of power, which violate the moral and bodily integrity of subjects capable of speech and action, are objectionable for Foucault, too (*Habermas 1987: 284*).

Like Habermas, Nancy Fraser has argued that whilst Foucault claims to bracket off questions of epistemic justification and of validity in relation to his criticism of modern society, at the same time he implicitly makes use of the very normative categories he claims to have foresworn. To illustrate this point, Fraser cites

Foucault's use of the terms domination, subordination and resistance. In interviews, Foucault claims that he studies power strategically and militarily, not normatively. The perspective of war, with its contrast between struggle and submission, takes the place of the liberal, juridical perspective of right and its contrast between legitimacy and illegitmacy. However, as Fraser points out, although the use of military terms such as domination and submission is intended to be value neutral, Foucault himself calls in no uncertain terms for resistance to domination, which implies that at a certain level, he is making some kind of value judgement about the legitimate uses of power. As Fraser puts it, 'why ought domination to be resisted? Only with the introduction of normative notions of some kind could Foucault begin to answer such questions. Only with the introduction of normative notions could he begin to tell us what is wrong with the modern power/knowledge regime and why we ought to oppose it' (Fraser 1989: 29).

Fraser suggests that one way of interpreting the aporia that arise from Foucault's assumption that critique can be engaged but not normative is that he does not bracket off every normative framework, but only the liberal one based on legitimacy. In this case, it is necessary to discover what alternative framework he presupposes. However, this suggested interpretation becomes increasingly tenuous when one reads a work like *Discipline and Punish*, which tacitly appeals to liberal notions of the legitimate and illegitimate uses of power and an associated cluster of concepts such as autonomy, dignity and human rights. For example, Foucault argues that the struggle against disciplinary power should be conducted in the name of an alternative system of rights: 'If one wants ... to struggle against disciplines and disciplinary power, it is not towards the ancient right of sovereignty that one should turn, but towards the possibility of a new form of right, one which must indeed by anti-disciplinarian, but at the same time liberated from the principle of sovereignty' (Foucault 1980: 108).

It seems that Foucault makes tacit use of the humanist rhetoric that he claims to be rejecting and delegitimizing. On the one hand, he attacks the idea of rights or sovereignity because its myth of the free individual acts as a smoke screen for the insidious implementation of modern disciplinary power. The anachronistic language of rights has the contemporary ideological function of masking disciplinary domination, and thereby contributes to it. Yet on the other hand, whilst Foucault accuses humanism of complicity with disciplinary techniques of power, the very force of Foucault's reading comes from an assumed familiarity on the part of the reader with the ideals of autonomy, reciprocity, dignity and human rights. As Fraser argues, when one considers what is so shocking in Foucault's vision of a caceral society, Kantian notions come to mind: 'When confronted with the treatment of persons solely as means that are causally manipulated by various institutions, one cannot help but appeal to such concepts as the violation of dignity and autonomy. But again, these Kantian notions are clearly related to the liberal norms of legitimacy and illegitimacy defined in terms of limits and rights' (Fraser 1989: 30).

Fraser concludes that Foucault does not just contradict himself, but rather that he misunderstands, in relation to his own critical standpoint, the way that norms function in social description. His assumption that norms can be isolated and bracketed off from the larger cultural and linguistic matrix in which they are situated is misleading. Fraser claims that: 'He fails to appreciate the degree to which the normative is embedded and infused throughout the whole of language at every level and the degree to which, despite himself, his own critique has to make use of modes of description, interpretation and judgement formed within the modern Western normative tradition' (Fraser 1989: 30–1).

CONTROL OF LIBERATION

Habermas and Fraser discuss the problem of cryptonormativism in relation to the middle period of Foucault's work up to the late 1970s. I argue, however, that in relation to his final work, this ambivalence around the questions of norms and validity, far from being resolved, becomes increasingly pronounced.

In many respects, Foucault is more aware in his final work that one cannot simply step outside a tradition of inquiry into normative concepts that have framed types of social critique and questions of social change. As we have seen, in relation to Foucault's discussion of the concept of truth, he recognizes that one cannot outrightly reject the notion of the 'obligation to truth' which he sees as structuring the will to knowledge in Western culture because it provides the most effective and powerful discourse within which to mobilize resistance to domination. Also, Foucault does not appear to make use of a value-free military terminology when he speaks of domination, subordination and resistance. His shift from neutrality to engagement is illustrated in his statement that the 'domination of truth' must be resisted and that it is the political obligation of individuals to interrogate governments in the name of free speech; there is 'the parrhesia (free speech) of the governed, who *can and must* summon in the name of knowledge and their experience and *because they are citizens* the government to answer for what it does' (Foucault 1989: 314; my italics). Furthermore, Foucault states that it is the duty of philosophy to challenge 'all phenomena of domination at whatever level or under whatever form they present themselves' (Foucault 1988b: 20).

Clearly, Foucault has moved a long way from his earlier position of impartial observer of social phenomena towards a position of engaged political critique. However, at the same time he constantly retreats from having to make explicit the alternative normative framework within which he works. This ambivalence permeates his later writing, particularly his interviews. It has already been noted, with regard to the concept of free speech of which Foucault makes use, that he defines it as a practice, not as a right, because, as he frequently states, the liberal discourse of rights and limits needs to be jettisoned. However, when Foucault exhorts individuals to challenge governments in the name of free speech, it is difficult to see how his definition of free speech as a practice substantially differs from the liberal notion of free speech defined as a right. The difference appears to be rhetorical rather than substantive.

Foucault's reluctance to make explicit his normative standpoint can be illustrated further by examining the distinction that he makes between practices of liberty and liberation. Pracitces of liberty, he argues, require a certain degree of liberation before they can be implemented. Liberation however, although a precondition of practices of liberty, is not itself a fixed state and it must be sustained through practices of liberty. Foucault maintains that there is an interdependence between the two phenomena. To illustrate his argument, Foucault gives the example of sexuality. In order for people to freely choose different types of sexual behaviour, there needs to be in place first a certain state of liberation, that is, a loosening of the code of 'compulsory hetereosexuality'. However, the emergence of alternative sexual practices is not indicative of a fixed, final state of liberation. Rather, these practices have to be ceaselessly worked upon and modified in order to ensure the continuation of a state of liberation: 'This liberation does not manifest a contented being, replete with a sexuality wherein the subject would have attained a complete and satisfying relationship. Liberation opens up new relationships of power, which have to be controlled by practices of liberty' (Foucault 1988b: 3–4).

Foucault goes on to state that these practices of liberty which 'control liberation' constitute ethical behaviour. However, when pressed to elaborate exactly what kind of ethical behaviour safe-guards a certain kind of liberty, he persistently avoids the question. At times, Foucault acknowledges that some kind of guidelines or 'rules of law' need to be established to ensure that the games of liberty can be played in a non-dominatory manner, but he never proceeds to define what kind of validity judgements these rules or law should be based on:

> I don't believe there can be a society without relations of power, if you understand them as means by which individuals try to conduct, to determine the behaviour of others. The problem is not of trying to dissolve them in a utopia of a perfectly transparent communication, but to give one's self the *rules of law, the tech-niques of management* and also the *ethics* . . . the practice of self, which would allow these games of power to be played with a minimum of domination (*Foucault 1988b: 18; my italics*).

In other words, when pressed to make explicit the normative assumptions that underlie his conception of progressive, non-dominatory behaviour, Foucault refuses to do so. He replies that it is not the task of the intellectual to tell individuals what to do, but rather to provide them with the knowledge of the way in which certain social mechanisms work, and thereby open up for these individuals the possibility of self-determination and the choice of their own existence. Practices of liberty cannot be determined in advance but only arrived at within the specific context (Foucault 1989: 395).

Whilst Foucault's desire not to legislate for others is understand-able, he does not distinguish clearly enough between an *a priori* legislation of acceptable and non-acceptable behaviour and the establishment of certain political aims against which one can evaluate behaviour. Whilst the former is to be avoided, it is neces-sary to retain some broader political aims, such as the establish-ment of non-exploitative social relations, if progressive political change, rather than an anarchic free-for-all is to be established. It is clear from both his political sympathies and from the examples of domination which he gives in his work that Foucault views ethics of the self as a form of progressive individualism based on tolerance and respect for the subject's chosen way of living. Yet by refusing to define what could be considered legitimate behaviour and what non-legitimate, by failing to elaborate on the normative assumptions underlying the anticipatory element of his critique,

Foucault's theory borders on a libertarianism which does not distinguish between acts that are predatory and oppressive in relation to others and actions that are genuinely progressive.

THE DISSOLUTION OF THEORY INTO PRACTICE

The problems that arise from the failure to outline certain normative standards against which behaviour can be assessed politically are illustrated by Foucault's neglect to explain how the individual evaluates his/her ethical reinvention of the self. Foucault says:

> It is true that we have to give up hope of ever acceding to a point of view that could give us access to any complete and definitive knowledge of what may constitute our historical limits. And from this point of view *the theoretical and practical experience* that we have of our limits and the possibility of moving beyond them is always limited and determined; thus we are always in a position of beginning again (*Foucault 1984a: 47; my italics*).

Whilst it is not possible for the individual to assume a total or complete perspective on how it is possible to go beyond established forms of subjectivity, Foucault suggests, nevertheless, that the individual retains some critical standards against which to evaluate the potentiality of new subject positions as opposed to the actuality of existing ones. Without some normative standards, it is not possible for the individual to distinguish between an arbitrary stylization of life and the development of genuinely oppositional subject positions. In order to resist the 'government of individualisation', individuals strategically select different forms of behaviour which will reveal the artificiality of what is hegemonically defined as 'normal' behaviour, and thereby indicate potential points of change:

> This work done at the limits of ourselves must, on the one hand, open up a realm of historical inquiry and, on the other, put itself to the test of reality, of contemporary reality, both to grasp the points where change is possible and desirable, and to determine the precise form this change should take (*Foucault 1984a: 46*).

However, despite implying that the individual has the capacity for autonomous critical reflection, Foucault undercuts this notion of autonomy by working with an oversimplified idea, inherited from his earlier work, of knowledge as the material effect of dominant power regimes. In his earlier work Foucault defined power as a phenomenon with purely material effects, exemplified in the image of the physical inscription of power upon the human body. As we saw in the first chapter, Foucault counterposed his material account of power to understandings of power as primarily a process of the ideological manipulation of consciousness. According to Foucault, these latter notions rely on a purely negative account of power as a repressive entity. They also imply that beyond the realm of false consciousness or ideology there is a realm of truth or objectivity, e.g. the mode of production, inner nature, and so on (Foucault 1980: 121–2). For Foucault, power is a positive, productive phenomenon which produces and incites effects in the social realm rather than simply repressing and denying.

One consequence of Foucault's material and positive theory of power is that knowledge of all kinds is reduced to the level of positivity; that is, it is regarded as both the material instrument and effect of different power regimes: 'power produces positive effects at the level of desire and also at the level of knowledge' (Foucault 1980: 59). Systems of power bring forth different types of knowledge which, in turn, produce effects in the bodies of social agents that serve to reinforce the original power formation. Theoretical knowledge is, for Foucault, not a disinterested, abstract realm of inquiry but an instrument of social control and discipline:

> We should abandon a whole tradition that allows us to imagine that knowledge can exist only where the power relations are suspended and that knowledge can develop only outside its injunctions, its demands and its interests . . . We should admit rather that power produces knowledge . . . that power and knowledge directly imply one another; that there is no power relation without the correlative constitution of a field of knowledge, nor any knowledge that does not presuppose and constitute at the same time power relations. (*Foucault 1977a: 27*).

The indissoluble link that Foucault establishes between knowledge and power is typified in his idea of the 'dispositif' or discursive formation. A discursive formation consists of practices and institutions that produce knowledge claims that the system of power finds useful. A discourse serves what Sheldon Wolin calls a 'maieutic function', in that it brings objects into being by identifying them and delimiting their field, e.g. homosexuality as a deviant phenomenon brought out by the medicalization of discourses on sexuality during the nineteenth century. As Wolin puts it, 'a discursive formation unites thought and practice in a seamless and circular web: practices set the conditions for discourse and discourse feeds back statements that will facilitate practice. Discourse appears completely incorporated into practice. It has no autonomous identity or distance (S. Wolin 1988: 184).

The problems of this undialectical conception of the relation between knowledge and power are passed on to Foucault's later work on the self and it precludes an understanding of how the individual may reflect on his/her own behaviour to assess its validity in relation to a politics of self-transformation. As we have seen, Foucault defines practices of the self as a set of socially defined techniques which, when selected by the individual, provide a set of meanings or 'truths' with which the individual can interpret and understand his/her behaviour:

> One cannot care for self without knowledge. The care for self is of course knowledge of self . . . but it is also the knowledge of a certain number of rules of conduct or of principles which are at the same time truths and regulations. To care for self is to fit one's self out with these truths. That is where ethics is linked to the game of truth' (*Foucault 1988b: 5*).

There are two crucial aspects to this process in which the individual fits him/herself out with truths. Firstly, the knowledge that one gains of oneself is primarily a practical rather than a theoretical knowledge. In other words, as in Foucault's earlier work, knowledge is reduced to a level of positivity in so far as it is understood as the instrument and effect of a given set of power relations. This symbiosis of the theoretical with the concrete is manifested in different ways. Practices of the self are defined as primarily concrete techniques of self-fashioning, rather than as forms of self-representation or ideological images of the self. Foucault states quite clearly that practices of the self are not intended as 'a history of the successive conceptions of desire, of concupiscence, or of libido', but rather as an analytical tool with which to interpret the material practices 'by which individuals were lead to focus on themselves as subjects of desire' (Foucault 1985a: 5). The merging of the theoretical with the practical is further exemplified in Foucault's use of the terms 'techniques' or 'technologies' of existence, which imply the application of knowledge for practical ends. When theory becomes inseparable from practice it becomes 'techne' (S. Wolin 1988: 193).

Secondly, because knowledge of the self is inseparable from its practical application, individuals are not necessarily completely aware of nor able to articulate the full implications or meaning of their practices. Thus Foucault writes vaguely: 'In studying this aspect of morality, one must determine how and with what margins of variation or transgression individuals or groups conduct themselves in reference to a prescriptive system that is *explicitly or implicitly* operative in their culture, and of which they are *more or less aware*' (Foucault 1985a: 25–6; my italics). It is clear that practices of the self constitute a primarily practical and intuitive knowledge, rather than a theoretical and critical knowledge. In other words, Foucault still works with his earlier understanding of knowledge which can only be measured by its level of positivity or practical effects. Knowledge appears to have no autonomous status from practice.

A problem with Foucault's reduction of discourse to the level of positivity is that a certain critical moment which is inherent to the separation of theory from practice is effaced. Considering *Discipline and Punish*, Sheldon Wolin argues that theoretical discourse has never achieved the 'perfect symbiosis' with practice that is implied in Foucault's notion of discursive practices of the self. At the very heart of the theoretical project as a practice is a certain autonomy from the political even when it is prescribing the political. It is in this distance between the theory of politics (the political) and the practice of politics (politics) that a necessary analytical distance or space of self-reflection is established. Wolin illustrates the nature of theoretical discourse by refering to Plato's Republic. In response to Socrates' question:'Is it possible for anything to be realized in deed as it is in spoken words, or is it the nature of things that action should partake of exact truth less than speech?' Plato formulates two examples. The first concerns the relationship between critical distance and failure. If theory is absorbed into the discourse of action so that it becomes inseparable, it becomes impossible to perceive when action has fallen short of what it should be. 'It is the nature of action to fall short of theory and it is the role of theory to declare that. Theory can only declare that critical function if it retains a separate identity. Otherwise theory becomes 'techne' and the theorist becomes indistinguishable from the technician of power' (S. Wolin 1988: 193). Thus, Plato declares that if a state were to come into being it would be only an approximation to the ideal and this necessary discrepancy would signify that theory remained distanced from power. Secondly, Plato argues that political practices do not simply apply ideal truths but diminish them. Practice does not merely use theory as it would technical knowledge, but uses it calculatingly. Wolin argues that the history of religious discourses exemplifies the betrayal of theory through political expediency; so too, collective life reflects the same experience, 'of justice systematically applied and individually denied, of revolutionary hopes frozen into a new establishment, of virtue smerched into realism' (S. Wolin 1988: 193).

Wolin's arguments are not intended as an apologetic for pure, abstact theory, or as an exoneration of theoreticians from the social and political implications of their work. Furthermore, Foucault's work on the interconnections between power and knowledge has been invaluable in highlighting how even the most speculative forms of thought have played a central part in techniques of social management and control. However, what Wolin objects to is that Foucault erradicates any distinction between theory and practice, and thereby erodes the autonomous perspective from which theory can both reflect critically upon itself and provide valuable critical insights into the practice of power. By denying theory any integrity, knowledge, for Foucault, can only serve as a form of domination rather than as a relatively independent system that may be betrayed in practice. Truth only becomes truth when it is integrated with practice and systems of power. As Foucault puts it:'Truth is a thing of this world: it is produced only by virtue of multiple forms of constraint' (Foucault 1977a: 27). The tensions and disjunctions between theory and practice have disappeared. 'At best any discrepancies appear as mere slippages, technical problems of ironing out applications of thought to practical realities, not as an ontological predicament' (S. Wolin 1988: 193).

REFLEXIVITY

By ironing out the distinction between theory and practice, it is unclear how it is possible for individuals to conduct a 'critical ontology' of themselves. For whilst an attitude of self-critique implies the ability to critically reflect on the significance of one's actions and deeds, Foucault's subordination of knowledge to the practical ends of self-mastery disallows the space that is necessary for critical reflection. This implicit ambivalence around the relation between theory and practice, self-knowledge and action, manifests itself in several points of tension in Foucault's work. On the one hand, maintaining the emphasis on practice in his ethics of the self,

Foucault explicitly argues against there being any moment of analysis or self-reflection in practices of the self: 'For centuries we have been convinced that between our ethics, our personal ethics, our everday life, and the great political and social and economic structures, there were analytical relations . . . I think we have to get rid of this idea of an analytical or necessary link between ethics and other social or economic or political structures' (Foucault 1984b: 350). Following on from this, he argues that ethics of the self is primarily a practical rather than reflective activity; the creation of ourselves as works of art.

Yet on the other hand, whilst Foucault argues against establishing an analytical link between general social structures and the practices of the individual, he goes on to introduce the problematic notion of reflexivity into the idea of the constitution of the self as an autonomous subject. In an interview with Gerard Raulet, he states that this process of constitution takes place within a reflexive relationship of the self to the self. He seeks to analyse 'forms of reflexivity – a relation of self to self – and, hence of relations between forms of reflexivity and the discourse of truth, forms of rationality and effects of knowledge' (Foucault 1983: 203). In the same interview, he states, 'my own problem has always been the question of truth, of telling the truth . . . what it is to tell the truth – and the relation between telling the truth and forms of reflexivity, of self upon self' (Foucault 1983: 204); and, 'I wish to know how the reflexivity of the subject and the discourse of truth are linked – "how can the subject tell the truth about itself?"' (Foucault 1983: 207).

Peter Dews points out that this admission of reflexivity as the defining attribute of autonomous subjectivity raises enormous problems which remain entirely unexplored in Foucault's later work. As Dews puts it, 'Foucault's contention is that ethical self-construction operates in a reflexive medium, yet at the same time he wishes to deny that this medium itself has any ethical relevance' (Dews 1989: 40). On the one hand, Foucault insists that we critically examine ourselves in order to establish how what passes as the universal and necessary is in fact based on the contingent and arbitrary. Thus, in the article 'What is Enlightenment?', Foucault says that it is necessary to consider our own identity in relation to dominant constructions such as sickness, health, madness, sanity, etc.:

> these historico-critical investigations are quite specific in the sense that they always bear upon a material, an epoch, a body of de-

termined practices and discourses. And yet, at least at the level of Western societies from which we derive, they have their generality, in the sense that they have continued to recur up to our time: for example, the problem of the relationship between sanity and insanity, or sickness and health, or crime and the law; the problem of the role of sexual relations (*Foucault 1984a: 49*).

Such an historico-critical investigation clearly involves making those analytical links between the individual subject and overarching social structures which Foucault, as we have already seen, elsewhere denies. Yet in the same interview, Foucault argues that the historico-critical analysis of identity must not turn into a project with 'global or radical' implications, but must confine itself to specific transformations and, as an example, he quotes the achievements of the feminist movement (Foucault 1984a: 46–7). Yet, the obvious point that Foucault fails to acknowledge is that the specific achievements of the feminist movement have been based, to a great extent, on making the necessary analytic links between what is regarded as the private and immutable realm of sexuality and overarching structures of male domination and gender inequality in society.

If knowledge is constituted within a specific form of power-knowledge, Foucault cannot explain how subjects can have another perspective on the same historical and social processes. Foucault asserts the autonomous perspective of subjects, but his assertion is undermined by his failure to explain theoretically how such autonomy is possible. His fundamental assumption that knowledge and power – invariably conceived as coercion – are indissolubly linked, dissallows the possibility of individuals being able to reflect critically on the disjunction between their experience and the categories of power-knowledge. In sum, the capacity for reflection still remains a product of a dominant power formation.

One possible way to reopen the gap between theory and practice and to restore the potential for autonomous thought is through the introduction of a notion of ideology. Commentators such as Dews and Spivak have argued that a theory of ideology allows for the possibility of a disjunction between the experiences of the oppressed and the inadequacy of the 'official' representation of those experiences disseminated by power (see Dews 1987: 186–92; Spivak 1988). In a study of Foucault's work on the self, Giles Deleuze suggests it is in the space of such a disjunction, in the interstices of experience and representation, that practices of the self are situated. Deleuze describes this disjunction in terms of relations of power folding back on themselves to create a space of autonomy: 'It is as if the relations of the outside folded back to create a doubling, allowing a relation to oneself to emerge, and constitute an inside which is hollowed out, and develops it own unique dimension' (Deleuze 1988: 100). Practices of the self implies such a theory of autonomy, but Foucault fails to explore the extent to which the legacy of his earlier theoretical positions – most notably, his abandonment of the concept of ideology because it implies an unjustifiable claim to possess a privileged access to truth on the part of the critic – disallows a cogent explanation of the possibility of autonomy. The relativist implications of Foucault's theoretical position undercut his commitment to a politics based on the autonomy of the individual.

As Dews puts it: 'To deny that political critique possesses an epistemological dimension is to be condemned either to a self defeating acceptance of the 'truth' of the contested perspective, or to resort to an appeal – of whose vunerability Foucault is well aware – to some 'prediscursive experience', or natural reality outside all perspectives' (Dews 1987: 189).

CONCLUDING REMARKS

The confusion that arises from Foucault's neglect to explain the normative underpinnings of his notion of ethics highlights shortcomings and difficulties in the current feminist debate on modernism and postmodernism. As we have seen, the feminist debate over difference has lead many feminists to endorse the postmodern rejection of generalized metanarratives and to argue for an emphasis on the specific and local. However, at the same time many feminists have acknowledged that the relinquishment of any generalizable theoretical perspective presents difficulties for feminism. Thus, on the one hand, some feminists are concerned that an overmonolithic model of sexual difference leads to a failure to consider other fundamental differences, such as race and class, which structure the social experiences of women. On the other hand, it is recognized that an extreme theoretical particularism may deprive feminists of the tools with which to examine how differences – especially sexual differences – are inevitably articulated into hierarchies of inequality. It seems, therefore, that whilst feminists must remain alert to issues of difference and specificity, it is also necessary for them to retain theoretical tools capable of analysing general structural tendencies in order to understand how difference becomes inequality.

By examining these ambivalences in the feminist position, it becomes apparent that the antagonism between theoretical meta-narratives and localized knowledge that is set up in the debate on modernity and postmodernity is an artificial and misleading approach to the whole issue of understanding difference. Rather than the polarized alternatives proposed by the postmodern debate, a potential alternative is to explore the extent to which theory is compatible with the local. As Wolin puts it, 'what follows is not that we should renounce theory to avoid its dominating discourse, rather we should find forms of theory that will be consistent with a localising . . . participatory, community oriented politics' (S. Wolin 1988: 199). Wolin argues that some generalizable theoretical perspective is crucial to the task of formulating a politics based on a respect for difference and locality. Theory helps to both 'locate' individuals and groups 'in relation to the more encompassing structures of power which are the hallmark of state-centred politics' and also to overcome the 'autistic tendencies of localism' and the 'self centred preoccupation of the postmodern individual' (S. Wolin 1988: 88).

Foucault's work oscillates between privileging a particularist perspective, in its stress on the individual's freedom of action, and retaining a more general political perspective committed to overcoming the government of individualization in the name of the individual's right to autonomy. Unlike the postmodern celebration of immanence, Foucault does not relinquish the hope of the transcendence of existing social relations for a more progressive and tolerant arrangement. However, he is reluctant to expand on the underlying normative assumptions that underlie his political goal. Clearly, Foucault makes such normative judgements when he uses concepts such as autonomy and domination, which rest on judgements about what constitutes legitimate and illegitimate uses of power. Foucault, however, is reluctant to be drawn on these issues because of a tendentious link that he makes between normativity and normalization, between totality and totalization. As a consequence, his position is more confused than a postmodernist one because he clearly works with a utopian image of transformed social relations, but he does not elaborate on the full implications of this image. This normative confusion, or 'cryptonormativism', manifests itself in his work in a circular and often elliptical logic and in an attempt to bypass the problems of the legitimation of action altogether. Foucault is unable to break out of this dilemma because he poses the problem of difference in terms of an antagonism between theory and decentralized politics, even though, on an implicit level, his work breaks down such antagonisms.

I think that the lesson of Foucault's work for feminists is that they must seek to take the debate over difference beyond the dichotomized options of theoretical metanarratives and localized knowledge and to explore how a respect for the particular can be incorporated into general theoretical perspectives. It is necessary to examine the exegetical clichés that normativity inevitably leads to normativism, and generalizations constitute a theoretical totalitarianism, in order to show that a clear statement of one's political aims and moral values need not necessarily conflict with the respect for individual difference. Nor need it necessarily close off, in advance, potential avenues of social change. From the opposite perspective, the category of difference needs to be carefully thought through by feminists in order to show that a respect for the unique can not be equated in a straightforward fashion with a politics of indifference or *laissez-faire*. In short, in order to respect difference and to incorporate this respect within a systematic programme of social transformation such as is demanded by feminism, it is necessary to work within some kind of normative framework. Postmodern theory does not provide such normative guidelines. This is not to dismiss the important insights of postmodern theorists, but rather to avoid falling into the polemical and over-simplified terms in which a large part of the Enlightenment/postmodern debate has been construed.

This issue of the incorporation of the category of difference within a theoretical framework which retains certain analytical and utopian metanarratives will be considered in more detail in the next chapter.

5

Self and Others

INTRODUCTION

In the previous chapter I argued that, without outlining some normative standards against which various techniques of existence can be assessed, Foucault's ethics slips into an unworkable relativism. Whilst this relativism may be an unintended consequence, Foucault needs to make more explicit his moral-political convictions to avoid such lapses.

In this chapter, I begin by considering the accusation that the normative confusion in Foucault's work results in a retreat to a form of aesthetics. Like Adorno, Foucault is accused of reducing politics to poetics and privileging an elitist notion of aesthetic practice. Whilst there may be some truth in these charges, I argue that a more central problem with Foucault's notion of an aesthetics of existence is that it privileges an undialectical and disengaged theory of the self. I argue that this privileging of the isolated self in the idea of an aesthetics of existence conflicts with recent feminist attempts to understand more fully the intersubjective dimension of social relations. With this in mind, I compare Foucault's aesthetics of existence with Habermas' notion of communicative action, which proposes a way of understanding how the identity and actions of an individual are always mediated through interaction with others. Such a notion of interaction provides the potential basis for a politics which combines a respect for difference with an idea of solidarity and collective political aims. Although Foucault's idea of an aesthetics of existence is informed by a respect for difference, without showing how a strategy of self-transformation relates to a politics of solidarity, it runs the risk of lapsing into an atomized politics of introversion.

As in the previous chapter, my conclusions on the tensions in Foucault's work relate, on a more general level, to the feminist debate on postmodernism. I argue that feminism should concentrate on the development of types of theory which can deal with difference, rather than trying to accommodate itself to a postmodernism which, in many respects, conflicts with some of the basic political assumptions and goals of the feminist movement.

THE RETREAT TO AESTHETICS

Some critics attribute the normative confusion underlying the idea of care of the self to the primarily aestheticist stance Foucault takes. It has already been noted how, following Baudelaire, Foucault envisages a contemporary ethics of the self as primarily an aesthetic experience. It is not the work of Baudelaire the poet that is of interest to Foucault, but the figure of Baudelaire the dandy who makes of 'his body, his behaviour, his feelings and his passions, his very existence, a work of art'. As the paradigmatic modern individual, the dandy is 'the man who tries to invent himself' (Foucault 1984a: 41). To be modern is, for Foucault, 'to take oneself as an object of complex and difficult elaboration', like a work of art. What interests Foucault in this idea of an aesthetic reinvention of the self are the moments when art passes over into the sphere of life. Foucault places great stress on Baudelaire's pan-aestheticism, where art no longer occupies its own private niche but where it gives birth to lifeforms directly. The exploration of the limits of subjectivity, central to what Foucault regards as a modern attitude, is primarily an aesthetic exploration. The reinvention of the self must resemble the creation of a work of art. Foucault describes it in the following terms:

> What strikes me is the fact that in our society, art has become something which is related only to objects and not to individuals, or to life. That art is something which is specialized or which is done by experts who are artists. But couldn't everyone's life become a work of art? . . . From the idea that the self is not given to us, I think that there is only one practical consequence: we have to create ourselves as a work of art (Foucault 1984b: 350–1).

Implied in the idea of creating one's life as a work of art is a notion of the active agent freely choosing modalities through which he or she constructs a relation with the self.

This idea of an aesthetics of existence, of turning one's lifestyle into a work of art and shaping it according to stylistic criteria, has been a source of considerable difficulties for many of Foucault's commentators. At a conference held in Paris in January 1988 on Foucault's work ('Michel Foucault, philosophe'), many speakers accused Foucault of retreating into an elitist and amoral aestheticism (see O'Farrell 1989: 127–9). The project of an aesthetics of existence was one which could only be indulged in by a privileged elite who do not have to face the harsh political and material realities of life, an elite who 'can employ all their energy in perfecting the refinement of their lifestyle' (Rochlitz quoted in O'Farrell 1989: 128). Richard Rorty accuses Foucault of failing to see that his own inner search for moral autonomy is both irrelevant to the aims of most people's lives and also, if adopted on a mass scale, could have undesirable social and political consequences (Rorty quoted in O'Farrell 1989: 128).

Richard Wolin (1986) argues that the primacy of aestheticist implications in Foucault's work leads to a normative stance based on decisionism. Wolin recognizes that aesthetics may have an important critical and utopian function. The aesthetic impulse may lead to the imaginative creation of alternative worlds which, 'by virtue of their anticipatory, utopian qualities, their sheer 'being other', are able to present a powerful indictment of the existing world in its present indigent state' (R. Wolin 1986: 85). However, it is crucial that the aesthetic realm interpenetrates with other realms, such as the ethical and cognitive, in order to ensure that its insights do not remain abstracted and elitist. Foucault, however, prioritizes the aesthetic realm over everything else and, as a result, produces an undemocratic and irrational Nietzschean ethics.

According to Wolin, Foucault wants to restore aesthetics to a position of 'unmitigated cultural primacy'. As a result of this aestheticist prioritization, the specific content of action becomes a matter of indifference because exclusive emphasis is placed on action or 'choice', rather than on the justification of action in relation to wider political aims. In a purely decisionistic ethics, 'good acts' are determined through a demonstrative assertion of the individual's volition or will to act. The problem with this aestheticist emphasis on form over content is that action *per se* is prioritized over the validity of action, the adoption of any non-conventional subject positions is endorsed, rather than trying to specify what subject positions should be adopted. The only criteria for action within this aesthetic decisionism is that acts 'must be performed taste-fully: with due respect for stylistic concerns which elevate such actions above the mundane actions of the vulgar "many"' (R. Wolin 1986: 84).

Wolin concludes that Foucault's aesthetics of existence provides no distinction between practices of the self that are manipulative and predatory in relation to other individuals, and the adoption of subject positions that are progressive in that they serve to break down what Foucault regards as oppressive forms of identity. He argues that Foucault revels in having 'severed all links with a "metanarrative of justice"' and that his standpoint favours 'either an attitude of narcissistic self-absorption or one of outwardly directed, aggressive self-aggrandizement' (R. Wolin 1986: 85). He states that in Foucault's ethics there is not a 'discernible trace of human solidarity, mutuality, or fellow feeling'. His ethical universe is an aesthetic game of one-upmanship which is deeply anti-pathetic to any kind of collective politics such as feminism.

Whilst Wolin is correct to point out a link between the aestheticist prioritization in Foucault's work and its normative ambivalence, I do not agree with his unsympathetic conclusion that, as a result of his desire to break entirely with Enlightenment notions of ration-ality, Foucault retreats into an elitist and irrationalist decisionism. We have already seen, from a close reading of Foucault's texts, that his relation with Enlightenment thought and some of its central concepts is more complex than Wolin is prepared to admit. Further-more, in some senses Foucault's prioritization of the aesthetic as the realm for contemporary action takes up a theme that is already predominant in a tradition of thought on modernity. This tradition runs from Nietzsche, who emphasized a process of 'creative de-struction' in order to affirm the self in a fragmented world (see Harvey 1989), through Simmel, who emphasized the notion of the stylization of life in order to escape the homogenizing tendencies of modern culture,[1] to Adorno, who stressed the potentiality of the modernist work of art to transcend the commodifying forces which dominate modern mass culture.

In *Sources of the Self*, Charles Taylor demonstrates how the modern sense of the self is deeply underpinned by an aesthetic expressivism which was most intensely realized in the Romantic epoch. By expressivism Taylor means the idea that arose in the late eighteenth century that each individual is different and original and that this originality determines how he or she ought to live. There is an obligation on each of us to live up to our originality.

Along with this expressive view of human life arose a new under-standing of art. Art was seen as the activity *par excellence* through which the expression of the self was achieved. The aesthetic was no longer understood as *mimesis* or imitation, but as expression: 'it makes something manifest while at the same time realizing it, completing it' (Taylor 1989: 377).

Taylor goes on to show how the Romantic notion of aesthetic expressivism is still central to the modern understanding of identity, although it has shifted from an emphasis on the relation between self and nature to a more reflexive stress on the self's relation with the self via the work of thinkers such as Baudelaire and Nietzsche. However, according to Taylor, even the most recent theories of the decentred subject are informed by the essentially Romantic urge to retrieve a form of experience or type of creative activity which has been occluded by an instrumental and industrialized world (Taylor 1989: 461–2). Even the most anti-subjectivist modernism shares, indeed accentuates, the Romantic emphasis on the poet or artist as a paradigm human being (Taylor 1989: 481).

Given the predominance of this strand of aesthetic expressivism in modern understandings of the self, it seems strange then to accuse Foucault's work of an elitist aestheticism. Rather, following Taylor, it may be more interesting to view Foucault's work as yet another variation of the Romantic/modernist quest to retrieve a more intense or worthwhile form of experience which escapes the deadening effects of the instrumental rationality which pervades contemporary culture. From this more constructive point of view, the main problem with Foucault's work on the self is not so much its aestheticism as its intense subjectivism.

In order to draw out more clearly this point about the subjectivist tendencies of Foucault's work, it is helpful to compare Wolin's criticism of Foucault's work with similar criticisms made of Adorno's work: that he reduces critical theory to aesthetics. As we saw in the previous chapter, commentators have noted that in relation to his critical standpoint, Foucault's work suffers from the same contradiction as that of Adorno's and Horkheimer's in *Dia-lectic of the Enlightenment*.[2] Habermas' critique of *Dialectic of the Enlightenment* is well known. He argues that in their total critique of instrumental rationality, Adorno and Horkheimer fail to ap-preciate the complex internal dynamic of modern society, and instead produce a 'flattened out' or one-dimensional account of modernity. This partial vision does not explain the conflictual nature of many aspects of societal modernization, or what Habermas calls the 'paradox of rationalisation', where rationalization connotes both emancipation and reification at the same time. Thus Adorno and Horkheimer cannot explain how, for example, the legal and democratic political structures of modern society both threaten and uphold the freedom of the individual. Judicial mechanisms, for instance, entail not only legal prohibitions, but also legal rights; not only types of exclusion, but also forms of entitlement. This partial vision also does not explain how it is that the academic disciplines do not simply produce technologically exploitable knowledge, but also contribute to an internal critique of the institutions of modern society. 'In the welfare-state democracies of the West, the spread of legal regulation has the structure of a dilemma, because it is the legal means for securing freedom that themselves endanger the freedom of their presumptive beneficiaries' (Habermas 1987: 291).

The ultimate irony of Adorno and Horkheimer's total critique of modern rationality is that it undermines the very position from which they produce their criticisms. Either their analysis forms part of the bankrupt and instrumental strand of modern rationality or, as Habermas points out, they implicitly retain a notion of a salvagable rationality that is necessarily embodied in their thought:

> Horkheimer and Adorno find themselves in the same predicament as Nietzsche: if they do not want to give up their goal of an ultimate unmasking and want to carry on their critique, then they must preserve at least one standard for their exploration of the corruption of all reasonable standards. In the face of this paradox, the totalising critique loses its direction' (*Habermas 1982: 28*).

The encroachment of instrumental rationality and an attendant identity logic upon all realms of social experience is so total that, for Adorno, the immanent potential for emancipation is an impossibility. The only realm in which Adorno sees the utopian glimmer of emancipation, in the form of the vestiges of a non-identity logic, is in the realm of the aesthetic. Adorno claims that the autonomous, modernist artwork is capable of both resisting assimilation into mass culture and also of revealing, in a negative way, the reality of cultural production and society in general. Radical avant-garde art communicates a shock of unintelligibility. Its very incoherence and fragmentation negatively reflects the irrationality underlying rationalized capitalist society (Adorno 1984: 321). Adorno's critics claim that through this manoeuvre emancipation is reduced to an aesthetic issue and not a social or moral one. Revolution is reduced to poesis.

In *Critique, Norm and Utopia*, Selya Benhabib takes a stand against some of Adorno's critics by arguing that it is trivial to criticize

Adorno for reducing critical theory to aesthetics. She claims that it is more interesting to ask why it is that he cannot conceive of a non-repressive and non-regressive autonomy as a moral or political state, but only as an aesthetic one. Her answer is that although his work produced a devasting critique of some of the problematic unifying and essentialist assumptions of the philosophy of the subject[3] upon which Marxist philosophy rested, he ultimately could not provide a real alternative to the philosophy of the subject.

Adorno replaced the philosophy of the subject with what he called 'the priority of the objective', a materialist category that maintains the priority of historically accumulated conditions over and against the illusions of a completely self-determining subject. Benhabib argues that this priority of the objective does not, however, present a real alternative to the philosophy of the subject. It may show the limits of revolutionary, optimistic thinking and also that thought remains determined by non-thought, the subject by the non-subject and necessity by contingency, but ultimately it remains the abstract negation of the philosophy of the subject and not its transcendence: 'this negation does not allow us to thematize what this philosophy really precluded: above all, plurality and being-with-the-other in the sense of being-with-an-other-like-myself' (Benhabib 1986: 214).

This brings us to the central problem with Foucault's notion of ethics of the self, which is not so much, as Wolin suggests, that he reduces politics to an aesthetic indecisionism, although this is an effect of his position. Rather, Foucault is unable to present a fully worked-through alternative to either Enlightenment rationality or to an indiscriminate postmodern celebration of difference. With respect to the former position, Foucault contests the idea that there can be one universal form of rationality that can ground theories of emancipation; he states straightforwardly: 'The search for a form of morality acceptable to everyone in the sense that everyone should submit to it, strikes me as catastrophic' (Foucault 1988a: 253–4). In its place, he argues for multiple rationalities and strategies of resistance. However, with respect to the second, postmodern position, Foucault does not want to relinquish some notion of political engagement in favour of an uncritical, extreme particularism. Foucault remains, therefore, in a cleft stick attempting to negotiate a way between a refusal to outline a normative basis for action in so far as it may become normalizing and a reluctance to endorse an entirely deregulated libertarianism. His failure to find a way of negotiating this dilemma stems from the fact that, ultimately, his ethics privileges a notion of the self establishing a relation with the self, rather than understanding the self as embedded in and formed through types of social interaction. As Foucault puts it: 'One must not have the care for others precede the care for self. The care for self takes moral precedence in the measure that the relationship to self takes ontological precedence' (Foucault 1988b: 7).

The problem, then, with Foucault's work is not the notion of aesthetics *per se*, but rather the emphasis placed on the idea of an isolated process of self-stylization as the basis for a modern ethics of existence. Even within the problems explicitly posed by Foucault's own work, the idea of the formation of the self as a work of art is an inadequate solution. Thus, as we saw in the previous chapter, Foucault argues that in order to explore fully new realms of experience, it is necessary to get rid of the idea of 'an analytical or necessary link between ethics and other social or economic or political structures', (Foucault 1984b: 350). According to Foucault, the idea that our personal lives are inextricably bound up with overarching social and political structures has been used to discourage individuals from radical experimentation in their own lives. Sexual deviancy becomes linked with social anarchy. As an indication of the type of self-liberation we should be aiming for, Foucault cites the ancient Greeks: 'Individual liberty was very important to the Greeks ... not to be a slave (of another city, of those who surround you, of those who govern you, of one's own passions) was an absolutely fundamental theme ... in Antiquity, ethics, as a deliberate practice of liberty has turned about this basic imperative: "Care for yourself"' (Foucault 1988b: 5).

In the same interview, however, Foucault goes on to acknowledge that the Greeks' preoccupation with the self and the stylization of one's life was, in fact, guided by wider social, cultural and political imperatives: 'Ethos implies a relation with others to the extent that care for self renders one competent to occupy a place in the city, in the community or in interindividual relationships which are proper' (Foucault 1988b: 7). Although Foucault explicitly rejects the idea that the practices of the ancient Greeks should serve as a blueprint for contemporary behaviour, he nevertheless argues that they provide important insights for a modern ethics. Yet Foucault seems to produce a very selective interpretation of ancient ethics. For whilst the Greeks may have exercised a degree of liberty in the control of their daily lives, this liberty was nonetheless embedded in a network of social and political obligations. In other words, the ancient Greek sense of the self was always informed by those 'analytical and necessary' links that Foucault wishes individuals in contemporary society to divest themselves of. It seems, then, that in his presentation of the ancient notion of the stylization of the self as a model for a contemporary ethics, Foucault filters out a more communal and interactional notion of the self held by the Greeks.

My intention is not to dispute the accuracy of Foucault's historical reading, but rather to question whether the idea of the formation of the self as a work of art, predicated on the severance of links between the self and other social structures, is really an adequate strategy with which to resist the government of individualization. According to Foucault, the government of individualization operates precisely through drawing out the individuality of the subject. Power, in the form of, for example, the confessional, draws out the idiosyncracies of individuals in order to regulate their behaviour more efficiently: 'power applies itself to immediate everyday life which categorizes the individual, marks him by his own individuality, attaches him to his own identity, imposes a law of truth on him which he must recognize and which others have to recognize in him' (Foucault 1982: 212). Given that power works through individualization, what guarantee is there that the creation of the self as a work of art is not merely another strategy through which power controls individuals? As Adorno remarks: 'Pseudo-individuality is rife . . . What is individual is no more than the generality's power to stamp the accidental detail so firmly that it is accepted as such' (Adorno and Horkheimer 1972: 154). Without an interactional notion of the self – that is, without making the analytical links between one's own actions and the social context – the individual cannot distinguish between what constitutes a radical exploration of identity and what is simply an arbitrary stylization of life. Without an understanding of how the individual's actions are constantly mediated through interaction with other individuals, Foucault cannot explain how the potential uncovered in the exploration of identity can be communicated to others in order to initiate progresive change at the level of the group, community or class. Foucault cannot produce a satisfactory answer to the dilemmas he himself poses because his theory of the self prioritizes an isolated individuality, rather than demonstrating how the construction of the self is inextricably bound up in various processes of social interaction.

THE PHILOSOPHY OF THE SUBJECT: SUBJECT AND OBJECT

One way of highlighting the inadequacies of Foucault's account of the individual is to compare it with Habermas' theory of

communicative reason, which enables an understanding of the individual in a dialogical and interactional context. In *The Philosophical Discourse of Modernity*, Habermas suggests that Foucault is
unable to solve some of the central problems in the tradition of
philosophical thought on modernity because his work remains
caught within some of its fundamental terms, especially the philosophy of the subject. For Habermas, Foucault's philosophical
project, which is, in certain respects, a continuation of the one initiated by the Frankfurt School, is aporetic because his critique of
instrumental reason is so total that he retains no form of rationality, apart from aesthetic rationality, on which to base a theory of
emancipation. The notions of aesthetic autonomy which both
Adorno and Foucault present as the only resistant mode to instrumental reason remain caught within a philosophy of consciousness
based upon the dominatory dynamic of the subject/object relation.
This is to say that the philosophy of the subject privileges an
objectifying attitude in which the 'knowing subject' regards its self
and other individuals as it would passive entities in the external
world.

In *Critique, Norm and Utopia*, Selya Benhabib expands on how the
Western philosophical tradition has always offered two models of
the self, both variations of the philosophy of the subject: the thinking, cogitative self (Hegel) and the active one appropriating and
transforming nature (Marx). Both approaches privilege the shaping consciousness, in that either a lonely self cogitates upon an
object or an active self shapes the world. Even when attempts are
made to understand intersubjectivity and the relations between
selves, they are construed in terms of the interaction of consciousness 'from *my* mind to *your* mind, from *my* consciousness to *your*
consciousness', rather than in terms of social and linguistic interaction which constitutes the self. In other words, in the philosophy
of consciousness, individuation precedes sociation, rather than
seeing individuation proceeding only under conditions of sociation.
(Benhabib 1986: 242–3).

For Habermas, it is ironic that Foucault attacks the philosophy of
the subject only to remain caught within its central terms of sub-
ject/object and the paradigm of the knowledge of others as objects.
As Habermas puts it: 'To the objectivism of self mastery on the
part of the human sciences there corresponds a subjectivism of self
forgetfulness on Foucault's part' (Habermas 1987: 294). Thus in *The
Order of Things*, Foucault is unable to approach the question of
the 'doubles' that structure modern thought – cogito/unthought,
transcendental/empirical, the return/retreat of the origin – in terms

other than a 'hectic to and fro', because he still remains caught within a philosophy of the subject. Habermas suggests that Foucault's argument that these doublings repeat themselves throughout modern thought is a sign of the exhaustion of the philosophy of the subject, which allows no mediation or alternative to this 'observer perspective' on the transcendental/empirical double of the relation to the self. Only when no other perspective is admitted save that of the observer 'does the subject have to view itself as the dominating counterpart to the world as a whole or as an entity appearing within it' (Habermas 1987: 297). Foucault's position ends in an 'unholy subjectivism' that precludes the possibility of resistance.

Habermas argues that a theory of communicative reason based on linguistic theory is the only way to overcome the normative deficiencies of totalized critiques of instrumental reason presented by Foucault (and Adorno). The model of the isolated autonomous subject proposed by both Adorno and Foucault is not a true negation of the government of individualization or identity logic, both of which preclude the recognition of radical difference in the form of the 'other'. Rather, what is required is a complete epistemological break, whereby the premises of a work model of activity are replaced by a model of communicative intersubjectivity. A model of linguistically generated intersubjectivity should be substituted for the objectifying perspective of the observing self:

> As soon as linguistically generated intersubjectivity gains primacy ... Then ego stands within an interpersonal relationship that allows him to relate to himself as a participant in an interaction from the perspective of alter. And indeed this reflection undertaken from the perspective of the participant escapes the kind of objectification inevitable from the reflexively applied perspective of the observer. Everything gets frozen into an object under the gaze of the third person, whether directed inwardly or outwardly. The first person, who turns back upon himself in a performative attitude from the angle of vision of the second person, can *recapitulate* the acts it just carried out. In place of reflectively objectified knowledge – the knowledge proper to self-consciousness – we have a recapitulating reconstruction of knowledge already employed (*Habermas 1987: 297*).

Foucault's idea of isolated, aesthetic self-transformation as the only possible form of resistance to the government of individualization would be replaced with an understanding of social relations

as a series of constantly mediated communicative exchanges between self and an other, understood not as an object but as an
irreducible subject. The objectifying attitude in which the knowing
subject regards itself as it would entities in the external world is no
longer privileged. Fundamental to the paradigm of mutual understanding is, rather, the performative attitude of participants in interaction, who co-ordinate their plans for action by coming to an
understanding about something in the world: 'When ego carries
out a speech act and alter takes up a position with regard to it, the
two parties enter into an interpersonal relationship. The latter is
structured by the system of reciprocally interlocked perspectives
among speakers, hearers, and non-participants who happen to be
present at the time' (Habermas 1987: 296–7).

The conception of identity that this model proposes is one in
which identity is constructed through a process based not on solitary activity – as in Foucault's idea of the creation of oneself as
a work of art – but on interaction and the recognition of differences between the self and the other. The self is sustained by
the continuous redefinition of the boundaries between self and
other. In the philosophy of the subject, the relationship with the
other is understood in terms of an identity logic, that is, the other
is understood in terms of the cognitive categories of the self. The
effect of this model is to reduce the other to a projection or extension of the self, rather than as an independent being or another
self. In the interactional model proposed by Habermas, the other
is conceived of as another self who is capable of acting in a way
so as to disrupt the identity logic of the self. This model introduces difference, in the form of an independent self, into the process of interaction in which identity is established. As Benhabib
puts it:

> If identity logic is the attempt to blur limits and boundaries, then
> those limits can be re-established via the act of an other self who
> is capable of rejecting the narcissitic self-extension of the other.
> The true negation of identity logic would be an epistemological
> relation in which the object could not be subsumed under the
> cognitive categories of the self without that it – the object – could
> also regard these categories as adequate to capture its own dif-
> ference and integrity. Identity logic can only be stopped when
> difference and differentiation are internal to the very self-identi-
> fication of the epistemological object and subject, and this is only
> the case when our object is another subject or self (*Benhabib 1986:*
> 221).

FEMINIST CRITIQUE OF SUBJECT/OBJECT DYNAMIC

Habermas' model of communication based on the interaction between two selves, rather than on the notion of a solitary self cate-
gorizing the objectified world, has proved suggestive to feminists
who seek an alternative model of social relations. The feminist
critique of the subject/object dynamic is too varied to be gone into
in any detail here (for example, Hekman 1990: 73–94), but it will
be schematically outlined. The basic insight that animates the critique of the subject/object dualism is straightforward in that it is
argued that throughout the history of Western thought men have
been defined as subjects, women as objects. In Enlightenment epistemology the subject/object dualism is the central structure around
which knowledge is defined in terms of absolute truths which are
acquired by individual autonomous subjects. The privileged element in this dualism, the abstract, knowing subject, is associated
with the masculine, the object of knowledge with the feminine
(Hekman 1990: 73; Moi 1989).

What feminists have found most problematic about this model is
its definition of the knowing subject as a disengaged self, or an
unencumbered subject. The subject/object model prioritizes the
abstract consciousness and activities of the individual without acknowledging the extent to which social relations – in particular, for
feminists, psychosexual relations – are constitutive of the individual.
Feminist theorists argue that the vision of the unencumbered self
is a masculine one because the degree of separateness and independence it postulates among individuals has never been the case
for women. Furthermore, such a perspective has the result of
trivializing or rendering irrational the perspective of women (see
Young 1987; Benhabib 1987).

As a result of these undesirable consequences, feminists have
sought to produce an alternative understanding of social relations
which escapes the dominatory logic of the subject/object model. In
The Pornography of Representation, Suzanne Kappeler has argued for
a model of intersubjectivity in order to transcend the limitations of
the subject/object dynamic characteristic of relations between men
and women. More recently, Toril Moi has suggested that a notion
of analytical dialogue suggested by psychoanalytic practice offers
the potential for an alternative modelling of social relations, According to Moi, the analytical situation radically questions the split
between active subject and passive object because the process of
transference and countertransference engages analyst and analysand

in a complex, differential set of interactions. As she puts it: 'Transference and countertransference turn the analytic session into a space where the two participants encounter each other in the place of the Other, in language' (Moi 1989: 197).

Another way to develop an alternative understanding of social relations has been suggested to feminists by Habermas' theory of communicative reason. The work of Habermas is seen as 'developing a conception of normative reason that does not seek the unity of a transcendent impartiality and thereby does not oppose reason to desire and affectivity' (Young 1987: 59). The process of communication offers no firmly established binary opposites, it cannot be gendered as either masculine or feminine, and therefore it offers women the opportunity to 'escape the patriarchal tyranny of thought by sexual analogy' (Moi 1989: 198). Habermas' idea of a non-adversarial dialogue, that is, the notion that forms of communication have a liberating potential once they have been freed from the distorting effects of conventional norms and modes of authority, accords with feminist attempts to formulate an ethics based on communication and the establishing of responsible relations between individuals.

FOUCAULT, HABERMAS AND THE ROLE OF THE OTHER

Foucault's emphasis on self-formation in his idea of aesthetics of existence is at odds with the recent feminist concern to develop a more adequate understanding of the intersubjective dimension of social relations. Habermas' argument that Foucault's work remains trapped within a philosophy of the subject is based on a reading of the work of his early and middle periods. The same critical insight, however, can be extended to Foucault's later work on the self. Although one of the principal aims of Foucault's work is a deconstruction of the philosophy of the subject which underlies Western thought (Foucault 1985b: 366), his alternative model of the self does not fully succeed in radically breaking with any of the dominant characteristics of the theory of the subject which he attacks. Just as in the work model of activity that underlies Marxist and existentialist conceptions of the subject, Foucault's model emphasizes the lone subject who acts upon the self in order to realize his/her identity, 'to constitute oneself as the worker of the beauty of one's own life' (Foucault 1988a: 259).

The central difference between Foucault's idea of the construction of the self as a work of art with the ultimate goal of attaining complete self-mastery, and other variations of the philosophy of the subject – Marxist, existentialist, phenomenological, etc. – is that Foucault stresses the anti-essentialist character of the subject. As Benhabib notes, the model of the isolated individual relied upon by Hegel, Marx, the Critical Theorists and others, is based around a notion of self-actualization. That is, in acting, an agent is said to unfold, enhance, manifest or express certain inherent potentialities. From this perspective, the object of work/work of art is seen as the embodiment of the potentiality of the agent. In his model of the self, Foucault refuses the idea that there is any presocial potentiality or inner nature that is necessarily expressed or realized through the individual's interaction with the world. He repeatedly emphasizes that identity is a radically contingent phenomenon constructed through social practices, rather than an expression of an inner nature revealed through engagement with the social. Thus, explaining the difference between his ethics of the self and a Sartrean existentialism, Foucault states:

> I think that from the theoretical point of view, Sartre avoids the idea of the self as something which is given to us, but through the moral notion of authenticity, he turns back to the idea that we have to be ourselves – to be truly our true self. I think that the only acceptable practical consequence of what Sartre has said is to link his theoretical insight to the practice of creativity – and not of authenticity. From the idea that the self is not given to us, I think that there is only one practical consequence: we have to create ourselves as a work of art (*Foucault 1984b: 351*).

On the one hand, then, Foucault criticizes the idea of an essential or pre-social identity proposed in the existentialist version of the philosophy of the subject. Yet on the other hand, Foucault's conception of the self still remains within its central terms of an active self acting on an objectified world and interacting with other subjects who are defined as objects or narcissistic extensions of the primary subject. Foucault's entrapment within the fundamental dynamic of the philosophy of the subject can be illustrated most clearly in his inadequate treatment of the category of the 'other', which is understood as a passive vector against which practices of the self are played out.

In response to the question about whether the idea of care of the self runs the risk of 'absolutizing' itself and whether this absolutization could become a domination of others, Foucault claims that if one cares for self 'correctly' then one cannot abuse an other. Care for the self necessarily incorporates care for the other:

> The risk of dominating others and exercising over them a tyrannical power only comes from the fact that one did not care for one's self and that one has become a slave to his desires. But if you care for yourself correctly, i.e. if you know ontologically what you are, if you also know of what you are capable, if you know what it means for you to be a citizen in a city . . . if you know what things you must fear and those that you should not fear . . . if you know, finally, that you should not fear death, well, then, you cannot abuse your power over others (*Foucault 1988b: 8*).

This passage makes clear that despite his argument that power permeates all social relations, practices of the self appear to be abstracted from any social context which may predetermine inequalities between the behaviour of individuals. This is to say that Foucault's faith that by caring for oneself correctly one automatically cares for another seems to overlook that a white/male/heterosexual caring for himself correctly may necessarily imply the domination of black/female/gay 'other' who, because of his/her relatively subordinate position in terms of access to resources and authority, does not have the power to resist such domination. Foucault might reply that the white/male subject was not practising liberty correctly, but until guidelines are laid down about what constitutes valid behaviour then Foucault's belief in the self-limiting nature of the care for the self seems untenable. Since Foucault declines to outline, even in the most general terms, what he considers to be a valid use of power and what constitutes an abuse, then there is no guarantee that care of the self would not lead to the domination or marginalization of the other.

Of course, Foucault acknowledges that there are states of domination within which 'the relations of power are fixed in such a way that they are perpetually asymmetrical and the margin of liberty is extremely limited' (Foucault 1988b: 12). As an example of such domination, Foucault refers to the marital relation of the eighteenth and nineteenth centuries, in which, although the women were not totally powerless, there was on the whole a fixed dynamic of domination. The wife could be unfaithful, she could extract money from her husband, she could refuse him sexually, but 'she was, however, subject to a state of domination, in the measure where all that was finally no more than a certain number of tricks which never brought about a reversal of the situation (Foucault 1988b: 12). For Foucault, such a disregard of the rights of the other amounts to an abuse of the care for self, resulting in the domination of others.

These states of domination are, however, on the whole, rare. In contemporary Western society, the care for the self is practised by and amongst 'free individuals': 'It is free individuals who try to control, to determine, to delimit the liberty of others and, in order to do that, they dispose of certain instruments to govern others. That rests indeed on freedom, on the relationship of self to self and the relationship to the other' (Foucault 1988b: 19–20). By freedom, Foucault means that individuals have the chance to resist the games played by others. The capacity for resistance ensures that care for the self does not turn into domination of others:

> There cannot be relations of power unless the subjects are free. If one or the other were completely at the disposition of the other and became his thing, an object on which he can exercise an infinite and unlimited violence, there would not be relations of power ... Even though the relation of power may be completely unbalanced or when one can truly say that he has 'all power' over the other, a power can only be exercised over another to the extent that the latter still has the possibility of committing suicide, of jumping out of the window or of killing the other. That means that in the relations of power, there is necessarily the possibility of resistance (*Foucault 1988b: 12*).

But what kind of resistance is suicide or murder? Defined in such general terms, the free individual's capacity for resistance is not a guarantee against the 'absolutization' of the care for the self, rather it simply represents a rather desperate way to escape from a state of oppression. To take a less extreme example, consider the kind of resistance that a woman at home with small children can put up against her violent husband. She can of course leave him, there is no longer a stigma attached to the breakdown of marriages. But unless she is fortunate enough to have a highly paid job to arrange child care, she will be dependent on meagre state benefits. In other words, unless the woman is prepared to give up a stable home and regular income for poverty, she has very few effective ways of resisting her husband's violence. It is not enough, therefore, for Foucault to assert that the capacity of free individuals for resistance ensures that care for the self will not turn into tyranny of others or that the care for the self necessarily includes a concern for others. Such statements are hollow unless accompanied by an awareness of the overarching structures of inequality and discrimination against which all relations between free individuals are played out.

Foucault's neglect to analyse the structural sources of inequality, influence, resource and power that overdetermine different types of care for the self indicates a somewhat naïve belief in a society as a harmonious whole. His idea that caring for the self necessarily incorporates a care for the other disregards the fact that within the type of hierarchical relations that structure modern society, caring for the self necessarily involves a struggle to delegitimize, overpower and silence the other. Selya Benhabib makes a similar criticism of Lyotard's notion of language games which assumes that they are games of perfect information rather than games of contradiction or struggle. Giving a concrete example, she argues,

> Lyotard cannot maintain that the current attempt of conservative, prolife groups to establish a 'new reverence for life and creation', to deny the moral legitimacy of abortion, to even ask science to provide exact criteria as to when the fetus becomes a person, are 'narratives' in our culture that point to a happy polytheism of language games (*Benhabib 1990: 123*).

The shortcomings in Foucault's treatment of the other highlight the inadequacy of the idea of the care for the self as a way of analysing existing social relations. In particular, Foucault's discussion of the other reveals the limitations of care of the self as a way in which to resist and overcome the government of individualization in contemporary society. Against the modern obsession with the self, Foucault poses a notion of isolated self-experimentation in which questions of social interaction and respect for others are effectively bypassed.

The scant attention accorded to the other in Foucault's notion of care for the self contrasts strongly with Habermas' model of intersubjective social relations where the other plays a central role in the constitution of the individual's identity. In a relational definition of identity, identity can only be attained through the recognition of difference and sustained via the continuous redefinition of the boundaries between self and other. According to the subject/object modelling of human interaction, which lies at the heart of the philosophy of the subject, emphasis is placed on a primary self's interaction with an objectified world and other selves construed as narcissistic extensions of the original self or objects.

Foucault's insistence that concern for others is derivative of care for the self indicates the extent to which he remains trapped within the terms of the philosophy of the subject. However, in Habermas' theory of linguistically mediated intersubjective relations, through which both identity and communication are established, the other is accorded a central and active role rather than a passive and subordinate one. For if the actions of every individual are linguistically mediated and interpreted, then the other has a crucial role to play in this process of interpretation. In other words, individuals constitute and reproduce their identity in relation to values, norms and meanings which define a socio-cultural system. A consequence of this position is that no matter how private and idiosyncratic the needs and desires of individuals may be, they are only meaningful if we also interpret them socio-culturally. An individual's actions are always subject to an interpretative indeterminacy in so far as a subject never simply acts through desires and potentialities, but rather the definition of his/her actions/desires are always subject to the interpretation of others. For Habermas, this socio-cultural process of interpretation is bound up with linguistically mediated intersubjective communication. In Benhabib's words:

> Human action is linguistically mediated, both for the actor and for others, who formulate their intentions and the definitions of what they do in linguistic terms. Such formulations are essentially contestable, by ego as well as by alter. The interpretative indeterminacy of social action is not an ontological shortcoming, but its constitutive feature. The model of communicative action ... emphasises that social action always entails linguistic communication, and that the interpretative indeterminacy is a constitutive feature of social action (*Benhabib 1986: 243*).

Foucault's idea of the self is caught within a subject/object dynamic in which the other is simply a narcissistic extension of the self – its difference subsumed under an identity logic – to the extent that his original idea of the social mediation of the self remains undeveloped and unexplained. Foucault's argument is that although practices of the self are freely selected by the individual, these practices are, at a basic level, defined and overdetermined by the social context. For Habermas, this process of mediation takes place in the communicative interaction between individuals and groups. This interaction necessarily involves the subject confronting difference, in the form of other individuals. From this perspective, identity is maintained via the continuous redefinition of boundaries between self and other. As Benhabib puts it,

> community and commonality arise and develop between us not, as Marx thought, because we are thrust into objectively similar life conditions. A common, shared perspective is one that we create insofar as in acting with others we discover our difference and identity, our distinctiveness from, and unity with, others. The emergence of such unity-in-difference comes through a process of self transformation and collective action (*Benhabib 1986: 348–9*).

In contrast, Foucault's intransitive model of the self provides no systematic framework within which to explain how the individual's practices are mediated through the social context and how this process of mediation introduces an element of indeterminacy into the individual's self-understanding. For Foucault, the individual is preoccupied with the attainment of a complete self-mastery or autonomy. As Charles Taylor observes, the problem with such an exclusively subjectivist outlook is that it encourages modes of life which tend towards a certain shallowness. Furthermore, 'the primacy of self-fulfilment reproduces and reinforces some of the negative consequences of instrumentalism. Community affiliations, the solidarities of birth, of marriage, of the family, of the polis, all take second place' (Taylor 1989: 507). Foucault does not hint at any mitigation of the extreme subjectivism that informs his ethics. In one of his final interviews, Foucault affirms the interviewer's statement that in practices of the self all knowledge is subordinated towards the practical end of self-mastery (Foucault 1984b: 361). Elswhere he argues: 'Liberty is . . . in itself political. And then, it has a political model, in the measure where being free means not being a slave to one's self and to one's appetites, which supposes that one establishes over one's self a certain relation of domination, of mastery' (Foucault 1988b: 6). The role of the other is reduced to that of passive receptacle or inert context. The interests of the other are derivative and secondary to the self: 'One must not have the care for others precede the care for self. The care for self takes moral precedence in the measure that the relationship to self takes ontological precedence' (Foucault 1988b: 7). However, as Habermas explains, it is possible to argue that the preoccupation with autonomy or self-mastery, which is also characteristic of the philosophy of consciousness, is simply a moment in the process of social interaction which has been artificially isolated or privileged:

'both cognitive-instrumental mastery of an objectivated nature (and society) and narcissistically overinflated autonomy (in the sense of purposively rational self-assertion) are derivative moments that have been rendered independent from the communicative structures of the lifeworld, that is, from the intersubjectivity of relationships of mutual understanding and relationships of reciprocal recognition' (Habermas 1987: 315).

TOWARDS A POLITICS OF DIFFERENCE AND SOLIDARITY

Perhaps the most serious drawback with Foucault's presentation of ethics of the self as a solitary process, rather than as socially inte-grated activity, is that it is unclear how such an ethics translates into a politics of difference that could initiate deep-seated social change. As Taylor puts it: 'A society of self-fulfillers . . . cannot sus-tain the strong identification with the political community which public freedom needs' (Taylor 1989: 508).

It is clear from his interviews that Foucault saw an ethics of the self as having implications that extend further than the limited arena of individual aesthetic self-formation. In one interview, he argues that although he is against consensus as a regulatory polit-ical principle, he is also against a notion of permanent dissensus. That is to say that individuals cannot remain locked exclusively within an atomized politics of the subject which privileges experi-mental self-expression over the formation of links with other indi-viduals and communities:

> It is perhaps a critical aim to maintain at all times: to ask oneself what proportion of nonconsensuality is implied in such a power relation, and whether that degree of non-consensuality is neces-sary or not, and then one may question every power relationship to that extent. The farthest I would go is to say that perhaps one must not be for consensuality, but *one must be against non-consensuality* (Foucault 1984c: 379; my italics).

It is also clear, from his radical sympathies and from the rela-tional definition of identity with which he works, that the ground-ing of an ethics in a theory of the self does not represent a retreat into an individualized private realm. Foucault is highly critical of the obsessive introspection or 'cult of the self' which predominates in so many Western lifestyles (Foucault 1984b: 362). Rather,

Foucault's particularist emphasis has more to do with his disillusionment with the public realm which he understands as composed of a network of controlling, disciplinary discourses: the
government of individualization. In this light, his ethics can be
understood as an inversion of the traditional liberal conception of
the relation between the private and public realms. Instead of conceiving of the private realm as that which contains the affective
and emotional aspects of existence and as that which is necessarily
excluded from the public, the private is defined as those aspects of
individuals' lives and activities that they have a right to exclude
others from. This definition of privacy is meant to emphasize the
direction of agency as the individual withdrawing, rather than being
kept out of the public realm. As Iris Young explains, 'with the
growth of both state and non-state bureaucracies, defense of privacy in this sense has become not merely a matter of keeping the
state out of certain affairs, but asking for positive state action to
ensure that the activities of nonstate organizations, such as cor-
porations, respect the claims of individuals to privacy' (Young
1987: 74).

This idea that ethics of the self is not intended as a retreat into
a form of privatized individualism, but rather represents an attempt to block the institutional regulation of individuality, is re-
inforced by Foucault's arguments on the abolition of legislation
pertaining to issues of sexuality. The contentious nature of
Foucault's arguments on the decriminalization of rape have been
discussed in the first chapter. The decriminalization of rape would
serve to further submerge issues connected to the social construction
of sexual difference upon which rape is based. Ultimately, therefore, decriminalization would help to reinforce and legitimize the
sexual oppression of women. However, despite these undesirable
consequences, Foucault was motivated by the contrary desire to
liberate sexuality from the legal control of the state. By breaking
the bond between sex and crime, sexual behaviour would be en-
franchised from legal punishment and the sexual sphere would be
rendered free from intervention by the state. It is the establishment
of a space free from such interventions that is one of the aims of
an ethics of the self.

However, if it is not to slide into a politics based on an isolated
individualism, the necessary complement to the notion of a strategic withdrawal of the individual from discourses which govern
individuality is that of a strategic intervention by the individual
into the wider social realm in order to transform it and render it
less exclusionary than it traditionally is. How is it possible to trans-

late the radical lessons of a deconstruction of the self to a more broadly based politics? It is these interrelated strategies of withdrawal from and intervention into the social/public realm that some feminists argue should form the basis of a feminist politics which is addressed towards difference but also committed to collective political action. For Iris Young, this dual strategy is implied in the feminist slogan 'the personal is political'. She argues that the slogan does not deny a distinction between public and private, but it does deny a social division between public and private spheres, with different types of institutions, activities and human attributes. Young argues that two principles follow from this slogan. Firstly, 'no social institutions or practices should be excluded a priori as being the proper subject for public discussion and expression'; i.e. feminism has shown how radical politics in contemporary life should, in part, consist in taking actions and activities commonly thought of as private, such as how individuals and enterprises invest their money, and make public issues out of them. Secondly, 'no persons, actions or aspects of a person's life should be forced into privacy'; that is, the modern conception of the public creates an image of citizenship which excludes from public attention most particular aspects of a person (Young 1987: 74). Public life is defined as indifferent to race, age, gender, etc., and everyone is supposed to enter the public realm on identical terms. Such a conception of the public has resulted, according to Young, in the exclusion of persons and concepts of persons from public life. She argues that a contemporary emancipatory politics should foster a conception of the public which, in principle, excludes no persons, aspects of persons' lives or topic of discussion, and which encourages aesthetic as well as discursive expression: 'In such a public, consensus and sharing may not always be the goal, but the recognition and appreciation of differences, in the context of confrontation with power' (Young 1987: 76; see also Felski 1989).

Although Foucault does not use the categories of public and private, he nevertheless counterposes an ethics of the self to the government of individualization in a similar fashion. However, if Foucault's ethics of the self is not to remain an introverted labour – indistinguishable in effect from what he sees as the regressive contemporary 'cult of the self' – then there needs to be a more clear indication of how the radical lessons drawn from a reinvention of the self can be used to break down more institutionalized cultural practices. It is even more necessary to elucidate this exchange between the processes of self-transformation and social transformation, given that Foucault frequently stresses the insidious capacity of forms of global domination to invest and annex even the most oppositional microstrategies of power (*see Foucault 1980: 99*).

Despite this, however, Foucault's ethics of the self only articulates the first moment of withdrawal by the individual from manipulative state structures. Because of the essentially monadic nature of his theory of the individual, Foucault fails to explain how the individual's actions may contribute to a radical reworking of the impoverished practices of the social/public. For Foucault, the political energies of the individual are directed exclusively inward towards the goal of an isolated aesthetic autonomy, rather than towards a more collective goal in which radical individual behaviour is incorporated into a progressive social framework based on solidarity and tolerance. This atomized politics of difference is the result of his failure to develop a theory of the individual which adequately counters or reworks the emphasis on self-realization in the philosophy of the subject.

As well as failing to link the individual's work on itself with a broader oppositional movement, the aestheticist stress of Foucault's ethics is also problematic for feminists because it reinforces a tendency within some forms of feminism to aestheticize problems related to the subordination of women. Notions of '*écriture feminine*' have been criticized by feminists not only for their essentialist underpinnings, but also because the stress that is placed on avantgarde practices of reading and writing as forms of opposition to patriarchy can be elitist and overlooks the varying degrees of dissent and resistance which have existed among women in different historical and cultural contexts. Furthermore, by emphasizing a purely aesthetic response to problems of oppression, feminists may be formulating powerful responses to issues of feminine identity and social attitudes towards female sexuality, whilst other institutionalized forms of social and economic exploitation, such as the increasing feminization of poverty, remain unaddressed (see Fraser 1989). As Kate Soper puts it,

> there are many material circumstances firmly in place which tend to the disadvantaging of women and whose correction is not obviously going to be achieved simply by a revaluation of theory on the part of a post-structuralising feminist elite. In fact there are some concrete and universal dimensions of women's lives which seem relatively unaffected by the transformation of consciousness already achieved by the women's movement (*Soper 1990: 16*).

An advantage with Habermas' approach is that his modelling of social relations along the lines of interaction, rather than on an idea of solitary activity, suggests a way of conceiving of a politics of difference which does not necessarily slide into an atomized politics, an attitude of *laissez-faire* or a simplistic celebration of difference *qua* difference. Instead, a theory of communicative action suggests the political aim of establishing a community based on the tolerance and protection of individual and group differences. Selya Benhabib expands on the implications of Habermas' work for an emancipatory politics. She argues that one of the central problems of late capitalist society is that public life is viewed exclusively in terms of a legalistic-juridical perspective, whilst the actual concrete needs and interests of individuals – 'the vision of a community of needs and solidarity' – is ignored and rendered irrelevant. Whilst protecting formal rights, the expansion of legislation to more areas of the lifeworld has the effect of impoverishing the lifeworld further by limiting, rather than enhancing, the possibilities for individual autonomous action; that is, it may foster attitudes of dependency, passivity and clientelism. A communicative ethics proposes to redress the impoverishing effects of an 'extended normalisation and juridicification' of the lifeworld by stressing a participatory rather than a bureaucratic model of decision-making and by counterposing the concrete interests and needs of individuals to a discourse of rights and entitlements. These two discourses of rights and entitlements and needs and solidarity are not exclusive but complementary. As Benhabib puts it:

> The perspective of the generalised other urges us to respect the equality, dignity and rationality of all humans qua humans, while the perspective of the concrete other enjoins us to respect differences, individual life-histories and concrete needs. Such communities . . . are not pregiven; they are formed out of the action of the oppressed, the exploited, and the humiliated, and must be committed to universalist, egalitarian, and consensual ideals (*Benhabib 1986: 351*).

A similar idea has been recently expressed by Agnes Heller and Ferenc Feher in *The Postmodern Political Condition*. Here Heller and Feher argue that whilst the postmodern stress on diversity and individual difference provides a salutory lesson for totalizing political projects, it does not necessarily preclude the emergence of a common ethos or values. Drawing on the Weberian notion of a dissatisfied society, Heller and Feher argue that the only way for the individual to derive meaning and satisfaction from an instrumentalized and contingent world is to adopt an attitude of self-determination. Self-determination helps the individual overcome the feelings of powerlessness and arbitrariness which arise from the increasing trend towards globalization characteristic of modern societies.[4] It is such a goal – the retrieval, at the level of the individual, of a sense of meaning and purpose from a devalued world – that Foucault approaches in the idea of an ethics of self-formation. However, unlike Foucault, Heller and Feher stress that self-determination need not necessarily slide into an exclusively subjectivist approach to life. They argue that whilst individual self-expression is important, it is also necessary to retain an attitude of 'modern humanism' emblematically expressed in what they call the 'universal gesture':

> Doing something in our capacity as 'human beings as such, doing it for others as for 'human beings as such, doing it together with others, in symmetric reciprocity, solidarity, friendship as 'human beings as such' – this is the meaning of 'universal gesture'. It is irrelevant from which source one draws the strength to do these things for what matters most is that one *does* such things (*Heller and Feher 1988: 58*).

Modern humanism entails, therefore, developing in ourselves the capacity to be good citizens – this is to say the capacities for 'radical tolerance, civic courage, solidarity, justice and the intellectual virtues of *phronesis* and discursive rationality' – in order to protect the universal values of freedom and respect for individual life (Heller and Feher 1988: 88).

HABERMAS VERSUS FOUCAULT

Although Habermas' notion of a discourse ethics has provided a significant input into feminist and other attempts to understand the intersubjective dimension of social relations, I do not wish to suggest that Habermas' own position, contra Foucault, is unflawed. Obviously, there is not space to consider Habermas' own work in detail here, nor to do justice to all the criticisms made of his work. However, it is worth referring to some of the debates around the concepts of 'universal pragmatics' and 'ideal speech situation', linked to Habermas' notion of communicative rationality, in order to indicate the problematic nature of aspects of his work.

According to the theory of universal pragmatics, anyone engaging in communication, in performing a speech act, necessarily raises validity claims and presupposes that they can be vindicated or justified when challenged. According to Habermas, this assumption of a claim to validity and its justification form the conditions of possibility for all speech acts or communication. On the basis of this assumption, Habermas derives the idea of an ideal speech situation, characterized as 'pure intersubjectivity', i.e. by the absence of any barrier which would hinder communication (see Thompson and Held 1982: 123–4). The ideal speech situation is a 'metanorm' in that it delineates aspects of an argumentation process – around the validity claims raised by speech – which would lead to a rationally motivated agreement, as opposed to a false or apparent consensus. In respect to this notion of rational consensus, the ideal speech situation rests on four conditions: first, each participant must have an equal chance to initiate and continue communication; second, each must have a chance to make assertions, recommendations and explanations, and to challenge justifications; third, all must have equal chances to express their wishes, feelings and intentions; finally, the speaker must act as if in contexts of action there is an equal distribution of chances to order and to resist orders, to be accountable for one's conduct and to demand accountability from others (see Benhabib 1986: 285; Thompson and Held 1982: 124).

Although actual speech situations rarely correspond to this ideal, nevertheless, such an ideal is always presupposed in all communication. It is on this notion of an ideal speech situation that Habermas rests his definition of truth. Truth is defined essentially in terms of rational consensus: 'The condition for the truth of statements is the potential consent for all others . . . Truth means the promise to attain a rational consensus' (Habermas quoted in Thompson and Held 1982: 124). Furthermore, Habermas links emancipatory critique to this notion of rational consensus. Emancipatory critique is governed by the idea that a rational consensus could be achieved not only with regard to problematic truth claims, but also with regard to problematic norms.

The programme of universal pragmatics and the notion of an ideal speech situation are far from uncontentious. For example, some critics have pointed out that Habermas' arguments are based on a conception of communicative action which is itself highly idealized and untypical of ordinary linguistic interaction (Thompson and Held 1982: 125–7). Gadamer claims that Habermas' notion of unlimited communication comes straight from a medieval theory of intelligence represented by the angel 'who has the advantage of seeing God in his essence' (Gadamer quoted in Warnke 1987: 130). For other critics, the ideal speech situation is a dangerous and totalitarian utopia that negates all existing institutional relations and that can only lead to a totalitarian politics if realized (Benhabib 1986: 285). Foucault himself points out the fundamental mis-guidedness and undesirability of a notion of rational consensus as the goal of progressive politics:

> The thought that there could be a state of communication which would be such that the games of truth could circulate freely, without obstacles, without constraint and without coercive effects, seems to me to be Utopia. It is being blind to the fact that relations of power are not something bad in themselves, from which one must free one's self. I don't believe there can be a society without relations of power, if you understand them as means by which individuals try to conduct, to determine the behaviour of others. The problem is not of trying to dissolve them in the utopia of a perfectly transparent communication, but to give one's self the rules of law ... which would allow these games of power to be played with a minimum of domination (*Foucault 1988b: 18*).

Other critics have argued that Habermas' notion that genuine consensus is attained by way of better argument overlooks other equally compelling factors which may bring about agreement – compassion for example, or commitment to a common goal (Thompson and Held 1982: 128–9). The recognition of other valid motivating forces behind agreement seriously undermines the whole notion of an ideal speech situation. Richard Bernstein (1983) argues that far from transcending the dichotomy of objectivism and rela-tivism, Habermas remains caught within it and speaks with two voices: the 'transcendental' and the 'pragmatic'. As Annemiek Richters puts it: 'The very way in which Habermas poses the basic issues seems to admit only two alternatives: either there is a communicative ethics grounded in the very structures of inter-subjectivity and social reproduction, or else there is no escape from relativism, decisionism and emotivism' (Richters 1988: 633).

Richters' comment draws attention to a central weakness of Habermas' work in regard to the concerns of this book. As a result of his dichotomized view of communicative reason versus relativ-ism, Habermas fails to understand the complex nature of Foucault's final work. Although more recently Habermas acknowledges that Foucault appears to be more sympathetic to Enlightenment thought,

on the whole he regards Foucault's work as 'anti-modern' because
he sees it as rejecting the political ideals of the Enlightenment and
the project of modernity. For him, Foucault is a 'Young Con-
servative' (Habermas 1983: 14). As Habermas sees it, Foucault's
blanket critique of modernity is both theoretically paradoxical and
politically suspect. It is theoretically paradoxical because it implicitly
presupposes some of the categories and attitudes it claims to have
bypassed. It is politically suspect because it aims less at dialectical
resolution of the problems of modern society than at a radical
rejection of modernity as such. However, by constructing Foucault
as his opponent and as the champion of relativism, what Habermas
fails to see is that, in his final work, Foucault operated very
much within the notion of 'modernity as an incomplete project'.
For Foucault, the blind spot of the European Enlightenment was
its inability to recognize heterogeneity, otherness and difference.
Foucault has attempted to remedy this failing with his notion of an
ethics of the self which takes away the fear of difference, indeterminacy, and thus the radical critique of identity. As Richters
puts it:

> Habermas recognizes the plurality of forms of life, but for him
> pluralism, with its own right of existence, involves a universalistic,
> but fallibilistic, grounding of variety. This latter enterprise has
> absorbed much of his attention, to the neglect in his theoretical
> construction of the recognition of empirical heterogeneity, other-
> ness and difference. With his theoretical constructs, Habermas
> has stressed the elimination of social exclusion, while Foucault in
> his 'literary approach' makes us aware of the threat of inclusion
> by describing the effects of numerous assimilation processes in
> Western society (*Richters 1988: 640*).

Whilst Habermas' modelling of social relations along the lines of
communicative interaction includes the recognition of otherness
and difference, the treatment of this issue remains essentially formal rather than substantive. This then is perhaps the central weakness of Habermas's position *vis-á-vis* Foucault's work on the self:
Habermas does not grasp the concrete and embodied aspects of
experience as forcefully as Foucault.

Whilst the normative grounding of Habermas' communicative
ethics is much clearer than that of Foucault's work, the pull towards
a Kantian universalism leaves his theory strangely empty in regard
to concrete experience. The formalistic nature of Habermas'
metaethics and his neglect of the more substantive content of ethics

has been noted by many commentators, who have, in different
ways, identified it as one of the costs of switching from a classical
Marxian analysis of social relations in terms of a 'production paradigm', to a communicative model. Alex Callinicos argues that whilst
the Marxist privileging of the relation between the acting subject
and manipulable worldly objects is not unproblematic, it nevertheless raises certain issues about the bodily and sensuous aspects of
human existence which Habermas' 'ethereal conception of rationality' is unable to address (Callinicos 1989: 113–14).

A similar point is made by Agnes Heller, who states that

> although the Feuerbachian element had faded in the work of the
> later Marx, its bittersweet taste could be felt right to the end. The
> sensuous, the needing, the feeling human being never ceased to
> be one of his main concerns. Habermasian man has, however, no
> body, no feelings; the 'structure of personality' is identified with
> cognition, language and interaction (*Heller 1982: 22*).

Again, according to Heller, the formalist emphasis in Habermas'
theory arises from the shift from a production paradigm to communicative ethics, which simultaneously involves a shift from a
particular to a universal addressee. The particular addressee of
Marx's theory was the proletariat: 'The basic assumption of Marxian
theory was the world historical role of the proletariat ... All specific theoretical problems were reflected upon in the light of this
premiss. The theory with practical intent is a theory constructed
for the addressee' (Heller 1982: 24). For Habermas, the addressee
of his theory is not a particular social class but rather the universal
category of human reason: 'According to Marx, the proletariat develops from a class in-itself to a class for-itself and thus realises its
historical mission. For Habermas, distorted communication is reason in-itself, domination-free argumentation is reason for-itself; the
second stage *means* the realisation of the historical mission of practical reason' (Heller 1982: 24). However, the substitution of a universal for a practical addressee brings with it certain difficulties.
One difficulty is that Habermas is compelled to disregard the whole
motivational system of human beings. For Heller, Marx was not
compelled to do so: he attributed many kinds of motivations to the
proletariat – they suffer, they feel unhappy in their alienation.

The failure of communicative ethics to grasp the motivational
elements of human existence emerges from a comparison between
Marx's and Habermas' treatment of the notion of inner nature.
According to Habermas, Marx draws upon the Aristotelean idea of
techne to define work as a goal-rational activity which follows

exclusively technical rules. Because of this, Marx's conception of work follows an instrumental rationality which neglects the social, interactive aspects of human existence. However, Heller argues that Aristotle's conception of *techne* is wider than Habermas allows (*banausis*, the work of slaves, is work that follows purely technical rules) and, accordingly, Marx conceives of work not purely as a technical activity but as a 'teleological activity, where the unity of *noiesis* and *poiesis* is achieved in the work process by the same individual' (Heller 1982: 34). Initially it seems strange that Marx should appropriate this ancient one man/one work model to explain the distinctly different processes of modern industrial production. However, this is explicable in the light of Marx's theory that under capitalism the division of mental from manual labour takes on a new form: the mental and manual aspect of the *same* process is divided. Production follows purely technical rules without any longer being goal-rational from the standpoint of the individual. This is to say that what is rational socially is no longer rational for the individual.

Heller argues that Marx's differentiation between goal rationality and instrumental rationality has many theoretical and practical advantages over Habermas' identification of work exclusively with instrumental rationality. Firstly, it provides a dual perspective from which to evaluate societies: production and the producers. Second, Marx's model allows us to argue against Habermas that 'goal-rationality is not concerned solely with the appropriation of outer nature, but that goal-rationality and value-rationality together accomplish the socialisation of our *inner nature* as well' (Heller 1982: 35). Habermas' claim that work does not socialize our inner nature is based on a narrow definition of work as it has developed under capitalism, in which productive activity has ceased to be goal-rational from the standpoint of the producers. Following Marx's broader definition of work, however, we can see that creative activity is as central to the socialization of inner nature as interaction. As Heller puts it: 'The need to "make sense" of our lives always includes the need for creativity. If this need is not met, then we are deprived of one of the greatest joys attained by effort; and being deprived is discomfort, or, worse still, misery. Even institutionalised discourse could not replace this need, which is basic in us' (Heller, 1982: 35–6).

Habermas' neglect of the affective and motivational aspects of human existence is also commented on by Joel Whitebook. Habermas' primarily linguistic model of interaction may offer, on the one hand, a powerful explanation of the way in which inner and outer, the private and the social are always intertwined through language and communication. Yet on the other hand, what Habermas does not envisage is that the inner and outer realms – the notion of individual happiness versus that of collective justice – may be fundamentally different in nature and that the hedonic cannot be assimilated so easily to the rational. It does not follow from the linguisticality of the socialization process that a harmony exists between society and inner nature. As Whitebook explains: 'It does not follow . . . from the fact that inner nature is amenable to linguistic mediation that it is linguistic *an sich*. The possibility of a completely public language is not entailed by the demonstration of the impossibility of a totally private language' (Whitebook 1985: 154–5). By suggesting that individual needs can be easily assimilated within a universal ethics of speech, Habermas blurs the distinction between the linguistic and the non-linguistic within humans. He slips into a Kantian dualism in which the formal side of his ethics takes precedence over the substantive issue of individual happiness in so far as the emotional is subsumed under the rational rather than vice-versa (see Habermas 1979: 90). Thus, Habermas loads his theory of communicative interaction with a utopian potential that it theoretically cannot always carry. As Taylor says: 'The fact that the self is constituted through exchange in language . . . doesn't in any way guarantee us against loss of meaning, fragmentation, the loss of substance in our human environment and our affiliations. Habermas . . . elides the experiential problem under the public' (Taylor 1989: 509–10). By eliding the experiential with the public, Habermas manages to avoid contemplating the possibility that a society may be emancipated with respect to morality and justice but, at the same time, be unhappy with respect to the good life of its members.

What Habermas' thought loses over that of Foucault – and indeed over that of his predecessors in Critical Theory – is a sense of the eudaimonic side of ethics and also a powerful understanding of the sacrifices, at the level of individual experience, that the process of modernity has involved. Habermas is right to argue, via his shift from instrumental rationality to communicative rationality, that the process of modernity has not been purely negative, that progress has been made especially in the moral realm. Yet his essentially formalist defence of modernity risks overstating this progress. As Heller says: 'In Habermas's work the concept of progress is not a tragic one; it is not conditional, it is absolute. For him, progress is a fact – at least he wants to persuade us that it is. We are developing splendidly' (Heller 1982: 37). Against Habermas,

Foucault sees modernity as entailing a levelling down and standardization of individual experience. This dark side to modernity is expressed most forcefully in *Discipline and Punish* and *History of Sexuality* where, under the illusion of greater freedom, the bodily existence of humankind is insidiously manipulated and normalized. Whilst Foucault's bleak vision of modernity is undoubtedly too one-sided, it is nevertheless a powerful argument against the forces of conformism and panoptical control that undoubtedly play a role in societal modernization. At the very least, Foucault's work is a vivid warning against placing too much faith in Enlightenment notions of progress and rationality. In his final work, Foucault presents a more positive approach to this situation in that it explores how an individual ethics of the self may transcend the impoverishing constraints of biopower on socio-cultural existence. Whilst in comparison with Habermas the normative basis of Foucault's ethics may be problematic, he nevertheless seeks to explore the concrete ways in which individuals may redefine their existences in an experientially impoverished world. The uncovering of the historically contingent and singular in what is given as the universal and necessary leads to a practical ethics of the self based on transgression and experimentation with established forms of identity: 'The point, in brief, is to transform the critique conducted in the form of necessary limitation into a practical critique that takes the form of a possible transgression' (Foucault 1984a: 45).

Foucault may remain trapped within a philosophy of consciousness, but his notion of a recreation of the self as a work of art tackles the human urge for creativity which, if Heller is right, is as fundamental to the development of individuality as interaction. Whilst Habermas' criticisms of Foucault are not without force, he fails to see that with regard to the issues of embodied existence and individual happiness, Foucault's work on the self fills in the gaps of his own essentially formalistic ethics. As Gary Gutting remarks: 'He [Foucault] abandons the venerable but empty pretension that philosophy provides a privileged access to fundamental truths. But, at the same time, he offers a more concrete and effective approach to the equally venerable goal of liberating the human spirit' (Gutting 1989: 3).

CONCLUDING REMARKS

My intention in comparing the work of Foucault with that of Habermas is not to suggest that the latter presents a definitive solution to the shortcomings of the former. It is clear that Habermas' own constructive position contains many difficulties and unresolved problems. However, the comparison serves to highlight an element of intersubjectivity which could form the basis of a politics of solidarity which is lacking in Foucault's work. Without such an element of intersubjectivity, it is unclear how, even despite his obvious commitment to a notion of radical politics and social progress, Foucault's idea of an ethics of the self could form the basis of a contemporary politics based on the recognition of difference. Like Benhabib, Foucault's notion that a contemporary ethics must take account of the individual's concrete needs and experiences is derived, in part, from a disillusionment with the legalistic-juridical perspective of modern society. However, unlike Benhabib, Heller and Wolin, Foucault fails to tackle the issue of how the individual's right to self-determination may be better protected within a general political project of fostering a social environment based on solidarity and tolerance. Foucault's non-dialogic conception of the individual leads to a false dichotomy between the individual and the social. The social realm is seen as invariably antipathetic to individual interest, rather than as a realm which both protects and threatens these interests and, therefore, as a realm of contestation and struggle.

The particularism of Foucault's stance also arises, in part, from the insight that late capitalist societies generate a 'pluralization of social victims' and that it is not up to one group, by virtue of their privileged standpoint in the social structure, to formulate the political struggles of other groups. This belief is expressed in discussion with Giles Deleuze, where it is stated that there is no longer a representing or representative consciousness in politics: 'Those who act and struggle are no longer represented, either by a group or a union that appropriates the right to stand as their conscience' (Foucault 1977b: 206). As Benhabib puts it: 'Genuine collectivities are formed out of struggle, not out of the logic of substitution that preempts the experiences of one social group with categories derived from a language of another' (Benhabib 1986: 352). This lesson about the pluralization of social victims is one that, recently, Western feminists have had to take on board. It has been learnt that the particular language of a Western middle class feminism, which claims that sexual inequality is the fundamental form of oppression, cannot be used to represent women's interests universally. As many feminists engaged in anti-imperialist struggles, for example, have remarked, such an insistence on the primacy of struggle against sexual oppression may at best seem secondary, and at worst irrelevant to their own experiences and political aims. It is such a lesson about the indignity and misguidedness of speaking for others that Foucault seeks to press home in his idea of an ethics of the self which privileges the individual's autonomy.

Despite the crucial importance of this insight, however, the recognition of plurality and difference in struggles against oppression need not necessarily entail a withdrawal from all political strategies based on collective action and with general political aims. The individual's right to autonomy is not necessarily ensured within a social environment based on a predatory and atomized individualism. It is such an environment to which Foucault's ethics of the self would surely lead without some kind of overarching regulative principles which would ensure freedom of expression for all individuals regardless of their position in society. Foucault recognizes the need for some collective political aims when he says that although he is against consensus as a regulatory political principle, he is also against any notion of permanent dissensus. Some kind of general collective political aims are needed, therefore, to call the 'self out of the self' and to bring the isolated individual 'to a plane of generality which reminds the self in its locality that other beings and other life forms inhabit public spaces and are bent on establishing their own collective identities' (S. Wolin, 1988: 199). However, as I have shown, the relativist legacy of Foucault's earlier work returns to conflict with his later, more politically committed work. So whilst, in principle, he may be against the idea of permanent dissensus, he remains unable to explain theoretically how the self may be called out of a politics of introversion.

Conclusion

There is no doubt that over the past two decades or so there has been a stimulating engagement between Foucault's work on power and the body and feminist theory. In this book, I have made the case that Foucault's final work on the self, which has received relatively little critical attention as yet, has similarly important implications for feminist theory. Indeed, in my view, Foucault's work on the self brings his thought closer to recent trends in some feminist theory than much contemporary poststructuralist thought.

Initially, the philosophical lessons of the post-structuralist deconstruction of the rational subject were enthusiastically taken on board by some feminists in order to combat tendencies towards over-generalization and essentialism in their own theory. However, now that the issue of difference is prominent in many feminists' minds, there has been, over the past few years, a second wave of concern about the implications of the 'death of the subject' for an understanding of political agency. For many feminists, it appears too easy to slide from a crisis of subjectivity into a void or irretrievable fragmentation of subject positions. Foucault, perhaps more than any of his contemporaries, has recognized the problematic position with regard to political agency to which the dissolution of a unified subjectivity leads. His work on the self represents an attempt to work his way out of this impasse and, as a result, establishes a further potentially productive point of convergence between his thought and feminist theory.

One reason why Foucault's work on the self may be more accessible to feminists than other poststructuralist thought is that, to a great extent, Foucault avoids the colonization of the 'feminine' which marks the work of thinkers such as Derrida and Baudrillard. The feminization of the realm of poststructuralist thought – a realm dominated by male thinkers – has been noted with suspicion by several feminist theorists. The critique of the privileged rational voice that has dominated Western philosophy has meant that some contemporary philosophers have turned to the philosophical 'other' as a way of legitimizing their discourses. 'Woman' is viewed as the other *par excellence* and concepts such as the feminine, 'becoming woman' or 'woman-in-effect' have become central terms in certain types of post-Hegelian philosophy. Whilst the challenge to the primacy of rationality is to be welcomed, many feminists are now questioning the precise nature of the relationship between the 'death of man' and reflection on the feminine. One feature of this relationship that has particularly attracted feminist criticism is that it is a highly figurative view of the feminine put forward by male theorists which triumphs over real women's living thought. The feminine is celebrated as a source of creativity whilst real women as revolutionary political beings are bypassed. The principal beneficiaries of this putting-into-discourse of the feminine are, therefore, not women but the male 'Cartesian orphans': 'The new rationality organizes a femininity without women; if the "self" is absent in it, it lacks the "she" still more' (Braidotti 1991: 138).

I have argued that such criticisms cannot be made so easily of Foucault's work on the self. Foucault's rejection of the 'literary turn' of much recent philosophy, his corresponding insistence on the historical specificity of his categories (Foucault 1980: 114) and his retention of a notion of the acting self, distances his work from that of other French philosophers. The exploration of identity proposed by Foucault is not simply an endless dispersal of the subject, or a celebration of heterogeneity *qua* heterogeneity, but is linked to the overall political aim of increasing individual autonomy, understood as a humanizing quality of social existence. Thus, Foucault's notion of the radical interrogation of identity converges with the internal feminist critique of essentialism while, at the same time, it retains a notion of agency upon which a politics of resistance could be articulated.

However, despite these advantages, I have also argued that Foucault's work on the self is not without its limitations in relation to a potential feminist appropriation. Far from seeking to present theories of the feminine, Foucault appears to be relatively uninterested in exploring the intersection of sexuality with an understanding of the self. As Meghan Morris has observed: 'any feminist drawn in to sending love letters to Foucault would be in no danger of reciprocation. Foucault's work is not the work of a ladies' man' (Morris 1988: 26).

Some critics have argued that rather than being a problem, Foucault's disregard of the issue of sexual difference is consistent with his strategy of desexualization or thinking in terms other than the polarities of masculine and feminine. This argument is not without force. Given that the construction of sexuality around sexual difference has been a powerful tool of subjection for centuries, an emancipatory strategy must aim towards a redefinition of the body and its pleasures beyond such rigid categories. As we have seen, Foucault believes that this move towards desexualized forms of thought has been one of the strengths of the feminist movement:

> The real strength of the women's liberation movement is not that of having laid claim to the specificity of their sexuality and the rights pertaining to it, but that they have actually departed from the discourse conducted within the apparatuses of sexuality. These movements do indeed emerge in the nineteenth century as demands for sexual specificity. What has their outcome been? Ultimately, a veritable movement of de-sexualisation, a displacement effected in relation to the sexual centering of the problem (*Foucault 1980: 219–20*).

However, I think that Foucault's evaluation of the successes of the women's movement would differ quite significantly from what many feminists perceive as its strengths. Whilst undoubtedly most feminists would argue for a destabilization of conventional sexual categories in some form or another, much of the work – both theoretical and practical – of the feminist movement has centred on analyzing specific aspects of the feminine condition. By measuring the success of the women's movement only in terms of its ability to move beyond the categories of masculine and feminine, Foucault deprives feminism of the very cohesive element – the fact of being sexed female and socially constructed as women – that allows it to exist as a movement.

Furthermore, what Braidotti calls Foucault's 'impersonal style' in politics has lead to more serious difficulties than an idiosyncratic assessment of the strengths of the feminist movement. As we have seen, Foucault's call for the decriminalization of rape on the grounds that it loosens the sway of the law in the realm of sexuality overlooks the fact that the crime of rape derives precisely from the social construction of sexuality. If rape were categorized simply as assault it would not result in a liberation for women, rather it would render a particularly brutal form of oppression socially invisible. For many feminists it is unacceptable that Foucault could persist in his call for a decriminalization of rape given its pernicious implications for women.

Even within the terms of his own ethics, Foucault's asexual perspective is problematic. The ultimate aim of Foucault's ethics may be a redefinition of the embodied structure of subjectivity away from sexual polarities; however, given his distrust of totalized schemas, the starting point of his ethics must be the specific embodied condition of the individual subject. In Foucault's own words, an ethics of the self is 'an exercise in which *extreme attention to what is real* is confronted with the practice of a liberty that simultaneously respects this reality and violates it' (Foucault 1984a: 41; my italics). It is paradoxical, then, that Foucault insists on analyzing the specific nature of the processes of embodiment at the heart of subjectivity and then fails to consider the effects upon the individual of one of the most important processes of subjectification: sexual difference.

This problem of a desexualized perspective is one that feminists have had to deal with in Foucault's earlier work on the body and will have to continue to do so if they are to make use of his final work on the self. Whilst most feminists would acknowledge that on a political level Foucault is sympathetic to their work, on a theoretical level many may be forced to conclude that his silence on the issue of sexual difference is not enough to absolve his thought of the charge of androcentrism. When Foucault talks of the body or the self it is a male version that is frequently implied and thus, albeit unintentionally, he perpetuates the patriarchal habit of eliding the masculine with the general.

These difficulties in Foucault's work in regard to the question of sexual difference indicates one of the more general arguments of this book: that there is a significant disjunction between theories of difference and those of sexual difference. This is not to deny that there has been and continues to be a stimulating crossover between the two areas of poststructuralism and feminist theory. However, I believe that at a fundamental level, both sets of theories have different underlying imperatives which establish important points of divergence between them. The poststructuralist deconstruction of the subject remains primarily a philosophical exercise, whereas for feminists this critique is invariably linked to theories of political agency and intervention. In de Lauretis' words, 'Feminism differs from philosophical antihumanism in that it remains very much a politics of everyday life' (de Lauretis 1986: 12).

This may be an obvious point, but it seems that in the last few years some feminists, who are anxious to overcome tendencies towards generalization and essentialism in their work, have assumed rather uncritically a basic homology between theories of difference and those of sexual difference. Furthermore, as other feminists have noted, there is a marked asymmetry in the overlap between the realms of difference and sexual difference. Whilst feminists have pursued and taken on board poststructuralist insights, poststructuralist theorists have remained largely indifferent to the details of feminist work (Braidotti 1991).

The lesson that must be drawn from this asymmetrical and ultimately dissonant relationship between poststructuralism and feminism is that in the final analysis, feminists must assume a greater critical distance from imported theories in order to make their own diagnosis of the crisis of modernity. As many feminists have observed, for the male theorist the dissolution of the rational, unified subject is, in some sense or another, a negative or nostalgic experience. Foucault may not employ the strategy of colonizing the 'feminine', but nonetheless, there is a certain ironic nostalgia in his ressucitation of the ancient themes of autonomy and self-mastery in order to bypass the challenge of modernity: the dissolution of the subject. For women, however, the collapse of the primacy of the male voice in philosophical discourse is a potentially positive experience given their traditionally marginalized positions. Given this potential for autonomy, I have argued that one set of interpretations of the crisis of modernity that feminists must critically scrutinize before use are theories of the postmodern. In particular, the notion of the obsolescence of the grand narrative which is seen to be central to postmodern arguments needs to be very carefully unpacked. From the postmodern perspective, types of social critique that are pitched at a general level are invariably insensitive to, and therefore repressive of individual difference. There are no transcendent or emancipatory values upon which to base a left-wing politics that are not themselves narrative illusions locked into the prejudices of identity thinking.

Whilst the postmodern insistence on individual difference is a partially valuable lesson, I believe that it is not desirable or, ultimately, even possible, for feminism to take on the postmodern rejection of metanarratives. Whilst feminism has to guard against the dangers of generalization, it nevertheless rests on the fundamental assumption that the inequality between the sexes is indefensible and unjust. Such an assumption informs feminist analyses of the position of women in society, it underlies their call for a global abolition of gender-related inequalities and establishes a basic standard against which actual and potential social reforms can be measured. Without some fundamental notion of what constitutes the legitimate and illegitimate uses of power in relation to the subordination of women, feminism would either run into normative confusion similar to that which pervades Foucault's work, or it could even cease to exist as an autonomous movement.

It is for these fundamental reasons that I believe that recent feminist attempts to formulate a postmodern feminism should be treated with caution. This is not to say that I completely reject the insights of postmodern theory in favour of a definition of feminism as an offshoot of Enlightenment modernity. Rather, what I dispute is the falsely polarized terms of the debate on modernity and postmodernity which results in misleading oppositions between difference and legitimation, theory and practice, the individual and the collective, the particular and the general. As Anthony Giddens puts it: '"Bigness" is not in itself either an enemy of the person or a phenomenon to be overcome in life politics. Instead, it is the coordination of individual benefit and planetary organisation that has to be the focus of concern' (Giddens 1990: 157–8). In my view, a key task for feminists in the future is to seek to transcend such polarized ways of thinking in order to explore, for example, how outlining basic normative standards need not necessarily threaten the autonomy of the individual; how individual difference is better protected in a social environment based on tolerance and certain collective standards, rather than on a *laissez-faire* individualism; how a politics of self-actualization need not lapse inevitably into introversion but may contribute to wider forms of progressive social change.

Whilst Foucault goes along with the postmodern rejection of metanarratives, I have argued that his work cannot be categorized as postmodern. Against the postmodern dissolution of the subject, Foucault retains a notion of the self and affirms autonomy as a worthwhile goal of emancipatory politics. It is these themes in Foucault's work which resonate with current feminist anxieties about the implications of the death of the subject for a politics of progression and personal emancipation. The problem that arises from Foucault's work for feminists is the clash between positing a politics of engagement without providing normative guidelines for action. In this respect, it is unfortunate that Foucault died so soon after introducing the category of the self into his work. It would have been interesting to see how his thought on the self developed and how, if at all, he dealt with the problem of justification and norms. Despite these limitations, I have tried to show how Foucault's theory of an ethics of self-actualization based on the independent use of reason reflects more accurately the current concerns of many feminist theorists than the work of other contemporary French thinkers. In this respect, Foucault's final work on the self can be seen as tentatively mapping out some of the contours for a renewed development of feminist theory and debate.

Notes

CHAPTER 1   POWER, BODY AND EXPERIENCE

[1] A similar point is made by the authors of *Changing the Subject*, who demonstrate the inadequacy of orthodox materialist approaches to issues such as women's desire to become mothers. Explanations of maternal desires in terms of oppressive social conditioning do not explain the complex and often contradictory ways whereby women internalize and construct their identities around dominant representations of the body and femininity. As they observe, left-wing critiques of the maternal instinct as an ideological myth bypass altogether how it is that desires and pleasures are instrumentalized in the context of social regulation in advanced liberal democracies (see Henriques et al. 1984: 219). Women can often feel attracted to images of femininity that they simultaneously recognize, on a more rational level, as being oppressive.

[2] For an assessment of Foucault's work on feminist theory see, for example, Diamond and Quinby 1988; Gallagher and Laquer 1987; Hekman 1990; Weedon 1987.

CHAPTER 2   FROM THE BODY TO THE SELF

[1] Foucault coins the term 'subjectivization' to refer to a procedure from which subjectivity is constituted as a possibility derived from self-conscious selection. See the interview 'The Return of Morality' in Foucault 1988a.

[2] Such a dynamic relation between structure and agency is suggested by Bhaskar, who argues that it is necessary to postulate an 'ontological hiatus between society and people' if one is to understand how it is that society is neither wholly a product of human actions since it pre-exists

them, nor a complete determinant of these actions since society would not exist without the actions of agents. The positing of an ontological gap between society and the person helps to explain how it is that causal laws or determining social structures cannot simply be read off, in a one-to-one relationship, from empirical manifestations. This is because social mechanisms operate in societies which are characterized as '... open, where no constant conjunctions of events obtain' (Bhaskar 1979: 12).

[3] This notion of incorporating an interpretative understanding of the motivations of social actors into sociological analysis touches on the debate between Gadamer and Habermas on the value of incorporating hermeneutics into the critique of ideology. For an outline of the issues involved see McCarthy 1979: x–xii; Warnke 1987: 107–39.

CHAPTER 3   ETHICS OF THE SELF

[1] For a detailed consideration of the different feminist critiques of Enlightenment rationality, see Hekman 1990: 30–61; Nicholson 1990.

[2] In order to illustrate how need is a discursively constructed category, Fraser draws on the distinction between 'thin' and 'thick' needs. Many theorists have noted that needs claims have a relational structure, i.e. *a* needs *x* in order to *y*. This structure poses no problems in the consideration of 'thin' needs such as food or shelter. It is uncontroversial to say that homeless people need shelter to live. However, as soon as we get to a lesser level of generality, the level of 'thick' needs claims, things are more controversial. For example, what kind of shelter do homeless people need? What kind of strategies should governments adopt in order to help homeless people? See Fraser 1989: 163.

[3] For such criticisms see Braidotti 1989; Di Steffano 1990; Fraser and Nicholson 1988; Harstock 1990.

[4] Michèle Barrett points out that it is in the work of Gayatri Spivak that the convergence between the political recognition of differences of power and resources between women and the more philosophical critique of the integrity of the category of 'women' is most apparent. Spivak establishes this link when she writes that, 'in order to learn enough about Third World women and to develop a different readership, the immense heterogeneity of the field must be appreciated, and the First World feminist must learn to stop feeling privileged *as a woman*' (Spivak 1987, quoted by Barrett 1988: vi).

CHAPTER 4   THE PROBLEM OF JUSTIFICATION

[1] Geoff Bennington's remarks on the philosophical problems of the term 'poststructuralism' suggest a critique, along the same lines, of the term postmodernism (Bennington 1990: 122–4).

² Harding uses the term interpretationism rather than relativism because relativism is the consequence, but not always the intent, of interpretationism.

³ It is clearly difficult to argue that Foucault is not a postmodern thinker whilst pinning the label on other thinkers. However, given that, unlike Foucault, Baudrillard and Lyotard explicitly use the term 'postmodern' in their work, I think it is fair to regard them to an extent as theorists of the postmodern.

⁴ See also Laclau and Mouffe (1985: 115–16) on the idea of an 'essentialism of the elements'; also Adams and Minson 1978: 47.

⁵ On this point see Nancy Fraser's article 'Foucault's Body-Language: A Post-Humanist Political Rhetoric' (1983). She argues that although Foucault never explicitly states these assumptions, they are clearly presupposed. Moreover, she points out that his teacher, Georges Canguilhem, attempted to demonstrate an internal relation between the normative and normalizing in medicine (Fraser 1983: 57–8).

CHAPTER 5   SELF AND OTHERS

¹ Simmel writes: 'The deepest problems of modern life derive from the claim of the individual to preserve the autonomy and individuality of his existence in the face of overwhelming social forces, of historical heritage, of social culture, and of the technique of life' (See Frisby 1985: 49–67). There are, in some respects, interesting similarities between Foucault's notion of an aesthetics or 'stylistics' of existence drawn from Baudelaire, and Simmel's use of Baudelaire to develop a notion of the stylization of life.

² Adorno and Horkheimer's argument is based upon the thesis that 'Myth is already enlightenment; and enlightenment reverts to mythology'. Traditionally Enlightened thinking has been understood as a contrast to myth and as a force opposing it: as a contrast, because it counters the 'authority of tradition' with the non-coercive idea of the better, more rational argument; as an oppositional force because it 'breaks the collective spell of mythical powers by means of individually acquired insights which gain motivational strength. In this manner, the Enlightenment was supposed to contradict myth and thereby escape from its power' (Habermas 1982: 14). Adorno and Horkheimer reject this idea of the alleged superiority of rational Enlightened thought over mythical, 'non-rational' thought, arguing instead that the very process whereby rationality dominates myth is also the process by which Reason destroys itself. A totally rationalized society leads to the alienation of individuals from an objectified nature and also from their own inner selves. Individuality in modern society is regressive and alienated from itself and others. Just as in his earlier work Foucault establishes indissoluble links between the growth of the human sciences and the ubiquitous disciplinary power which totally dominates and orders modern society, so Adorno and Horkheimer regard rationality as a means of domination devoid of any validity claims: 'In cultural

modernity, reason is stripped of its validity claims and is assimilated to sheer power. The critical ability to take a 'yes' or 'no' stand is undercut by the unfortunate fusion of power and validity claims' (Habermas 1982: 18).

[3] 'The four presuppositions of the position described as 'the philosophy of the subject' were: a) a unitary model of human activity defined as 'externalisation' or 'objectification'; b) a transsubjective subject; c) the interpretation of history as the story of transsubjectivity; and d) the identity of constituting and constituted subject' (Benhabib 1986: 213).

[4] On the globalization of modernity see Anthony Giddens, *The Consequences of Modernity*. Giddens uses the image of the juggernaut to illustrate the feelings of ontological insecurity and 'existential anxiety' which characterize the individual's experience of modernity: 'a runaway engine of enormous power which, collectively as human beings, we can drive to some extent but which also threatens to rush out of our control and which could rend itself asunder. The juggernaut crushes those who resist it, and while it sometimes seems to have a steady path, there are times when it veers away erratically in directions we cannot foresee' (Giddens 1990: 139).

Bibliography

Adams, P. and Minson, J. 1978. The 'subject' of feminism. *m/f*, 2, 43–61.

Adams, P. 1989. Of female bondage. In T. Brennan (ed.), *Between Feminism and Psychoanalysis*. London: Routledge.

Adorno, T. and Horkheimer, M. 1972. *Dialectic of Enlightenment*. New York: Herder and Herder.

Adorno, T. 1984. *Aesthetic Theory*. London: Routledge and Kegan Paul.

Arac, J. (ed.) 1988. *After Foucault: Humanistic Knowledge, Postmodern Challenges*. London: Rutgers University Press.

Arendt, H. 1958. *The Human Condition*. Chicago: Chicago University Press.

Arthur, M. 1984. The origins of the western attitude towards women. In J. Peradotto and J. Sullivan (eds), *Women in the Ancient World: the Arethusa papers*. New York: New York University Press.

Barrett, M. 1980. *Women's Oppression Today: Problems in Marxist Feminist Analysis*. London: Verso.

—— 1987. The concept of difference. *Feminist Review*, 26, 29–41.

—— 1988. *Women's Oppression Today: the Marxist/Feminist Encounter*. Introduction to revised edition. London: Verso.

Bartkowski, F. 1988. Epistemic drift in Foucault. In I. Diamond and L. Quinby (eds), *Feminism and Foucault: Reflections on Resistance*. Boston: Northeastern University Press.

Bartky, S. 1988. Foucault, femininity and the modernisation of patriarchal power. In I. Diamond and L. Quinby (eds), *Feminism and Foucault: Reflections on Resistance*. Boston: Northeastern University Press.

Baudrillard, J. 1983. The ecstasy of communication. In H. Foster (ed.), *Postmodern Culture*. London: Pluto Press.

—— 1984. Game with vestiges. *On the Beach*, 5, 19–25.

Beechy, V. and Donald, J. (eds) 1985. *Subjectivity and Social Relations*. Milton Keynes: Open University Press.

Benhabib, S. 1986. *Critique, Norm and Utopia: A Study of the Foundations of Critical Theory*. New York: Columbia University Press.

—— 1987. The generalised and the concrete other: the Kohlberg-Gilligan controversy and feminist theory. In S. Benhabib and D. Cornell (eds), *Feminism as Critique: Essays on the Politics of Gender in Late Capitalist Societies*. Cambridge: Polity Press.

—— 1990. Epistemologies of postmodernism: a rejoinder to Jean-Francois Lyotard. In L. Nicholson (ed.), *Feminism/Postmodernism*. London: Routledge.

Benhabib, S. and Cornell, D. (eds) 1987. *Feminism as Critique: Essays on the Politics of Gender in Late Capitalist Societies*. Cambridge: Polity Press.

Benjamin, J. 1978. Authority and the family revisited: or, a world without fathers?. *New German Critique*, 13, 35–57.

—— 1982. Shame and sexual politics. *New German Critique*, 27, 151–9.

Bennett, F., Coward, R. and Heys, R. 1980. The limits to 'financial and legal independence': a socialist feminist perspective on taxation and social security. *Politics and Power*, 1, 185–202.

Bennington, G. 1990. Postal politics and the institution of nation. In H. Bhabha (ed.), *Nation and Narration*. London: Routledge.

Bernauer, J. and Rasmussen, D. (eds) 1988. *The Final Foucault*. Cambridge, Mass.: MIT Press.

Bernstein, R. 1983. *Beyond Objectivism and Relativism*. Oxford: Basil Blackwell.

Bhabha, H. (ed.) 1987. *Identity*. London: ICA.

—— 1990. *Nation and Narration*. London: Routledge.

Bhaskar, R. 1979. *The Possibility of Naturalism: A Philosophical Critique of the Contemporary Human Sciences*. Brighton: Harvester.

Bland, L. 1981. The domain of the sexual: a response. *Screen Education*, 39, 56–68.

Bleir, R. 1984. *Science and Gender: A Critique of Biology and its Theories on Women*. New York: Pergamon Press.

Blonsky, M. (ed.) 1985. *On Signs: A Semiotics Reader*. Oxford: Basil Blackwell.

Bordo, S. 1990. Feminism, postmodernism, and gender-scepticism. In L. Nicholson (ed.), *Feminism/Postmodernism*. London: Routledge.

Bouchard, D. (ed.) 1977. *Language, Counter-Memory, Practice: Selected Essays and Interviews*. New York: Cornell University Press.

Bourdieu, P. 1984. *Distinction: A Social Critique of the Judgement of Taste*. London: Routledge and Kegan Paul.

Boyne, R. and Rattansi, A. (eds) 1990. *Postmodernism and Society*. London: Macmillan.

Braidotti, R. 1989. The politics of ontological difference. In T. Brennan (ed.), *Between Feminism and Psychoanalysis*. London: Routledge.

—— 1991. *Patterns of Dissonance: A Study of Women in Contemporary Philosophy*. Cambridge: Polity Press.

Brennen, T. (ed.) 1989. *Between Feminism and Psychoanalysis*. London: Routledge.

Butler, J. 1987. Variations on sex and gender: Beauvoir, Wittig and Foucault. In S. Benhabib and D. Cornell (eds), *Feminism as Critique: Essays on the Politics of Gender in Late Capitalist Societies*. Cambridge: Polity Press.

—— 1990a. *Gender Trouble: Feminism and the Subversion of Identity*. London: Routledge.

—— 1990b. Gender trouble, feminist theory and psychoanalytic discourse. In L. Nicholson (ed.), *Feminism/Postmodernism*. London: Routledge.

Callinicos, A. 1989. *Against Postmodernism: A Marxist Critique*. Cambridge: Polity Press.

Cameron, D. 1984. *Feminism and Linguistic Theory*. London: Macmillan.

Carby, H. 1982. White women listen! Black feminism and the boundaries of sisterhood. In Centre for Contemporary Cultural Studies (eds), *The Empire Strikes Back: Race and Racism in 70s Britain*. London: Hutchinson.

Cassirer, E. 1955. *The Philosophy of the Enlightenment*. Boston: Beacon Press.

CCCS (Centre for Contemporary Cultural Studies) (eds) 1978. *Women Take Issue: Aspects of Women's Subordination*. London: Hutchinson.

—— 1981. *Unpopular Education: Schooling and Social Democracy in England since 1944*. London: Hutchinson.

—— 1982. *The Empire Strikes Back: Race and Racism in 70s Britain*. London: Hutchinson.

Chodorow, N. 1978. *The Reproduction of Mothering: Psychoanalysis and the Sociology of Gender*. Berkley: University of California Press.

Christian, B. 1988. The race for theory. *Feminist Studies*, 14, 67–9.

Connell, R. 1983. *Which Way is Up: Essays on Class, Sex and Culture*. London: George Allen and Unwin.

Daraki, M. 1986. Foucault's journey to Greece. *Telos*, 67, 87–110.

De Beauvoir, S. 1972. *The Second Sex*. Harmondsworth: Penguin.

De Lauretis, T. (ed.) 1986. *Feminist Studies/Critical Studies*. London: Macmillan.

De Lauretis, T. 1987. *Technologies of Gender: Essays on Theory, Film and Fiction*. London: Macmillan.

Deleuze, G. 1988. *Foucault*. Trans. S. Hand. Minneapolis: University of Minnesota Press.

Delphy, C. 1987. Protofeminism and antifeminism. In T. Moi (ed.), *French Feminist Thought: A Reader*. Oxford: Basil Blackwell.

Derrida, J. 1981. *Positions*. Chicago: University of Chicago Press.

Dews, P. 1987. *Logics of Disintegration: Post-structuralist Thought and the Claims of Critical Theory*. London: Verso.

—— 1989. The return of the subject in late Foucault. *Radical Philosophy*, 51, 37–41.

Diamond, I. and Quinby, L. (eds) 1988. *Feminism and Foucault: Reflections on Resistance*. Boston: Northeastern University Press.

Di Stefano, C. 1990. Dilemmas of difference: feminism, modernity and postmodernism. In L. Nicholson (ed.), *Feminism/Postmodernism*. London: Routledge.

Dreyfus, R. and Rabinow, P. 1982. *Michel Foucault: Beyond Structuralism and Hermeneutics*. Chicago: Chicago University Press.

Felski, R. 1989. Feminist theory and social change. *Theory, Culture and Society*, 6, 219–40.

Ferry, L. and Renaut, A. 1990. *French Philosophy of the Sixties: An Essay on Antihumanism*. Trans. M. Cattani. Amherst: University of Massachusetts Press.

Flax, J. 1990. Postmodernism and gender relations. In L. Nicholson (ed.), *Feminism/Postmodernism*. London: Routledge.

Forrester, J. 1980. Michel Foucault and psychoanalysis. *History of Science*, xviii, 286–303.

Foster, H. (ed.) 1983. *Postmodern Culture*. London: Pluto Press.

Foucault, M. 1972. *The Archaeology of Knowledge*. Trans. A. Sheridan. London: Tavistock.

—— 1977a. *Discipline and Punish: the Birth of the Prison*. Trans. A. Sheridan. Harmondsworth: Peregrine.

—— 1977b. Intellectuals and power. In D. Bouchard (ed.), *Language, Counter-Memory, Practice: Selected Essays and Interviews*. New York: Cornell University Press.

—— 1978a. *The History of Sexuality: An Introduction*. Trans. R. Hurley. Harmondsworth: Penguin.

—— 1978b. Politics and the study of discourse. *Ideology and Consciousness*, 3, 7–26.

—— 1979. Governmentality. *Ideology and Consciousness*, 6, 5–29.

—— 1980. *Power/Knowledge: Selected Interviews and Other Writings, 1972–1977*. C. Gordon (ed.). Brighton: Harvester.

—— 1982. The subject and power. In H. Dreyfus and P. Rabinow, *Michel Foucault: Beyond Structuralism and Hermeneutics*. Chicago: Chicago University Press.

—— 1983. Structuralism and poststructuralism: an interview with Michel Foucault. *Telos*, 55, 195–211.

—— 1984a. What is Enlightenment? In P. Rabinow (ed.), *The Foucault Reader*. Harmondsworth: Penguin.

—— 1984b. On the genealogy of ethics: an overview of work in progress. In P. Rabinow (ed.), *The Foucault Reader*. Harmondsworth: Penguin.

—— 1984c. Politics and ethics: an interview. In P. Rabinow (ed.), *The Foucault Reader*. Harmondsworth: Penguin.

—— 1984d. Polemics, politics and problematisations: an interview with Michel Foucault. In P. Rabinow (ed.), *The Foucault Reader*. Harmondsworth: Penguin.

—— 1984e. Nietzsche, genealogy, history. In P. Rabinow (ed.), *The Foucault Reader*. Harmondsworth: Penguin.

—— 1985a. *The Use of Pleasure*. Trans. R. Hurley. Harmondsworth: Penguin.

—— 1985b. Sexuality and solitude. In M. Blonsky (ed.), *On Signs: A Semiotics Reader*. Oxford: Basil Blackwell.

—— 1986. *The Care of the Self*. Trans. R. Hurley. Harmondsworth: Penguin.

—— 1988a. *Politics, Philosophy, Culture: Interviews and Other Writings, 1977–1984*. L. Kritzman (ed.). London: Routledge.

—— 1988b. The ethic of care for the self as a practice of freedom. In J. Bernauer and D. Rasmussen (eds), *The Final Foucault*. Cambridge, Mass.: MIT Press.

—— 1989. *Foucault Live: Interviews, 1966–1984*. New York: Semiotext (e).

Fraser, N. 1983. Foucault's body-language: a post-humanist political rhetoric. *Salmagundi*, 61, 55–70.

—— 1984. The French Derrideans: politicizing deconstruction or deconstructing politics. *New German Critique*, 23, 127–54.

—— 1987. What's critical about critical theory? The case of Habermas and gender. In S. Benhabib and D. Cornell (eds), *Feminism as Critique: Essays on the Politics of Gender in Late Capitalist Societies*. Cambridge: Polity Press.

—— 1989. *Unruly practices: power, discourse and gender in contemporary social theory*. Cambridge: Polity Press.

Fraser, N. and Nicholson, L. 1988. Social criticism without

philosophy: an encounter between feminism and postmodernism. Theory, Culture and Society, 5, 373–94.

Frisby, D. 1985. Georg Simmel: first sociologist of modernity. *Theory, Culture and Society*, 2, 49–67.

Fuss, D. 1989. *Essentially Speaking: Feminism, Nature and Difference*. London: Routledge.

Gallagher, C. and Laquer, T. (eds) 1987. *The Making of the Modern Body: Sexuality and Society in the Nineteenth Century*. Berkeley: University of California Press.

Gatens, M. 1991. *Feminism and Philosophy: Perspectives on Difference and Equality*. Cambridge: Polity Press.

Giddens, A. 1979. *Central Problems in Social Theory: Action, Structure and Contradiction in Social Analysis*. London: Macmillan.

—— 1984. *The Constitution of Society*. Cambridge: Polity Press.

—— 1990. *The Consequences of Modernity*. Cambridge: Polity Press.

Gilligan, C. 1982. *In a Different Voice: Psychological Theory and Women's Development*. Cambridge Mass.: Harvard University Press.

Green, G. and Kahn, C. (eds) 1985. *Making a Difference: Feminist Literary Criticism*. London: Methuen.

Grimshaw, J. 1986. *Philosophy and Feminist Thinking*. Minneapolis: University of Minnesota Press.

Grossberg, L. and Nelson, C. (eds) 1988. *Marxism and the Interpretation of Culture*. London: Macmillan.

Gutting, G. 1989. *Michel Foucault's Archaeology of Scientific Reason*. Cambridge: Cambridge University press.

Habermas, J. 1979. *Communication and the Evolution of Society*. London: Heinemann.

—— 1982. The entwinement of myth and Enlightenment: re-reading Dialectic of Enlightenment. *New German Critique*, 26, 13–30.

—— 1983. Modernity: an incomplete project. In H. Foster (ed.), *Postmodern Culture*. London: Pluto Press.

—— 1987. *The Philosophical Discourse of Modernity*. Cambridge: Polity Press.

—— 1989. *The New Conservatism: Cultural Criticism and the Historians' Debate*. Cambridge: Polity Press.

Hall, S. 1987. Minimal Selves. In H. Bhabha (ed.), *Identity*. London: ICA.

Harding, S. and Hintikka, M. (eds) 1983. *Discovering Reality: Feminist Perspectives on Epistemology, Metaphysics, Methodology and Philosophy of Science*. London: D. Reidel.

Harding, S. (ed.) 1987. *Feminism and Methodology*. Bloomington: Indiana University Press.

—— 1990. Feminism, science and the anti-Enlightenment critiques. In L. Nicholson (ed.), *Feminism/Postmodernism*. London: Routledge.

Harstock, N. 1990. Foucault on power: a theory for women? In L. Nicholson (ed.), *Feminism/Postmodernism*. London: Routledge.

Hartmann, H. 1981. The unhappy marriage of Marxism and feminism: towards a more progressive union. In L. Sargent (ed.), *Women and Revolution: A Discussion of the Unhappy Marriage of Marxism and Feminism*. London: Pluto Press.

Harvey, D. 1989. *The Condition of Postmodernity: An Enquiry into the Origins of Cultural Change*. Oxford: Basil Blackwell.

Hassan, I. 1985. The culture of postmodernism. *Theory, Culture and Society*, 2, 119–29.

Hekman, S. 1990. *Gender and Knowledge: Elements of a Postmodern Feminism*. Cambridge: Polity Press.

Held, V. 1987. Feminism and moral theory. In E. Kittay and D. Meyers (eds), *Women and Moral Theory*. Totowa, NJ: Rowman and Littlefield.

Heller, A. 1982. Habermas and Marxism. In J. Thompson and D. Held (eds), *Habermas: Critical Debates*. London: Macmillan.

Heller, A. and Feher, F. 1988. *The Postmodern Political Condition*. Cambridge: Polity Press.

Henriques, J. et al. (eds) 1984. *Changing the Subject: Psychology, Social Regulation and Subjectivity*. London: Methuen.

Hill, T. 1987. The importance of autonomy. In E. Kittay and D. Meyers (eds), *Women and Moral Theory*. Totowa, NJ: Rowman and Littlefield.

Holloway, W. 1984. Gender difference and the production of subjectivity. In J. Henriques et al. (eds), *Changing the Subject: Psychology, Social Regulation and Subjectivity*. London: Methuen.

Horkheimer, M. 1972. Authority and the Family. In M. Horkheimer, *Critical Theory: Selected Essays*. New York: Herder and Herder.

Hoy, D. (ed.) 1986. *Foucault: A Critical Reader*. Oxford: Basil Blackwell.

Hoy, D. 1988. Foucault: modern or postmodern? In J. Arac (ed.), *After Foucault: Humanistic Knowledge, Postmodern Challenges*. London: Rutgers University Press.

Husseyn, A. 1986. *After the Great Divide: Modernism, Mass Culture and Postmodernism*. London: Macmillan.

Jaggar, A. 1983. *Feminist Politics and Human Nature*. Brighton Harvester.

Jameson, F. 1983. Postmodernism and consumer society. In H. Foster (ed.), *Postmodern Culture*. London: Pluto Press.

Jardine, A. 1985. Gynesis: Configurations of Woman and Modernity. Ithaca, New York: Cornell University Press.

Johnson, P. 1988. Feminism and Images of Autonomy. *Radical Philosophy*, 50, 26–30.

Jones, A. 1985. Inscribing femininity: French theories of the feminine. In G. Greene and C. Kahn (eds), *Making a Difference: Feminist Literary Criticism*. London: Methuen.

Kappeler, S. 1986. *The Pornography of Representation*. Cambridge: Polity Press.

Kellner, D. 1988. Postmodernism as social theory: some challenges and problems. *Theory, Culture and Society*, 5, 239–69.

Kittay, E. and Meyers, D. (eds) 1987. *Women and Moral Theory*. Towtowa, NJ: Rowman and Littlefield.

Laclau, E. and Mouffe, C. 1985. *Hegemony and Socialist Strategy: Towards a Radical Democratic Politics*. London: Verso.

Lash, S. 1985. Postmodernity and desire. *Theory and Society*, 14, 1–33.

—— 1990. *Sociology of Postmodernism*. London: Routledge.

Leclerc, A. 1987. Parole de femme. In T. Moi (ed.), *French Feminist Thought: A Reader*. Oxford: Basil Blackwell.

Lovibond, S. 1989. Feminism and Postmodernism. *New Left Review*, 178, 5–28.

Lyotard, J. 1984. *The Postmodern Condition: A Report on Knowledge*. Manchester: Manchester University Press.

McCarthy, T. 1979. Introduction. In J. Habermas, *Communication and the Evolution of Society*. London: Heinemann.

Martin, B. 1982. Feminism, criticism and Foucault. *New German Critique*, 26, 3–12.

Merquior, J. 1985. *Foucault*. London: Fontana Press/Collins.

Moi, T. 1985. *Sexual Textual Politics: Feminist Literary Theory*. London, Methuen.

—— (ed.) 1987. *French Feminist Thought: A Reader*. Oxford: Basil Blackwell.

—— 1989. Patriarchal thought and the drive for knowledge. In T. Brennan (ed.), *Between Feminism and Psychoanalysis*. London: Routledge.

Moore, H. 1988. *Feminism and Anthropology*. Cambridge: Polity Press.

Morris, M. 1988. The pirate's fiancée: feminists and philosophers, or maybe tonight it'll happen. In I. Diamond and L. Quinby (eds), *Foucault and Feminism: Reflections on Resistance*. Boston: Northeastern University Press.

Nicholson, L. 1986. *Gender and History: The Limits of Social Theory in the Age of the Family*. New York: Columbia University Press.

—— (ed.) 1990. *Feminism/Postmodernism*. London: Routledge.

O'Brien, P. 1978. Crime and punishment as historical problem. *Journal of Social History*, 11, 508–20.

—— 1982. *The Promise of Punishment: Prisons in Nineteenth Century France*. Princeton: Princeton University Press.

O'Farrell, C. 1989. *Foucault: Historian or Philosopher?* London: Macmillan.

Owens, C. (ed.) 1983. *Postmodern Culture*. London: Pluto Press.

Pateman, C. and Grosz, E. (eds) 1986. *Feminist Challenges: Social and Political Theory*. Boston: Northeastern University Press.

Peradotto, J. and Sullivan, J. (eds) 1984. *Women in the Ancient World: the Arethusa Papers*. New York: New York University Press.

Plaza, M. 1978. Phallomorphic power and the psychology of 'Woman'. *Ideology and Consciousness*, 4, 4–36.

—— 1980. Our costs and their benefits, *m/f*, 4, 28–39.

Pollock, G. 1982. Vision, voice and power: feminist art, history and Marxism. *Block*, 6, 2–21.

Poster, M. 1984. *Foucault, Marxism and History*. Oxford: Basil Blackwell.

—— 1986. Foucault and the tyranny of Greece. In D. Hoy (ed.), *Foucault: A Critical Reader*. Oxford: Basil Blackwell.

Rabinow, P. (ed.) 1984. *The Foucault Reader*. Harmondsworth: Penguin.

Rajchman, J. 1985. Ethics after Foucault. *Social Text*, 13, 165–183.

Ramazanoglu, C. 1989. *Feminism and the Contradictions of Oppression*. London: Routledge.

Rasmussen, D. 1985. Communicative action and the fate of modernity. *Theory, Culture and Society*, 2, 133–44.

Richters, A. 1988. Modernity-postmodernity controversies: Habermas and Foucault. *Theory, Culture and Society*, 5, 611–43.

Riley, D. 1988. *'Am I That Name?': Feminism and the Category of Women in History*. London: Macmillan.

Rose, N. 1982. The pleasures of motherhood: discussion of Elizabeth Badinter's *The Myth of Motherhood: An Historical View of the Maternal Instinct*. *Ideology and Consciousness*, 5, 5–68.

Rose, G. 1984. *Dialectic of Nihilism: Post-structuralism and Law*. Oxford: Basil Blackwell.

—— 1988. Architecture to philosophy – the postmodern complicity. *Theory, Culture and Society*, 5, 357–71.

Rose, J. 1986. *Sexuality in the Field of Vision*. London: Verso.

Ruddick, S. 1987. Remarks on the sexual politics of reason. In E. Kittay and D. Meyers (eds), *Women and Moral Theory*. Totowa, NJ: Rowman and Littlefield.

Sargent, L. (ed.) 1981. *Women and Revolution: A Discussion of the Unhappy Marriage of Marxism and Feminism*. London: Pluto Press.

Sawicki, J. 1988a. Identity politics and sexual freedom. In I. Diamond and L. Quinby (eds), *Feminism and Foucault: Reflections on Resistance*. Boston: Northeastern University Press.

—— 1988b. Feminism and the power of Foucauldian discourse. In J. Arac (ed.), *After Foucault: Humanistic Knowledge, Postmodern Challenges*. London: Rutgers University Press.

Schor, N. 1987. Dreaming Dissymmetry: Barthes, Foucault, and Social Difference. In A. Jardine (ed.), *Men in Feminism*. London: Methuen.

Segal, L. 1987. *Is the Future Female?: Troubled Thoughts on Contemporary Feminism*. London: Virago Press.

Sennett, R. 1980. Destructive gemeinschaft. In A. Soble (ed.), *The Philosophy of Sex and Love*. Totowa, NJ: Rowman and Allanheld.

Showstack Sassoon, A. (ed.) 1987. *Women and the State: The Shifting Boundaries of Public and Private*. London: Hutchinson.

Smith, P. 1988. *Discerning the Subject*. Minneapolis: University of Minnesota Press.

Smith-Rosenberg, C. 1986. Writing history: language, class and gender. In T. de Lauretis (ed.), *Feminist Studies/Critical Studies*. Bloomington: Indiana University Press.

Soper, K. 1989. Feminism as critique. *New Left Review*, 176, 91–114.

—— 1990. Feminism, humanism and postmodernism. *Radical Philosophy*, 55, 11–17.

—— 1991. Postmodernism, subjectivity and the question of value. *New Left Review*, 186, 120–8.

Spivak, G. 1987. *In Other Worlds: Essays in Cultural Politics*. London: Methuen.

—— 1988. Can the subaltern speak? In L. Grossberg and C. Nelson (eds), *Marxism and the Interpretation of Culture*. London: Macmillan.

—— 1990. Gayatri Chakravorty Spivak: an interview. *Radical Philosophy*, 54, 32–4.

Taylor, C. 1989. *Sources of the Self: The Making of the Modern Identity*. Cambridge: Cambridge University Press.

Thompson, J. and Held, D. (eds) 1982. *Habermas: Critical Debates*. London: Macmillan.

Waerness, K. 1987. On the rationality of caring. In A. Showstack Sassoon (ed.), *Women and the State: The Shifting Boundaries of Public and Private*. London: Hutchinson.

Warnke, G. 1987. *Gadamer: Hermeneutics, Tradition and Reason*. Cambridge: Polity Press.

Weedon, C. 1987. *Feminist Practice and Poststructuralist Theory*. Oxford: Basil Blackwell.

Weeks, J. 1985. *Sexuality and its Discontents: Meanings, Myths and Modern Sexualities*. London: Routledge and Kegan Paul.

Whitebook, J. 1985. Reason and happiness: some psychoanalytic themes in critical theory. In R. Bernstein (ed.), *Habermas and Modernity*. Cambridge: Polity Press.

Willis, E. 1988. Comment. In L. Grossberg and C. Nelson (eds), *Marxism and the Interpretation of Culture*. London: Macmillan.

Winship, J. 1978. A woman's world: woman an ideology of femininity. In CCCS (eds), *Women Take Issue: Aspects of Women's Subordination*. London: Hutchinson.

Wright, I. 1986. The suicide of the intellectuals. *The Times Higher Educational Supplement*, 24 October.

Wolin, R. 1986. Foucault's aesthetic decisionism. *Telos*, 67, 71–86.

Wolin, S. 1988. On the theory and practice of power. In J. Arac (ed.), *After Foucault: Humanistic Knowledge, Postmodern Challenges*. London: Rutgers University Press.

Young, I. 1987. Impartiality and the civic public: some implications of feminist critiques of moral and political theory. In S. Benhabib and D. Cornell (eds), *Feminism as Critique: Essays on the Politics of Gender in Late Capitalist Societies*. Cambridge: Polity Press.

Index